KENT AIRFIELDS IN THE SECOND WORLD WAR

Robin J. Brooks

COUNTRYSIDE BOOKS
NEWBURY, BERKSHIRE

First Published 1998
© Robin J. Brooks 1998
Reprinted 1999

COUNTRYSIDE BOOKS
3 Catherine Road
Newbury, Berkshire

ISBN 1 85306 523 4

The cover painting is by Colin Doggett and shows Hurricanes of
No 32 Squadron at Biggin Hill in 1940.

Designed by Mon Mohan

Produced through MRM Associates Ltd., Reading
Printed by Woolnough Bookbinding Ltd., Irthlingborough

CONTENTS

KENT'S WORLD WAR II AIRFIELDS

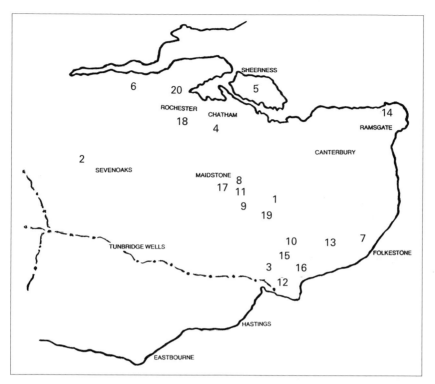

KEY TO MAP

1	Ashford	11	Lashenden
2	Biggin Hill	12	Lydd
3	Brenzett	13	Lympne
4	Detling	14	Manston
5	Eastchurch	15	Newchurch
6	Gravesend	16	New Romney: Honeychild
7	Hawkinge	17	Staplehurst
8	Headcorn (Egerton)	18	West Malling
9	High Halden	19	Woodchurch
10	Kingsnorth ALG	20	Rochester

INTRODUCTION

Christened 'Hell-fire Corner' during 1940 due to its geological position as the nearest landmass to the enemy, Kent's association with aviation began long before this. Taking the first infant steps in flying on the Isle of Sheppey during 1930, the county was called the 'cradle of aviation'. Pioneer aviators such as Sir Charles Stewart-Rolls, Lord Brabazon of Tara and Frank McClean flew from the airfield at Shellbeach near Leysdown and established the Royal Aero Club there with its first headquarters in a building known as Mussel Manor. Aircraft manufacturing began on the site when the Short Brothers established a company before moving their operation to nearby Eastchurch and producing their first biplane. At the same time, the first experimental deck landings were taking place off Sheerness.

The Second World War saw the county firmly in the front line with the Battle of Britain being fought in the skies above Kent. Airfields were in abundance over this period but today just one military site remains, this due to be closed by the year 2000.

This quotation from *A Writer's Notebook* by W. Somerset Maugham sets the mood for what is within these covers. 'At sunset over the slate-grey of the western clouds was spread a fiery vapour, a rain of infinitesimal tenuity, a great dust of gold that swept down upon the silent sea like the train of a goddess of fire. With almost a material effort, it seemed, it pushed aside the obstructing clouds, filling the whole sky with brilliancy, and then over the placid sea was stretched a broad roadway of flame upon which might travel the passionate souls of men, endlessly, to the source of deathless light.' I dedicate this book to all who died or were injured whilst serving at one of the Kent airfields.

Robin J. Brooks

I
SETTING
THE SCENE

Had it not been for the rapid expansion plans of the military during 1938/9, things today may well have been very different for this country and, indeed, the world. When there seemed little doubt that war would come once again, Britain's aircraft industry began doubling its efforts to produce monoplane fighters and bombers in order to compete with the vast German war machine. The RAF around this time still possessed obsolete biplane fighter aircraft but the brilliant design of Sydney Camm, the Hawker Hurricane, was being produced as quickly as possible. With the first production aircraft flying on 12th October 1937,

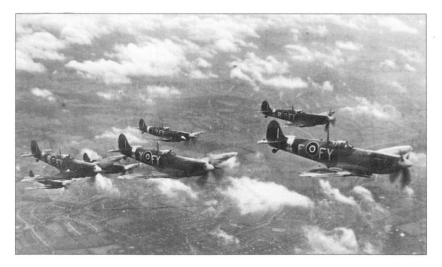

Spitfire IXs of 611 (West Lancashire) Squadron airborne over Kent. (MAP/RAF Museum)

Britain's first early warning system – the concrete disc at Hythe with stethoscope in the centre. (R. J. Brooks)

the first squadron to exchange their aging Gloster Gladiator biplanes for the new monoplane was No 111 then stationed at Northolt. A success story had just begun.

In Kent, many small civil airfields were requisitioned by the military during this expansion period. They were enlarged and became in the main, fighter airfields. Some were already operational by the time war broke out but others, such as West Malling, were still in the course of construction during the Battle of Britain. All of the airfields were just grass in 1939/40 but as more powerful and heavier aircraft were developed, so the need arose for tarmac or concrete runways and taxi areas. These were slow in coming and even when the war ended in 1945, some airfields such as Detling, Hawkinge and Lympne had no such facility.

Also considered for use during this expansion period were the AA Landing Grounds. In 1932 the Automobile Association had a register of sites to cater for the private pilot as well as the motorist. The *AA Register of Aircraft Landing Grounds* detailed suitable places where a permanent aerodrome had not yet been established. Basic in the range of services, they were usually situated near large country retreats in order to cater for the discerning customer. When war began, the AA handed all this information over to the military who inspected every site but found very few suitable for their purpose. None were chosen in Kent.

By September 1939, 116 airfields were ready for operations countrywide. Kent saw the fighter airfields of Biggin Hill, Manston, Hawkinge and Gravesend fully operational. Lympne, although built, was in 1939 only classed as an emergency airfield, and was to join Fighter Command some time later. Detling and Eastchurch were Coastal Command airfields and West Malling, as mentioned, was still under construction. Rochester was the home of Short Brothers where the Stirling bombers and, further down on the River Medway, the Sunderland were under construction. All of the airfields with the exception of Rochester had been visited by the Air Ministry's Directorate-General of Works, a technical branch of the Civil Service which was responsible for supplying airfields to the RAF's requirements. Despite objections from landowners, the Air Ministry had the power to requisition any land under the Emergency Powers (Defence) Act of 1939. In almost every case of airfield expansion, this had to be used.

Plotting the enemy's course in one of the Chain Home radar stations situated along the coastline. (Kent Messenger)

The Dover radar towers under attack in 1940. (Kent Messenger)

Behind the scenes further developments were taking place. Huge aerials began to appear all along the Kent coast about which very little was known by the general public. They were in fact the successors to the huge concrete slabs that can still be seen today at Lydd and high on the cliffs above Dover and Hythe. These were then called 'sound mirrors' and were used to detect aircraft engines as they crossed the Channel. By the late 1930s, a new name and installation had appeared. Radar, the initials standing for Radio Direction and Range, gave the first warning of enemy aircraft in a far more sophisticated way and was a major contributor to the RAF's success in the air. At various places across Kent, direction finding huts and installations began to appear. One of the main places for ASR detection of aircraft down in the Channel was at Wittersham near Rye. Though the operators of the equipment could not communicate with the pilots that they listened in to, they were able to get a bearing on where they had come down in the sea and thus aid a quicker rescue either by the ASR Squadron based at Hawkinge or by summoning one of the ASR launches from Dover or Ramsgate.

So the scene was set for the greatest aerial battle in history. In order to get as many airfields as possible ready for the onslaught, buildings were hastily erected and followed a very similar pattern on most of the sites.

Airfield Buildings

For the expansion to go ahead at an accelerated pace, the same designs for buildings were used. Plans for these were subjected to approval by the Royal Fine Arts Commission and also the Society for the Protection of Rural England, a rather strange formality perhaps considering war was imminent. One of the more noticeable buildings of this period was the hangar. Most First World War airfields and those that were built between the wars, had the 'A' Type hangar. The RFC had used a large wooden shed with a gabled front and sliding doors and the more familiar canvas Bessoneaux hangar. By 1937 these had been supplemented by a new design known as the Aeroplane Shed Type 'C'. This was a large construction with what appeared to be a flat roof but which was really a series of gable sections. None of this type were erected on airfields in Kent, nonetheless they are worthy of mention to see how hangar design changed. More familiar on the Kent airfields was the Bellman Transportable hangar. These were produced to meet the changing conditions on airfields and were so easily erected and disman-

Obstacles were placed in fields to prevent paratroops and aircraft landing.
(Kent Messenger)

11

tled that many that were in use during the war now reside on industrial sites. Measuring 180 feet long with a span of 95 feet and a 25 feet door height, they were a steel framework covered in corrugated iron sheeting.

To succeed these came the 'T' Type Transportable Shed, many of which can still be seen today on the wartime airfields of the county. Designed and built by the Tees Side Bridge and Engineering Works, like the Bellman, they were steel framed with a corrugated iron covering. They have lasted very well to this day although much of the covering has now rusted. It is, however, the Blister hangar that provides the most poignant memories of an airfield at war. Over 3,000-plus were erected on all types of airfield. Designed and made by C. Miskin and Sons, it was trialled at Biggin Hill in January 1940 and immediately proved a success for the poor ground crews who had previously had to endure servicing aircraft in the open. By 1942 many had been removed from the fighter airfields and placed on training bases as more modern designs came along. Although the earlier models just had curtains at one end for protection, later types were bricked in and were far more draught-proof.

The technical and domestic buildings followed a similar set pattern. The same materials were used in each case with the buildings usually being sited some distance away from the landing area. Likewise the huts used for accommodation and various departments such as stores, armouries, equipment etc were quickly and easily erected. At the beginning of the war, the most widely constructed hut was the 'B' Type, a prefabricated wooden building. By 1940, timber had become in short supply and new and cheaper materials were used. Included in these new huts were the Ministry of Supply Timber Hut, the Laing Hut (designed and constructed by John Laing and Sons, the builders) and the Maycrete Hut, composed of concrete slabs with an asbestos roof. Some of the latter are still around today being used for a variety of purposes. The same applies to the famous Nissen Hut, designed by Colonel P. Nissen. Large numbers of these were built and most have stood the test of time and are still in use.

The Watch Office or Control Tower evolved out of necessity as more and more aircraft were moved about a station and in the air. Prior to 1939, air traffic control was non-existent, there was just a duty pilot to log aircraft in and out. With the expansion came a special building situated alongside the landing area or in some cases, attached to the end of a hangar. After the Battle of Britain there was a need for more sophisticated buildings and a design known as Air Ministry drawing No 518/40 led to the first of many two-storey concrete control towers being built. By 1943, the Type 12779/41 had appeared at many airfields, many of these remaining in use to this day.

Defences

The fall of France caused the Air Ministry to look at the entire airfield defence system. When it became obvious that the Battle of Britain was about to begin and that fighter airfields would surely come under attack from the Luftwaffe, a succession of large scale projects got underway.

A Bofors gun manned to protect a bridge at Maidstone during Army manoeuvres. (Kent Messenger)

Pillboxes were hastily built around the airfield perimeter, some with sandbags, others with bricks. At first it was the army that was mainly detailed to defend the sites with assistance from RAF gunners but later it became the sole duty of the RAF Regiment. Guns ranged from machine-guns to Bofors down to hand pistols, which many airmen fired at enemy aircraft attacking their airfields out of sheer indignation and desperation! With the Regiment came better guns and better training for the gunners but in 1940, this was still some way off. With the threat of invasion a distinct possibility, ingenuity became the name of the game with the adapting of motor vehicles to carry guns.

In the haste to defend the airfields, many inventions and ideas were trialled at several of the airfields. One of the more interesting and yet bizarre defence ideas was the Pickett-Hamilton Retractable Gun Turret. Invented by a Kentish man, Francis Norman Pickett, it was a 'pop-up' pillbox that was sunk into the grass beside the main runway areas. The

The entry hatch to a Pickett-Hamilton Retractable Gun Turret at West Malling. (R. J. Brooks)

pillbox was circular, made of concrete and measured some 6 feet in diameter. Inside this circular concrete tube was placed another smaller tube thereby allowing it to rise above the main one. A pumping device was installed in the centre of the inner ring and this moved the pillbox up and down. The raising could either be done by a compressed air cylinder or by means of a pneumatic hand pump operated by one of the three occupants inside the pillbox. Entry was by a metal hatch in the top and the men, once inside, would fire their weapons through slits in the concrete. Immediately after the action, they would lower the fort down to grass level thus denying the enemy the opportunity of capturing them. The idea certainly attracted the attention of Winston Churchill who wrote to General Ismay on 12th July 1940 stating: 'I saw these pillboxes for the first time when I visited Langley Aerodrome last week. This design appears to afford an admirable means of anti-parachute defence and it should surely be adopted. Let me have a plan.' In the event, most of the Kent airfields had at least three sited around the landing areas and although a good idea, constant flooding made them most uncomfortable for the occupants and as no invasion by the enemy ever took place, there is no record of them ever being used.

The same lack of success dogged the PAC system. Installed at some of the Kent airfields, the Parachute and Cable device was intended to bring down enemy aircraft. Fired from a tube, the rockets would reach about 2,000 feet when two parachutes would be deployed automatically. The larger one would carry away the rocket case whilst the smaller parachute had a 1,000 foot length of cable attached to it with a small mine on the end. It was hoped that the cable would catch any part of an enemy aircraft and drag the mine up to the aircraft with the desired results. The only record of it being fired was at Biggin Hill but as with the Pickett-Hamilton Turret, it was a wild idea hastily brought into use for a country badly prepared for war.

It was the Munich Crisis that brought the value of camouflage to the attention of the Air Staff. Whilst a large area such as an airfield could not be completely disguised, it was possible to blend it with the surroundings by using colour co-ordinations. It was also possible to paint black lines to simulate hedges across a vast landing area by using black emulsion paint. The trees and hedges surrounding most airfields were ideal natural camouflage when it came to dispersing aircraft. The hardstandings leading to these areas were coloured to blend in with the green foliage. Buildings, hangars and any of the domestic buildings were made to look as inconspicuous as possible by the painting of anything white either black or brown.

A road block along the Tonbridge Road at Maidstone. (Kent Messenger)

The last aspect that roughly comes under the heading of camouflage was the building and siting of decoy airfields. Intended to persuade the Luftwaffe to drop their bombs there instead of on the proper airfield, the most elaborate decoy was classified as a 'K' site. This had dummy aircraft and buildings and was laid out exactly as the mother site. Nighttime decoys were classed as 'Q' sites and were equipped with dummy Drem runway lighting. The first sites were operational by January 1940 and by August, 26 'K' and 56 'Q' sites were in use. The programme cost many millions of pounds but its success made the expense worthwhile. By 31st July 1940, 60 enemy attacks had been made on these sites in mistake for the real thing.

Royal Observer Corps

Although now stood-down as an active unit, the Corps played a valiant and vital part in our defence during and after the Battle of Britain and into peacetime. Its origins were back in the First World War when enemy airships flew over England unmolested and sometimes undetected. After a particularly nasty incident in May 1915 when a Zeppelin killed and maimed many civilians in the East End of London, a reporting system for enemy aircraft was set up by the local constabularies. Later years saw the London Air Defence Area established with Major-General E.B. Ashmore in command. Once again, special constables were employed as observers and experiments were carried out in Kent using a chain of reporting stations all over the county. These reports were received and assessed at a headquarters set up in a room above the post office in Cranbrook High Street.

From these humble beginnings, the Corps grew and was taken over by the Air Ministry in January 1929. By then, a countrywide chain of reporting posts were in position and by the time of the Munich Crisis were manned day and night by observers. Each county had a main headquarters where all the reported sightings and plots of enemy aircraft were collated. In Kent, the No. 1 Group Headquarters was in a large country house in London Road, Maidstone, the building where it was to remain until stand-down. With an RAF uniform and Observer Corps flashes being issued in March 1940, the corps went to war.

The system of reporting worked out over many years of peace worked superbly. When the radar stations were attacked and put out

A typical ROC plotting room. The table grid represents the south-eastern corner of the UK. (Kent Messenger)

Observers A. Wraight with binoculars and E. Woodland of ROC post Mike 1 at Dymchurch. They were the first to see and track the V1 Doodlebug. (Kent Messenger)

of use, it was the Observer Corps that continued to warn of enemy aircraft approaching. Throughout the Battle of Britain, the Blitz and the V1 campaign, the observers were out in all weathers and working under very primitive conditions. The Royal prefix was granted in 1941 and although the corps continued to serve until 1945, it was amazingly stood down at the cessation of hostilities. Not for long however as it was realised that the corps had a role to play during peacetime as an early warning and nuclear monitoring service. This continued until the 1980s when, with the threat of a nuclear war fast receding, the Royal Observer Corps was stood down for the final time.

This then was the scene as Kent prepared to go to war. As the corner of England closest to mainland Europe, it was known that when war came, this 'Garden of England' would take the brunt of enemy action. Though we were ill-prepared for such a battle, the few years of military expansion did go some way in helping the county to achieve a victory and allow Kent to emulate the county motto: 'Invicta - Unconquered'.

2
BIGGIN HILL

To Biggin Hill came the honour of the title 'The Strongest Link', words which were later to be incorporated in the station crest. It was a sector or controlling station in No 11 Group, Fighter Command commanding sector 'C' and as such, particularly during the Battle of Britain, it became world famous.

During the latter days of 1916, the land had already been earmarked as a night emergency landing ground when scientists from the Wireless Testing Park at Joyce Green near Dartford, looked at Biggin Hill with a view to using it for their experiments. They liked what they saw and the unit moved to Biggin Hill in February 1917. One year later the station had become included in the London Air Defence Area and No

The Aerodrome, Biggin Hill, Kent.

Biggin Hill c1925. The triple-bay hangar was the first to be built in 1917 and was destroyed in 1940. (J. Wise)

141 Squadron arrived with Bristol fighters. It soon became obvious that the airfield, perched high up on the North Downs, was in a prime position for the defence of the capital and an extensive rebuilding programme began. With most of the original buildings on the south side of the grass landing area, construction was to take place on the north side. Completed by 1930, the first squadrons to occupy the airfield were Nos 23 and 32. Empire Air Days and flying displays were the order of these inter-war years until the distant rumblings of another war about to break brought a further period of expansion.

Even at this early stage of its development, Biggin Hill was important to civil aviation as a weather reporting station on the Croydon-Le Bourget route. At 600 feet above sea level, it was often used by airliners who put down there when Croydon was fogbound. The daily Lufthansa service to Croydon passed directly over the airfield, an ideal opportunity to photograph the rebuilding programme.

By 1938 the expansion period was in full swing. Camouflage was applied to the buildings, air raid shelters were hastily dug and more importantly, the squadrons began to exchange their ancient biplanes for the new Hawker Hurricane monoplane. Still a grass airfield at this time, it was decided to construct a tarmac runway and work immediately started on a 4,800 foot by 150 foot strip. At last the military were taking the signs of war seriously and it was none too soon. The German military machine was continuing its onslaught on its near neighbours and despite Chamberlain's warning to Hitler that Britain would fulfil its guarantees to Poland, the German army marched into that country at 04.45 hours on 1st September 1939. On the 3rd, Britain declared war on Germany.

At Biggin Hill, Wing Commander R. Grice had arrived to command the station little knowing that he would lead 'Biggin on the Bump', as it had become known, through its most traumatic period. The Christmas of 1938 had been the first white one for many years. With no operations possible, the men and women at Biggin enjoyed what they all believed would be the last Christmas of peace. On 24th August 1939, the RAF was mobilised and the resident squadrons, Nos 32 and 79 (Madras Presidency) came to full readiness, being joined on the eve of battle by No 601 (County of London) Auxiliary Squadron who brought the first twin-engined aircraft to fly from the base, the Bristol Blenheim 1F.

Immediately after Mr Chamberlain's announcement that Britain was at war with Germany, Wg/Cdr Grice came on the tannoy to speak to all the station personnel. He uttered just one sentence, the rest of the speech was drowned by the sound of the local air raid sirens. It

79 Squadron Hurricanes up from Biggin Hill in 1939. (Kent Messenger)

appeared as though Hitler was wasting no time as the telephone rang in 32 Squadron's dispersal. The duty airman listened intently and shouted, 'Blue section patrol Gravesend 5,000 feet. Scramble.'

Falling over each other in their haste, three pilots raced to their waiting Hurricanes and took off. A few minutes later they were recalled when the 'hostile' aircraft was found to be a French transport aircraft heading for Croydon. Still it was all good practice for the real thing. Despite several other false 'scrambles', nothing much happened at Biggin Hill. The long awaited onslaught was some time coming.

This period of time did however allow the three squadrons to put in many hours of friendly interceptions with each other as well as exercising with local balloon and gun emplacements. Defence of the airfield had been entrusted to the 90th AA Regiment whilst the Queen's Own Royal West Regiment had provided 74 privates to stem any paratroop or saboteur attacks on Biggin. Not content with this, newly promoted G/Cpt Grice formed his own force by arming 70 of his airmen with rifles.

October 1939 proved a dismal month as the country entered the period now known as the 'Phoney War'. Despite all the prophecies of instant attack by the Luftwaffe very little happened. The only signs of confrontation were those of friendly rivalry that took place between the two regular squadrons and the auxiliary squadron.

601 were affectionately known as the 'millionaires' mob', for within their ranks were such gentry as Max Aitken, Loel Guinness, Roger Bushell and many others. They wore blue ties instead of the regulation black, lined their tunics in bright red silk and wore silk scarves inside their flying jackets. Nearly every officer owned a sports car and many of them their own private aircraft as well. Although branded amateurs by 32 and 79 Squadrons, they were later to prove themselves as equals.

November saw a slight improvement in the weather, allowing several suspect aircraft to be investigated by the Biggin squadrons but a real taste of the action to come did not happen until the 21st of the month. From early morning several of the coastal radar stations had picked up 'blips' on their screens. At 10 am, yellow section of 79 Squadron were ordered to the forward airfield at Hawkinge, just above the cliffs at Folkestone. This enabled them to make contact with a potential enemy aircraft that much sooner. Whilst a section usually consisted of three aircraft, engine failure on one of the Hurricanes meant that only two arrived to patrol the Dover area. The first contact that F/O Davies and F/Sgt Brown made was a friendly Avro Anson of Coastal Command. Then the vectors came in quickly as the two aircraft made for South Foreland. They did not have to wait long before the sinister sight of the Swastika and the Balkan Cross filled their gunsights. With a cry of 'Tally Ho', both aircraft dived on to their quarry, a Dornier 17, and opened fire at 60 yards. As pieces of the German aircraft flew off, one engine was seen to be on fire. Following through cloud, Davies and Brown had the satisfaction of seeing it drop into the Channel. First blood to 79 and Biggin Hill!

Eight days later it was the turn of 601 Squadron to go to war when six Blenheims were ordered to Northolt near London. Amidst intense security, the six aircraft joined with six Blenheims of 25 Squadron and carried out a devastating raid on the enemy seaplane base at Borkum in the Frisian Islands. All the aircraft returned to Debden safely with Fl/Lt Peacock receiving a DFC for his part in the operation.

'I say, old boy. Did you know that the Waafs have arrived?' The news spread like wildfire through Biggin Hill much to the annoyance of many of the wives. Mainly employed in the operations room, they gave a touch of glamour to every watch and many were to prove themselves as heroines during the blitz that was to come.

December again saw very little action. The winter was one of the severest on record with snow and hard frost being the norm. While this hampered any flying, it also kept the Luftwaffe at home.

At Biggin Hill, the new year brought several changes. 601 moved to

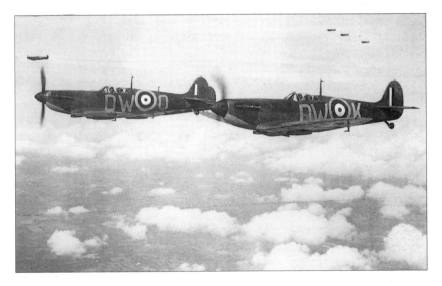

Spitfire Is of 610 Squadron.

'Scramble!' Pilots of 32 Squadron rush to get airborne. (Kent Messenger)

Tangmere, 79 to Manston and 32 to the satellite airfield at Gravesend. This was to allow for a further period of construction and expansion. For three months the workmen toiled at the base digging deep air raid shelters and finishing the concrete runway. Finally upon completion, 32 and 79 Squadrons returned to Biggin on the Bump after months of convoy escort duty without seeing a single German aircraft. Although they did not know it, things were about to change.

On 1st March 1940, Hitler issued invasion plans for Norway and Denmark and by 9th April, German forces had occupied the latter and were invading the former. By May, Norway too had surrendered and Hitler moved on to conquer Holland, Belgium and Luxembourg. As the troops pressed onward to France, it became obvious that a massive rescue operation had to be implemented for the British Expeditionary Force which, together with the French forces, had been attempting to slow the enemy advance in the hope that France might not be overrun.

It was in May that the greatest success of the war so far came to the Luftwaffe. The month also tested Fighter Command to the limit for the first time. It had long been obvious that the BEF was ill-equipped to defeat such a powerful army as the Germans. Even with the help of the RAF who had sent 400 aircraft in 25 squadrons to France, defeat was inevitable for many of the aircraft were slow and very vulnerable. Despite these obvious shortcomings, 79 Squadron were ordered to France, arriving at Merville on 10th May 1940. They were replaced at Biggin by No 610 (County of Chester) Auxiliary Squadron who moved down from Prestwick. Partnered by 32 Squadron, the pace of war quickened as both units began to carry the war across to the Low Countries. 32 themselves were ordered to strafe Ypenburg airfield in Holland where a large force of German troop carriers had assembled. Flying down to refuel at the forward airfield at Manston, twelve Hurricanes set off and flew directly across the Channel. Approaching Ypenburg, the aircraft slid into position and one by one, fired their guns in anger. The result was 16 burning Junkers 52 transports.

79 Squadron returned to their home base on 21st May having just got out of France in time before the Germans arrived. Biggin Hill was to play a definitive role in Operation Dynamo, the evacuation of the BEF from Dunkirk, but not so 32 and 79 Squadrons who were both sent away for rest periods, the former going to Wittering and the latter to Digby. Both stations were far from the battle front of South East England. Their replacements were Hurricane detachments of Nos 229 and 213 Squadrons and No 242 (Canadian) Squadron, the first of many Commonwealth squadrons to fly from Biggin. Briefings for the

evacuation were carried out under complete security as the squadrons prepared for the task ahead.

At 6.57 pm on 26th May, Vice Admiral Ramsay received orders for Dynamo to commence. The next day all three Biggin squadrons were in action and had many contacts with the enemy. Day one saw 213 and 242 on a joint patrol over Gravelines and shooting down two Me 109s for no loss. All of this changed on day two when 213 Squadron found themselves amongst a formation of Ju 88s and He 111s escorted by 109s. The bombers were attacking the rescue ships in Dunkirk Harbour and the shock of seeing the Hurricanes ensured that many of the bombs were jettisoned into the sea. From this fight, 213 shot down a Me 109 and damaged a Ju 88 for the loss of two Hurricanes. Sgt Boyd bailed out from his aircraft and was picked up in the sea, being back at Biggin Hill within 24 hours.

610 had moved over to Gravesend for Dynamo. Their Spitfires were in action over the beaches from day one dispatching three Me 109s into the Channel. As they flew over the hundreds of craft either crossing the Channel or anchored just off Dunkirk Harbour, the pilots could not help but feel a pang of admiration for these brave sailors. In amongst the larger naval craft were little seaside boats, yachts, trawlers, in fact every type of boat imaginable. On the beach itself they could see the beleaguered army, looking like a trail of ants, wading out to the waiting boats. Overhead the Luftwaffe were bombing and machine gunning the troops for Goering had promised Hitler that he would prevent the Dunkirk evacuation by air assault rather than risk a tank attack getting caught in boggy ground.

The weather deteriorated on 28th May but still the Biggin squadrons were airborne to cover the retreating troops. From the 26th, aircraft from 11 Group flew 321 sorties against superior German formations. By the 30th, the weather had got worse, keeping most of the Luftwaffe at home. This enabled 68,014 troops to be evacuated from the beaches but with the better weather on 1st June, the attacks began in earnest once again. More battles involving the Biggin squadrons came on 2nd June and the next day saw the remainder of the French troops taken off the beaches. Finally at 2.23 am on the 4th, the Admiralty reported that Dynamo had been completed: 224,585 British and 112,546 French and Belgians had been evacuated. At the conclusion of the operation, Churchill stated to the nation: 'Wars are not won by evacuations. But there was a victory inside this deliverance which should be noted. It was gained by the Royal Air Force.'

In June 1940, Biggin's home squadrons, Nos 32 and 79, returned after their brief spells of rest whilst the Dunkirk squadrons departed to other airfields. There was, however, no rest for Fighter Command as it continued to cover the withdrawal of the last remnants of the BEF. In addition the Hurricanes of both squadrons carried out escort duties to the Blenheims bombing enemy-held harbours. The month also brought further bad news when on the 10th, Italy declared war on Britain and France and Norway capitulated. By the 14th, the German army had entered Paris and it became obvious that they would not stop there. The next inviting conquest was Great Britain.

'What General Weygand called the Battle of France is over. I expect the Battle of Britain is about to begin. Upon this battle depends the survival of Christian civilisation.' So spoke Winston Churchill. He continued, 'Let us therefore brace ourselves to our duties and so bear ourselves that, if the British Empire and its Commonwealth last for a thousand years, men will still say: This was their finest hour.'

On this side of the water and at Biggin Hill in particular, it was realised that the odds were stacked against us. Although the output of new aircraft was rising steadily, Fighter Command only had 57 squadrons totalling 600+ fighters to combat the German menace. It was also known that the fiercest fighting would be over Kent with No 11 Group, consisting of 21 squadrons, in the forefront of the forthcoming battle. At Biggin Hill, 610 left Gravesend to join 32 Squadron whilst their comrades of 79 moved down to Hawkinge. The airfield also played host to many dignitaries including the Prime Minister and the King, all of them anxious to wish the squadrons the very best of luck in their fight against a superior force of aircraft.

On 8th July, 610 moved back to Biggin Hill with Spitfire Is and on the 10th were joined by No 141 Squadron equipped with the Boulton Paul Defiant fighter. As Sqd/Ldr Richardson led his aircraft down from Turnhouse in Scotland he felt excited that at last his squadron was to meet the enemy. The Defiant had introduced a new tactical concept in two-seat fighters whereby no forward firing guns were fitted. All offensive power was concentrated in the rear cockpit by a four-gun, power-operated turret. 264 Squadron had taken the Defiant into battle on 12th May 1940 with splendid results. On the 29th of that month the squadron destroyed 37 enemy aircraft in one operation, the Germans mistakenly identifying the Defiants as Hurricanes and diving on their supposedly defenceless tails. By the 31st, Defiants had shot down 65 enemy aircraft and were thus dubbed infallible.

By 18th July 141 were ready for operations and although the squadron had settled in the south camp at Biggin Hill, the aircraft were to be flown to West Malling, a satellite airfield to Biggin Hill. The first scramble came the next day when the twelve Defiants flew to the forward airfield at Hawkinge. By mid-day they were at readiness and were airborne at 12.32pm, when only nine of the aircraft took off. Engine trouble kept two on the ground whilst the third could not complete his take-off run.

They were assigned to patrol a line south of Folkestone at a height of 5,000 feet, reaching this just as the sirens around the area began to wail. The Luftwaffe were bombing Dover Harbour escorted by a force of Me 109s of the second Gruppe of Jagdgeschwader 51 operating from St Omer. Given a new course, 141 Squadron had been vectored to a point off Cap Gris Nez when Fl/Lt Loudon in Defiant L7001 saw the 109s diving out of the sun. Flying in sections of three line astern, the Defiants opened out to bring their guns round to deliver a beam attack. Unfortunately, since the last contact with the Defiants, the German pilots had realised the most vulnerable spot on this aircraft was its belly. The 109s therefore dived past the Defiants and came up underneath them where they knew the power-operated turret could not bear down on them. In seconds, two Defiants were going down in flames into the Channel. P/O J.R. Kemp with his gunner Sgt R. Crombie and P/O R.A. Howley with Sgt A.G. Curley were never seen again. Minutes later P/O R. Kidson and Sgt F.P.J. Atkins were also lost at sea. The slaughter continued as a fourth Defiant was hit. P/O J.R. Gardner, although wounded, managed to bale out before the aircraft hit the sea. His gunner, P/O D.M. Slater, was sadly lost.

With 141 Squadron trying desperately to fire at the 109s, the German pilots regrouped for a second attack as a fifth Defiant with Fl/Lt M.J. Loudon and P/O E. Farnes was hit in the engine. Managing to evade his aggressor and although wounded in the arm, Fl/Lt Loudon told his gunner to abandon the aircraft as he attempted to reach Hawkinge. He crashed just short of the airfield but lived. His gunner also survived, having been picked up by the Air Sea Rescue service in the Channel.

The carnage continued when a sixth Defiant crashed at Elmsvale Road, Dover. Fl/Lt I.D.G. Donald DFC and P/O A.C. Hamilton were killed outright as the seventh aircraft, although badly hit, managed to crash-land at Hawkinge. Tragically the pilot, P/O I.M. McDougall had advised his gunner, Sgt J.F. Wise, to bale out when the aircraft lost power. Although the engine was emitting black smoke and glycol was streaming out, it picked up sufficiently for the pilot to attempt to make Hawkinge. After seeing that his gunner was swimming strongly for the shore, he headed for the airfield. Sgt Wise was never seen again.

Only two intact Defiants returned to Hawkinge and they themselves may not have made it but for the timely intervention of 111 Squadron with their Hurricanes. For the Luftwaffe it was a triumph even though one 109, flown by Feldwebel Heilmann, was damaged by a Defiant and crashed on return to St Omer, killing him.

For 141 Squadron, its first action of the war had ended in tragic circumstances with six aircraft lost, four pilots and five gunners killed and the other aircraft badly damaged. The squadron was released from operations straightaway and sent to Prestwick for conversion to night fighting duties. At Biggin Hill, the rumour had got around that the entire squadron had been wiped out. The fact that this was not entirely true did nothing to bring a glimmer of light to the entire sad affair. The operation justly earned the title 'the slaughter of the innocents'.

The rest of the month saw 32 and 610 Squadrons covering the Channel convoys and coming into daily contact with the enemy as the Luftwaffe continued to probe our defences. Along the coasts of Kent and Sussex, the Chain Home and Chain Home Low radar stations were operational from dawn to dusk. Together with the Observer Corps, they tracked every enemy and friendly aircraft that entered their range. The 32 Squadron diary for 20th July 1940 gives a vivid account of an everyday operation from Biggin Hill.

'Great morning, noisy afternoon. Hawkinge again responsible. Squadron patrol Dover below low cloud. Red Knight [pilot's nickname] unwisely said he saw something above cloud. Green section went to see. Didn't. Pancake all. Just doing so when we saw a barbecue in progress over Dover. Interest immediately revived and we tore back to have a "butchers". Red section nominated a Me Jaguar, chased it through spray and tipped it into the sea. Received unwelcome attention of another Jaguar.

'Later we intercepted, without any exaggeration, a total of at least 20,000 assorted Huns! The following tipped stuff into the drink: Hector, Pete B, Sgt Higgins, Humph and Red Knight. The Mandarin converted three non-smoking Ju 87s into smoking 87s but earned the attention of at least 4 squadrons of 109s to such an extent that he just couldn't make the drome (fan stopped). He forced landed in a field, 2532 caught fire and burnt out. Mandarin jumped out with cuts and a string of language which did justice to his high position.'

The date set for the commencement of the annihilation of the RAF was Saturday, 10th August 1940 but bad weather prevented any flying by either side over the next two days. Therefore it was on Monday, 12th August that 'Adlertag' or 'Eagle Day' began.

At Biggin Hill it was the turn of 610 Squadron to be at dawn readiness. The ground crews had been up since before first light ensuring that all the Spitfires were serviceable. With a full complement reported, the pilots had nothing to do but sit around the dispersal hut until the scramble came. On the opposite side of the Channel it was the same situation. Early morning mist had prevented the assault from beginning directly it became light and this had enabled Goering to pass a message to his bomber force that he was confident that air superiority would be gained in four days!

On the coasts of Kent and Sussex, the radar stations had first picked up signs of activity in the Pas de Calais region around 7am. From there, the enemy movements were passed onto Fighter Command Headquarters 11 Group and seven sector stations of which Biggin Hill was one. Twenty minutes later the telephone in the 610 dispersal hut rang. The duty orderly answered it, turned round and yelled, 'Squadron scramble. Dungeness at 2,000 feet.' In one rush the pilots raced to their waiting aircraft where their ground crews were ready to strap them in. In three minutes, all the Spitfires were airborne and Sqd/Ldr Ellis of 610 Squadron was talking calmly to the controller back at Biggin Hill.

Crossing New Romney and approaching Ashford, the nine Do 215s with their escorting Me 109s were spotted. With a cry of 'Tally Ho', indicating to the controller that the enemy had been sighted, the Spitfires of 610 Squadron fell upon the enemy formation.

Immediately the 109s broke rank and came at the Spitfires. In a matter of minutes or maybe seconds, the sky was a mass of screaming engines and staccato gun-fire. In the ensuing battle, two 109s were confirmed shot down with six damaged. Although it was first blood for 610 Squadron, P/O E.B.B. Smith in Spitfire L1044 was shot down but managed to bale out and land in the sea whilst Spitfires P6806 and R6621 were damaged but repairable, with P9495 crashing somewhere over Romney Marsh. All the pilots baled out safely although there were injuries to P/O Smith and F/O F.T. Gardiner.

Suddenly the sky was empty of enemy aircraft, for it must be remembered that the Germans had a limited time over Britain before low fuel demanded they return to their French airfields. The bombers however had hit their target, a radar station on the Kent coast. Sqd/Ldr Ellis led his eleven Spitfires back to Biggin Hill, well pleased with the squadron's first contact with the enemy.

In the afternoon it was the turn of 32 Squadron who had flown down to Hawkinge at noon. Scrambled at 2.30 pm, it was found to be a false call but another at 4.50 pm saw a formation of Do 215s again escorted by Me 109s intent upon an attack on Dover. Led by Sqd/Ldr Michael Crossley, 32 Squadron had the upper hand as they downed eleven enemy aircraft for the loss of Hurricane N2596 which crashed near the airfield. Its pilot, P/O A.R.H. Barton was unhurt.

Hawkinge had been on the receiving end of the bombers and although technically out of action, the Hurricanes of 32 managed to land. Just as they were being refuelled, another attack materialised over the airfield. Looking skywards, the ground crews nervously continued to fill the aircraft until the Station Commander roared over the tannoy for everyone to take cover. Hurriedly turning off the fuel bowsers, the crews joined all but the essential personnel in the shelters. Five minutes later they emerged to find the station a total mess yet with not one Hurricane touched. Commenting that 'Hawkinge was too blitzy', 32 Squadron flew back to Biggin Hill.

Both squadrons were stood down for the day at sunset as the Station Intelligence Officer summed up the day's achievements. The squadrons had flown 36 sorties with five enemy casualties confirmed, 16 unconfirmed and four probables with damage. All the Biggin pilots were safe with one in hospital. Not a bad day's score. If only the rest of the battle could be the same!

Though scheduled for Monday, 12th August, historians now denote Tuesday, 13th August 1940 as 'Eagle Day'. Again, the real thrust of 'Adlerangriff' came in the afternoon due to the fact that mist and fog in the morning was slow to clear in the Channel. Despite this, formations did take off in the morning but were recalled personally by Goering. Three units however had faulty radios and did not receive the signal. They pressed on to bomb Eastchurch, Odiham and Portland.

At midday on the 14th, 610 Squadron gave chase to a formation of Ju 87 Stukas and Me 109s, claiming six confirmed with seven probables. Having shot down a 109, Sgt B.E.D. Gardiner flying Spitfire K4997, was forced to land at Wye at around 12.30 pm. He was admitted to Ashford Hospital with gunshot wounds in his arm but his aircraft was repairable. At the same time, Spitfire L1009 was damaged in combat but landed back at Biggin Hill to fly another day. 32 Squadron had similar luck when they were scrambled 30 minutes after 610. Two Hurricanes were damaged with another written off but all three pilots were safe including P/O Barton who had force-landed at Hawkinge again. That night it was tales of heroism and luck in the bar of the White Hart at nearby Brasted.

Thursday, 15th August dawned fine and warm as a ridge of high

An airman with a red flag guides aircraft clear of unexploded bombs as Hurricanes of 32 Squadron come in to land on 15th August 1940. (Chaz Bowyer)

pressure arrived over the country. With this forecast, the Luftwaffe prepared for a major assault on the airfields and radar stations. The raid was also aimed at bringing as many British fighters as possible into the battle with the object of destroying them. The second phase of the battle was about to begin.

The early hours were quiet enough but from 11.00 am onwards five main attacks developed. At Biggin Hill both 32 and 610 Squadrons were at readiness from first light but not until 2.30 pm did the scramble come. 32, who were already at Hawkinge, were airborne in minutes but were mystified when the controller sent them to Harwich. Seeing a gaggle of Me 109s in front of them heading for home, they realised why and rapidly caught up with them. A ferocious dogfight followed with Hurricanes and Me 109s trying to get the better of each other. During the battle, 32 lost Hurricane N2459 when it was shot down and crashed at Pye Sands, Pennyhole Bay just south of Harwich. P/O D.M. Grice, no relation to the Biggin Hill station commander, baled out but was badly burned. He was rescued from the sea by an MTB and taken to the naval hospital at Shotley. In the same action, P/O B. Wlasnowalski had to force-land with a glycol leak but his aircraft was deemed repairable. The enemy, however, suffered badly at the hands of 32, losing several 109s.

Running low on fuel, 32 Squadron flew back to Biggin Hill only to be scrambled 90 minutes later to a position over Selsey Bill. Three hundred enemy aircraft were approaching Hampshire and Dorset as 32 once again threw themselves at the enemy. Leading red section, Mike Crossley soon despatched two Ju 88s into the sea as the enemy formation, surprised at the ferocity of the attack, dropped their bombs at random. Several other Me 109s and 110s were seen to be in flames but with so many aircraft in so little airspace, it was difficult to keep an accurate account. In this attack however, Hurricane P3552, was damaged but repairable with Sgt B. Henson unhurt.

The fifth and last assault of the day came at 6.15 pm when enemy formations headed for Biggin Hill and Kenley, another Fighter Command airfield just a short distance away. Both Biggin squadrons were airborne with 610 making their presence felt by downing two Do 17s, whereupon the escorting 109s turned and fled for home. The German formation became so split up that they missed their original targets and instead bombed West Malling, a grass airfield still under construction.

Whilst all this was going on, a second formation had bombed Croydon airfield. As 32 Squadron were returning to Biggin Hill, they noticed the large columns of black smoke coming from the area. The squadron diary says it all: 'We turned and beat it for Croydon as fast as we could. Sure enough when we approached, we saw a large party in progress. Masses of Me 110s were dive-bombing the place. As they did not appear to notice our approach, we steered straight past them with the object of getting between them and the sun.'

It was the perfect end to a hectic day as 32 Squadron downed three Do 17s, two Ju 88s and four Me 109s. The squadron had been scrambled three times together with all the 21 squadrons of Fighter Command. The cost to the Luftwaffe on this day was 72 aircraft, a grievous loss. The British casualties were 34 aircraft lost, 17 pilots killed and 17 wounded. Whilst this may seem a lot of aircraft and pilots to lose, in comparison the Luftwaffe had flown 1,786 sorties with nearly every available fighter being used in an attempt to destroy Fighter Command. Despite all this, no real success was achieved by the enemy. Later in the day, Goering issued an order prohibiting the presence of more than one officer in any single air crew. It was an attempt to reduce the officer casualties on bombers which by now had reached serious proportions.

The nine o'clock news that night caused a hush in the bar of the White Hart. The same was happening at the Old Jail and the Black Horse at Biggin Hill, another two favourite watering holes for the squadrons. The news of great losses for the Luftwaffe was met by clapping and loud cheering and it was long after closing time when pilots and ground crew stumbled out into the warm night and made their way back to the airfield.

The next day, a Friday, also proved successful for the Biggin squadrons with 32 claiming nine destroyed and 610 claiming three probables. With another warm sunny day in prospect, readiness was from first light despite the celebrations of the night before. Once again the enemy chose the airfields of West Malling, Hornchurch and Tangmere as the main targets. Sadly, Fl/Lt W.H.C. Warner flying Spitfire R6802 was lost when he failed to return from a dogfight with 109s over Dungeness. Another 610 Spitfire was also damaged in the same fight but P/O D.McT. Gray managed to land back at Biggin Hill.

The past two hectic days of effort by Luftflotten 2 and 3 had taken its toll on men and machines and in contrast, Saturday, 17th August was limited mainly to reconnaissance sorties. Likewise it gave Fighter Command a brief respite to take stock for whilst the command had lost aircraft, it was the shortage of pilots that was causing Dowding most concern. He had suggested taking Fairey Battle pilots from the light bomber squadrons to fill the gaps and although the Air Staff at first refused his request, they later agreed to take pilots from the Battle squadrons and from the Army Co-Operation Lysander squadrons. The loss of aircraft, however, was grossly exaggerated by the Luftwaffe who had confidently stated that 372 Spitfires, 179 Hurricanes, 9 Curtiss Tomahawks and 12 Defiants had been destroyed. They further calculated that Fighter Command only possessed 300 serviceable aircraft whereas the figure was really 700. It said much for the enemy intelligence service!

With the attacks on most of the other Kentish airfields, everyone at Biggin Hill felt that they must be the next on Goering's list. They did not have to wait long for just as the good people of Kent were leaving church on Sunday, 18th August, the sirens began to wail. Hurrying to the nearest shelters, they looked anxiously up at an increasingly cloudy sky but as yet saw no enemy aircraft. The Biggin squadrons were at top line readiness but were kept on the ground whilst squadrons from other airfields attacked the German formations. First it was Kenley's turn to receive about 100 bombs, which caused total devastation. Then attention was turned to Croydon and another load of accurate bombs rained down. West Malling suffered a further blow and as the scenario unfolded, everyone felt sure Biggin was next. The plots on the sector room table showed 50+ bandits coming in over Tunbridge Wells and Sevenoaks. There was no doubt. At last the dispersal telephones rang. '32 and 610 Squadrons scramble – protect base.'

Twelve Hurricanes of 32 and fifteen Spitfires of 610 Squadrons were airborne in minutes, engine boosters at full power to gain as much height as possible. A short distance away, aircraft of Kampfgeschwader 76, a crack bomber unit based at Beauvais, Creil and Croneilles-on-Vexin in France were heading for Biggin Hill. Comprising Ju 88s and Do 17s, the crews were ticking off the twelve minutes or so it would take them to reach their target.

Back on the ground, the tannoy ordered all non-essential personnel to don their tin hats and take cover. The 58th Heavy AA Regiment on airfield defence duties trained their guns skyward, eager to get in their shots and perhaps down one or two bandits. The Biggin Hill contingent of the Home Guard made sure their rifles had ammunition and were fully cocked, they too intent on giving the enemy a bad time. The duty controller at Biggin knew what was about to happen. 'Enemy approaching base – Angels 12, attack imminent.' As he spoke the words, the airfield came within the sights of the enemy at the same time as 32 and 610 Squadrons came out of the sun at them. The first bombs fell on the eastern side of the airfield causing little damage, but in the shelters the women and men could not believe the sound of exploding bombs could be so penetrating through the thick shelter surround.

One by one the enemy aircraft dropped their bombs with deadly accuracy. Thirty one Dorniers led by their Commandant, Oberst-leutnant Frohlick, were intent on wiping Biggin Hill from the map. One particular aircraft piloted by Oberleutnant Rudolph Lamberty came in at zero feet and after dropping his bombs was met by a fusillade of Bofors and small arms fire. In his own words: 'Half-way across the airfield all hell broke loose.' In addition to the gunfire, the PAC (Parachute and Cable) defence system had been fired and Lamberty had collided with one of the wires which tore a hole in the leading edge of one wing. One of the Bofors shells also hit the port wing, blowing a sizeable hole in it. Struggling to gain control, Lamberty shouted to his crew to prepare for a crash landing. Seeing the bomber coming in low over Leaves Green, the Home Guard raised their rifles as one man and fired at the stricken bomber. Brushing a hedge at the end of a field, the Do 17 clipped the branches of several trees and with flame and smoke streaming from its port engine, settled down on the grass in a wheels-up crash landing.

Meanwhile overhead the Biggin squadrons had achieved success with Ju 88s, Do 17s, Do 215s and Me 109s falling to the guns of 32 and 610. The former had lost seven Hurricanes but with no loss of life although several of the pilots were badly wounded; 610 had fared a little better losing two aircraft, both pilots shaken but not injured. The airfield itself had suffered very badly with numerous craters around the runways. There were various injuries and two airmen were killed. For a raid that had only lasted ten minutes, 500 bombs had been dropped with one direct hit on the MT sheds damaging several vehicles beyond repair. For many of the personnel it was the first taste of fire. Despite this, the Waafs displayed tremendous courage throughout the raid and this resulted in the first of three Military Medals to be awarded to the Waafs at Biggin Hill whilst under attack.

It was at a very battered Biggin that 32 and 610 Squadrons landed, carefully avoiding the large craters. Immediately the pilots joined all the other personnel in filling them with whatever hard materials they could find. In late afternoon, 32 were scrambled again as a large enemy force attacked the Thames Estuary airfields. The squadron accounted for five Me 109s.

That evening in the bars of the White Hart, the Old Jail and Black Horse, and especially the Crown at Leaves Green, the talk was of the captured German airmen and just who did deal the fatal blow to the Dornier. A report in the *Daily Telegraph* dated 20th August 1940 gives credit to the Home Guard but this is thought to be a very good piece of propaganda rather than actual fact. Intelligence reports after the incident give equal credit to the ground defence guns, the Home Guard and two pilots from No 111 Squadron, then operating from Croydon, who fired and hit the enemy aircraft. The argument was to continue for many more weeks to come!

The next few days proved a welcome break from constant action as cloud covered the country keeping the Luftwaffe at home. With a break in the cloud on the 22nd, a British convoy code-named 'Totem' was passing through the Straits of Dover when it came under attack from the German long range guns situated along the Pas de Calais. At 12.40 pm, the Luftwaffe were bombing the ships and 610 Squadron were ordered off to provide protection. Tangling with a bunch of 109s, Sgt D.F. Corfein's Spitfire R6695 was shot down but he managed to crash-land at Hawkinge unhurt. 32 had been ordered off to Hawkinge at mid morning but P/O J. Peiffer crashed on landing at the grass airfield. He was, however, unhurt and his Hurricane, P3205, was repairable.

The full force of the Luftwaffe returned on 24th August, now recognised as the beginning of the third phase of the battle. Both 32 and 610 were scrambled at various times during the day. In the morning sorties, 32 lost five Hurricanes with only three injured pilots whilst 610 lost four Spitfires with, again, only three pilots slightly injured. Once again, the battle was entering a very crucial phase but it was the number of pilots that was still causing Dowding the most concern. The second phase of the battle (8th to 18th August) had cost Fighter Command 94 pilots either killed or missing with 60 wounded. Those that had survived were very tired and in need of rest periods. Replacing them with new and raw pilots, as yet untried in battle, seemed to Dowding at least, as though he were feeding the Christians to the lions but what choice did he have? Only battle experience would ensure that somehow they survived.

Rest periods did indeed come to all the squadrons including No 32, by now nicknamed 'The Pursuit'. The news of a move to Acklington, far from the battle front of Kent, was a tonic. On 27th August they flew their Hurricanes from Biggin Hill for the last time. 'So long Biggin. No, we would not have you again for worlds but we would not have missed you. You made men out of boys and we're grateful. 32 Squadron will never forget you.' So wrote the squadron diarist. For nine years 32 had flown from the 'Bump' and at present was the top scoring squadron of Fighter Command with 102 enemy aircraft to its credit and one DSO and five DFCs awarded to its pilots. Their last sortie from Biggin Hill on Sunday, 25th August however had ended in tragedy when P/O K.R. Gillman, a very popular member of the squadron, failed to return from a sortie over Dover at 7 pm. Neither his body nor his aircraft were ever found but his name lives forever on the Runnymede Memorial. He was just 19 years old.

79 (Madras Presidency) Squadron flew their Hurricanes down from Acklington as soon as 32 had departed. Glad to be back at Biggin, Sqd/Ldr J.H. Heyworth led his Hurricanes carefully in, noting the damage that had been done to his old base. They had time only to refuel before being scrambled to Hawkinge on instant readiness.

Thirty minutes after landing, the squadron was airborne again meeting the enemy half-way across the Channel. In as many minutes they had gained four probables and shot down a He 59 Seaplane. Just for good measure they sank two E-boats with machine gun fire as they raced out from Calais to rescue the unfortunate German pilots bobbing up and down in the Channel swell. All of this took place within the view of the Prime Minister who that day was in a control centre dug out of the Dover cliffs. 79 Squadron had returned home!

The stubborn resistance put up by Fighter Command over the past few weeks had caused a delay in the German plans for an invasion of England. Although the German-held French ports were full of invasion barges, Goering could not yet report to Hitler that the skies belonged to his Luftwaffe. Thus, the German High Command would not give the order for the invasion to begin. The next few days however, were to see Fighter Command come its closest to total defeat.

Friday, 30th August 1940 also very nearly saw the demise of Biggin Hill. It began with a renewal of the shipping raids in the Channel. At 10.30 am, the Chain Home radars picked up three waves totalling 100 aircraft at 15,000 feet. It became obvious to the Sector controller at Biggin that this force was intending to attack the fighter airfields, including his own! Sixteen squadrons were scrambled from various bases, including 79 and 610. As if they knew their very existence was at stake, the pilots threw their aircraft into the fray. The sky became criss-crossed with vapour trails as several furious dog-fights were fought out. 79 Squadron lost two Hurricanes with another two damaged but repairable, the most spectacular escape being that of P/O E.J. Morris who collided with a He 111 of 10/KG1 during a combat over Reigate. Managing to bale out safely, he saw his beloved P3203 break into a thousand pieces and fall to earth. With the German formation in disarray, the bombs fell wide of the airfield but sadly landed in the vicinity of Keston and Biggin Hill villages. 79 and 610 Squadrons shared ten victories between them, which could have been more had they not been forced to land at Biggin Hill due to low fuel.

The second attack of the day came at 1.30 pm when a large armada crossed the coast between Dover and Dungeness. Once over the coast it split and various aircraft headed for Biggin Hill, Kenley, North Weald and Tangmere. Whilst the Biggin Hill attack failed, the radar stations at Dover, Pevensey, Rye, Foreness, Fairlight and Beachy Head were all put out of action. The advance warning of attack had virtually gone.

At 6 pm the same day, the sirens in Biggin Hill village began to wail again. On the airfield the evening meal had just started as the melancholy sound filled the ears. This time the enemy had caught Biggin Hill without any prior warning as a group of Ju 88s split from the main force following the Ashford railway line. Carrying 1,000 lb bombs, the Ju 88s swept in at low level and had the sky to themselves. The damage they inflicted this time nearly put the station out of action. Workshops, the transport section, stores, barracks, the armoury, the WAAF quarters and a hangar all disappeared under the deluge of bombs. The noise was indescribable as explosion after explosion rent the air. In the shelters, the crump, crump of detonating bombs sounded as though they were coming through the roof. Some of the Waafs and the men began to pray out loud as the devastation continued. At ground level, the power, gas and water mains were all severed with the main GPO telephone link damaged in three places, thus no link was possible with headquarters 11 Group. Two aircraft were destroyed in the hangar which received a direct hit, but worst of all was the bomb which hit one of the shelters crammed full with airmen. As the roof and sides caved in, 40 lost their lives. In a Waaf shelter, a bomb which had landed nearby blew the door in and entombed the girls in dust and rubble. Choking and crying at the same time, many started pulling the bricks and mortar away in an attempt to get out.

Suddenly it was silence as the enemy raced for home. 610 were already airborne fighting elsewhere when the attack happened but 79 Squadron had just managed to get six Hurricanes off in time to defend the airfield. They got two probables for the loss of one Hurricane, P/O P.F. Mayhew being unhurt. Ironically, Sqd/Ldr Mike Crossley, who had flown down in a 32 Squadron Hurricane to visit his old base, lost his aircraft in the attack. Looking sadly at the battered remains, he shook his head. 'This would never have happened if 32 was still here,' was his comment!

Late into the night, recovery was still going on. The dead were laid out in neat rows for identification whilst the injured were rushed to local hospitals. Section Officer Felicity Hanbury, in charge of the Biggin Hill Waafs, made her way among the dead girls. Visibly shaking, she pulled a cigarette out of her coat pocket. A voice some distance away shouted at her. 'Put that cigarette out before you blow us all to bits. Can't you smell the ruddy gas?' Nervously, she threw the unlit cigarette on the ground and moved on to comfort the injured as best she could. Never had she seen such devastation or death on such a scale.

As dawn broke over the airfield, heralding another fine day, work was still going on to supply essential services. The GPO engineers had worked all through the night to repair the broken cables for it was essential that contact with 11 Group headquarters and the other airfields in the sector was re-established. This was also the day that 610 Squadron were to be rested as the Spitfires and crews prepared to leave after breakfast for Acklington. Since 8th July 1940 they had flown from the Bump and seen action nearly every day. There was not one man who did not want a rest from constant battle. They were to be replaced by No 72 (Basutoland) Squadron who brought their Spitfires down from Acklington.

The first of the day's raids were picked up by radar shortly after 8 am leaving the French coast. Biggin Hill was not on their list of targets then, but by midday, as over 100 aircraft crossed the coast at Dungeness, it became obvious that this time it was. Dropping their bombs safely from 12,000 feet, the Do 215s had it all their own way. Once again the runway was peppered with craters rendering it unusable whilst further damage was done to hangars, the married quarters and the officers' mess. 79 Squadron who had flown to the defence of Dover, attacked by the same raid, were forced to land at Croydon. G/Cpt Grice had every available man and woman put to filling in the craters and by teatime, one runway was in use allowing 72 Squadron to fly in from Acklington.

During the afternoon there were sporadic raids over Kent and both squadrons were kept busy. The duty controller over this period, Sqd/Ldr Roger Frankland, noted that a small formation of Ju 88s were flying along the line of the Ashford/Redhill railway line. He was in no doubt of the intended target! 'Tin hats on everybody, please. Those not essential take cover.' Just as he finished, ten Ju 88s arrived overhead and in five minutes had demolished practically all that was left standing of Biggin Hill. This time it was a direct hit on the operations block which once again severed all the good work that the GPO engineers and many other people had done over the past two days. The first bomb cut all the telephone lines connecting the ops room to the rest of the station. Only the direct line to Uxbridge, the 11 Group headquarters remained

CO Gp/Capt Grice congratulates three Waafs awarded the Military Medal, including Sgt Elizabeth Mortimer, Cpl Elspeth Henderson (now Section Officer) and Sgt Emily Turner. (IWM)

intact manned by two Waafs, Sgt Emily Turner and Cpl Elspeth Henderson. They vehemently refused to leave their posts knowing that they were the only connection with the outside world. When at last, Sgt Turner was dragged protesting from her switchboard, it was none too soon as a 500 lb bomb ripped through her position. It exploded in the Defence Teleprinter Network Room. G/Cpt Grice, who was in the ops room at this time, was cut about the face and head by the flying debris. The shock of the blast sent his beloved pipe flying but groping around in the dark and rubble he retrieved it. Shoving it into his mouth, he rushed to assist Cpl Henderson, knocked down by the explosion.

Biggin Hill was indeed a sorry sight with the station armoury ablaze, four Spitfires burnt out and many other buildings on fire. Despite the devastation, only one death was reported, that of a local Boys Brigade bugler who was on loan for signal duties. Sadly, he died from his injuries several days later. The local emergency services rushed to the airfield to assist the RAF fire and ambulance teams. The injured were taken to the sick quarters and Bromley hospital as every able bodied man and woman once again set to in an attempt to clear up the mess that was their station. The day also saw Fighter Command's heaviest losses with 39 fighters shot down and 14 pilots killed. Although the enemy lost 41 aircraft over the day's attacks, the odds were still very much against Fighter Command being able to hold out. With Manston on the Thanet coast already out of action and West Malling, Lympne and Hawkinge in nearly the same position, the enemy only had to repeat what had happened to Biggin Hill at Kenley, Tangmere, Croydon and Gravesend and no station south of London would be serviceable.

With no ops block to control two squadrons, 72 were forced to move to Croydon whilst 79 were to be controlled from a makeshift ops room set up in a shop in Biggin Hill village. Engineers once again toiled all night to make sure telephone lines to all the essential services and establishments were operating in the temporary room. By morning, although very battered, the station was again operational.

The next day, 1st September, was a Sunday and arrangements had been made to bury those killed in the past week's raids in the cemetery just beyond the airfield. Fifty coffins were laid neatly alongside 50 newly dug graves. By noon, the relatives and friends of the dead were gathered around the cemetery whilst the station was represented by G/Cpt Grice and Section Officer Hanbury. Under a cloudy grey sky, the Padre commenced his service just as the sirens in Biggin Hill and Keston began to wail accompanied by the roar of Merlin engines as 79 Squadron were scrambled to protect their base. Looking skywards, the Station Commander advised everyone to take cover before the service could continue. Only when the last civilian had taken to the shelters did he ask the Padre, now flanked only by himself and S/Officer Hanbury, to continue.

Overhead, Do 17s of Luftflotte 2 attacked the airfield for the sixth time in three days. As the noise of exploding bombs made both officers wince and wonder at what further devastation the enemy could bring to their airfield, the Padre, hesitating now and then, attempted to make himself heard above the noise of aircraft and explosions. In minutes however, the attack was over and as silence once again fell over the mournful scene, the civilians came out of the shelters and Biggin Hill's dead were buried in peace at last.

To say that Biggin Hill was a shambles was to put it mildly. Had Goering and his Luftwaffe been able to see it from where G/Cpt Grice stood, they would have realised just how close they were to gaining command of the skies. Luckily, they could not, despite the fact that the station received further attacks from the 1st September to the 4th. Over this period, only one Hurricane, P3676, of 79 Squadron was lost. The pilot, Sgt J. Wright, survived the crash but died of his wounds the next day. Tuesday, 5th September saw a further Hurricane, P5207, flown by Fl/Lt G.O.L. Hayson, damaged but with skill he managed to land it back at base where it was deemed repairable.

Although not many buildings were left standing at Biggin Hill, it mystified the station commander just why the Luftwaffe kept bombing his station. Taking a look for himself from the air, he felt convinced that whilst any one single structure was left intact, the attacks would continue. From the air, one of the hangars appeared untouched even though it was just a shell. Taking it upon himself, G/Cpt Grice felt that it must be razed to the ground and proceeded to lay explosive charges all around it. He had planned to detonate the hangar during the usual 6 pm evening raid but on this occasion, the Luftwaffe declined to co-operate.

Realising that the expected raid was not going to materialise, he advised the ground crews to take cover and pressed the plunger. The resulting explosion was the loudest heard to date on the Bump and in one swoop, the entire hangar disintegrated. Shoving his pipe into his mouth, the station commander announced to all personnel that the destruction of Biggin Hill was complete! Sometime later the Group Captain was subject to a Court of Enquiry regarding his actions but nothing further was heard. Whether this was influenced by the fact that the major raids on the base suddenly ceased has never been established. This was, however, the beginning of the fourth phase of the Battle of Britain. The airfields were to be left alone at the expense of an intensive bombing campaign against London and the major cities. The Blitz proper had begun.

For Biggin Hill, the change of tactics was the answer to many people's prayers. The warm September weather allowed repair work to the runways and essential services to continue apace. The temporary ops room in the shop was still in operation but plans were hastily made to requisition a country house named Towerfields and turn it into a new operations room. On 8th September, 79 Squadron were posted away to Pembrey and in turn were replaced by No 92 Squadron. The Spitfire Is led by the CO, Sqd/Ldr P.J. Sanders, flew in at noon. With very little time to get used to the place, 92 were scrambled within hours and bagged an He 111 and two 109 probables to announce their presence. The next day they were again in action but lost three Spitfires in the last raid of the day. Spitfire L1077 crash-landed at Rye with P/O C.H.

Saunders admitted to hospital with shrapnel in his leg. P9372 was shot down at the same time, P/O W.C. Watling suffering bad burns to his face and hands as he baled out. Twenty minutes later, Spitfire R6596 returned to base badly damaged with P/O B. Wright unhurt.

The 12th of the month saw 72 Squadron return after their forced sojourn at Croydon. Work at repairing the runways and buildings on the Bump had progressed sufficiently to allow two squadrons to operate once again. The evening of the 12th saw both of them in the bar of the White Hart, battling for supremacy as the better squadron! By the time 92 arrived at Biggin Hill, their reputation had preceeded them. They enjoyed the high life and even had their own dance band made up of officers and other ranks. They were never without female company and many parties were held in the officers' mess, a large country house named Southwood. In addition, frequent trips to the London theatres and restaurants were very often the order of the day, lingering into the small hours when they staggered back to Biggin Hill ready to fight another day.

The timetable for the German invasion of England was once again postponed due to the resistance of the RAF during August. During the past two weeks the Luftwaffe had lost 107 bombers and two Stukas plus numerous 109s and 110s. Far from driving the RAF from the skies, the number of fighters never seemed to diminish. Little did the German High Command know that reserves were being brought to 11 Group from the other groups in different parts of the country. The Luftwaffe commanders decided that the only way to bring Britain to her knees was to strike at the heart of the country. London! Despite the capital being the main target of the Luftwaffe during September, Biggin Hill was still subject to raids. All of this was about to change however as dawn broke on Sunday, 15th September 1940, now known officially as Battle of Britain Day.

The German reconnaissance aircraft were about early. This usually indicated a day of big raids and although not known at the time, the day was to be a decisive one for the enemy. The 72 and 92 dispersals were alive early in the morning as ground crews checked, fuelled and re-armed the aircraft. In the dispersal huts themselves, large fires were burning as the pilots came in and threw themselves into chairs and sofas, determined to get the last minutes of sleep before the expected scramble came.

The hours passed slowly until 10.30 am when the first of the raiders came in over Kent. The plots began to show up thick and fast at the group operations room at Uxbridge. By coincidence, it was the day that the Prime Minister and Mrs Churchill had chosen to visit the operations room. Standing silently, they watched the scenario unfold in front of them. The first squadrons ordered up were 72 and 92 from Biggin. At the latter dispersal, twelve Merlin engines roared into life as the controller spoke to Brian Kingcome. 'Squadrons patrol Maidstone. Angels 120. Rendezvous with 72 over base.' Running down the well patched runway, they joined 72 in climbing as quickly as they could.

Meanwhile the enemy formation had spread out over Kent at heights ranging from 15,000 to 26,000 feet. As the enemy pilots saw the fighters approaching, all thoughts of formation flying and precision bombing left their heads. It was every man for himself! 72 and 92 Squadrons tore into the attack and in as many minutes had downed several Do 17s. Accurate bombing by the enemy was out of the question and so bombs were dropped at random all over south-east London. One heavy bomb damaged the Queen's private apartments in Buckingham Palace whilst others fell on the Royal lawn. By noon, the raid was over and both squadrons returned safely to Biggin Hill with no loss.

Scrambled again at 1.30 pm, 92 Squadron met the enemy over Canterbury. In a furious dogfight P/O Bob Holland's Spitfire, R6606, was hit and crashed near the coast but he managed to bale out, slightly injuring his ankle on landing. Two other Spitfires returned safely to the base although badly damaged.

For the Biggin squadrons it was a good day. Nine of the enemy confirmed destroyed plus a score of others damaged. That evening the bar of the White Hart was full as the pilots, in common with almost every family in the land, listened to the evening news bulletin. 'The RAF today shot down 185 enemy aircraft for the loss of 40 of our fighters, most of the pilots being saved.' Whilst the figures were later amended to 56 and 26, it was a much needed tonic and a triumph for Fighter Command. Two days later, Hitler decided to postpone Operation Sealion indefinitely.

The next day general cloud and rain precluded the enemy from launching any large scale raids although a small formation bombed East London, the Germans losing five aircraft for the loss of one fighter. On 13th September, 'B' Flight of No 141 Squadron flying the Boulton Paul Defiant flew into Biggin Hill. The type had now been relegated to night fighting duties since its disastrous time around the Dunkirk period.

141 were airborne as dusk fell on the 15th but found no success despite a renewed Luftwaffe night offensive against London. The next night proved to be exceptionally clear as P/O J. Waddingham with Sgt A.B. Cumbers as his gunner patrolled between Maidstone and

Sgts Laurence and Chard of 141 Squadron celebrate downing a Ju 88 over Bexley on 14th September 1940. (IWM)

Tonbridge. Thirty minutes into the patrol, Sgt Cumbers saw the silhouette of a Ju 88 standing out against the bright light of the moon. Searchlights were already combing the sky at the sound of aircraft engines and although these continually blinded both pilot and gunner, they got within 40 yards of the enemy without being seen. Six hundred rounds poured into the Ju 88 from the power-operated 0.303 Browning machine gun turret causing pieces to fly off the enemy aircraft. In seconds it went into an irreversible dive and crashed into the Kent countryside.

The next night, 'B' Flight scored another confirmed hit when Sgt Laurence and Sgt Chard shot down a Ju 88 over Bexley. Although the Defiants were flying in bad weather and had no airborne radar to guide them to their quarry, the combined talents of the air crew and the Biggin controllers usually brought success. Biggin Hill, however, was essentially a day fighter station and it was found difficult to operate both day and night fighter squadrons. Consequently, 141 moved over to Gatwick after five successful days and nights at Biggin.

With the Luftwaffe still losing aircraft at an alarming rate, 27th September 1940 saw further large scale attacks on London. Both Biggin squadrons were at dawn readiness and were scrambled shortly after 9.15 am. This time the Me 109 escorts to the main bomber force caught both 72 and 92 by surprise and in a space of five minutes, three Spitfires of 72 were shot down over Sevenoaks with two pilots, P/O E.E. Males and P/O P.J. Davies-Cooke killed and Sgt J. White force landing but unhurt. In the same action, 92 lost four Spitfires with two pilots, Fl/Lt J.A. Paterson and F/Sgt C. Sydney killed whilst P/O J. Mansel-Lewis and P/O T.S. Wade were unhurt. During the afternoon, a further two Spitfires of 92 were lost with Sgt T.G. Oldfield killed and Sgt H. Bowen-Norris unhurt. The enemy, however, also suffered grievously with 67 aircraft lost and over half this number of pilots killed.

At the end of September, the battle entered the fifth phase. Despite all the German efforts and the fact that they had lost 1,653 aircraft since the beginning of the battle, the Luftwaffe had achieved very little. To offset these tremendous losses, Goering resorted to using fighter/bombers operating at high altitudes rather than the mass aircraft formations of the past.

With 72 and 92 Squadrons still in residence, Biggin Hill continued its war. On 2nd October the airfield was attacked once again but damage was minimal. After what they had suffered, the men and women of Biggin treated it more as a nuisance than an air raid. The next few days saw raids over Kent and the major cities both by day and by night. 72 Squadron lost one Spitfire in another raid on Biggin on Sunday, 6th October and the next day, three were damaged in combat with Me 109s during a mid morning raid. 92 also suffered losses over this period with Sgt E.T.G. Frith baling out of his blazing Spitfire over Ashford on the 10th. Although admitted to hospital in the town badly burnt, he died from his injuries just over a month later.

The next day, Thursday, 10th October was a very sad day for 92 Squadron when two pilots were killed as the result of a mid-air collision. It was just after dawn that a section of the squadron were scrambled to intercept a lone Do 17 picked up by the radar stations just crossing the English coast. As far as Brian Kingcome and the rest of the squadron were concerned, six Spitfires could deal with one Do 17.

Thirty minutes after they had left, a lone Spitfire approached Biggin Hill. Landing and coming to a stop, 'Wimpey' Wade clambered out and unfolded a tragic story. Having found the enemy aircraft, it had been attacked by three of the Spitfires. During the attack, P/O D.G. Williams in Spitfire X4038 and F/O J.F. Drummond in Spitfire R6616 had collided. Whilst Williams was killed instantly, Drummond, wounded in the leg and arm, had baled out too low and was also killed. Both aircraft buried themselves deep in the Sussex soil near Tangmere airfield. Another Spitfire, X4557, flown by Sgt W.T. Ellis, was hit by return gunfire from the Do 17 and crash-landed near Poynings railway station. Although shaken, Sgt Ellis was unhurt.

The rest of 92 Squadron could not believe it. 'And to beat it all, the bastard got away,' was all 'Wimpey' Wade could say through a torrent of tears. The episode gave way to deep depression for the squadron which lasted for several days. On the 12th they were scrambled again as the enemy made for the capital. This time they shot down four 109s, rekindling their former glory and putting them back on form.

With a change of squadrons, 72 were posted up to Coltishall in Norfolk to be replaced by No 74 (Trinidad) Squadron who flew down from the same base two days later. Equipped with the Spitfire IIA, the 'Tigers' as they were known, were commanded by Sqd/Ldr A.G. Malan, DFC and Bar. Nicknamed 'Sailor', due to the fact that he went to sea aged 15 in South Africa, he was the first RAF pilot to collect and fly the production Spitfire. Since then, his love for the aircraft had never ceased.

Thursday, 17th October was a day of bright intervals and local showers. Soon after breakfast, 90 Me 109s and 110s raided towns in Kent. They were back again in the afternoon when 74 Squadron were sent into the attack. Catching the enemy over the Thames Estuary, they shot several down for the loss of Spitfire P7360. Flown by F/O A.L. Ricalton, it was shot down and crashed at Hollingbourne near Maidstone at 3.40 pm, killing the pilot.

The fighter/bomber raids continued throughout October despite the changing weather. By the 26th, the night blitz on London was at its worst and the German News Agency was able to boast that 'bombs fell all over the place'. Despite the bragging, the Luftwaffe were still losing a tremendous number of aircraft which fell foul of the fighters and the ack-ack barrage, which was strengthening all the time. However, the loss of British pilots and the fact that a rift was seen to be developing between Dowding and other leaders in Fighter Command was worrying. Whilst he proclaimed that the only way to hit the enemy was to scramble his squadrons in 11 Group as the radar stations picked up the plots and thus meet the enemy head on, the other leaders of the remaining groups insisted that their squadrons should be brought south immediately and not wait to be called for. This way the enemy would meet a big wing formation. Dowding did not agree with this policy and told the Air Ministry and Government so in no uncertain manner. This argument was to rage on long after the war had ended.

The German losses in October were 325 aircraft. According to Air Ministry figures, the total number of enemy aircraft downed between 10th July and 31st October was 2,698. This was later downgraded to 1,733. Even more exaggerated were the Luftwaffe claims which stood at 3,058 British aircraft. Once again, this was later reduced to 915. At Biggin Hill, the score for the station was approaching 600 kills and it had gained the unenviable title of 'the most raided station in Fighter Command'. Yet despite the destruction and devastation, like a certain well known London theatre, G/Cpt Grice could boast 'that we never closed!'

According to many historians, 31st October was the end of the Battle of Britain. With the dark nights and changeable weather closing in, the pattern of the Luftwaffe attacks was about to change again. November was still to see attacks on the airfields of 11 Group but with less frequency and ferocity. The North Camp at Biggin Hill was still a shambles from the August and September attacks and very little had been done to repair and improve it. Most of the essential offices and sections were operating from requisitioned premises in local villages surrounding the airfield. This obviously imposed great difficulties for the day to day running of the station, a situation that became visibly obvious when a delegation of top brass visited. Within days, workmen and lorries had arrived to begin work on the reconstruction. This progressed so well that it allowed another squadron, No 66, to fly in from water-logged West Malling on 7th November 1940.

The difference that they found between the two resident squadrons that they had now joined somewhat bewildered them. On the one hand there was 74 Squadron, a strict, disciplined unit under 'Sailor' Malan, who even insisted his pilots were in bed by 10 pm each night – and there was 92 Squadron! As opposite to 74 as you could ever get with their sophisticated outlook upon life. Fast powerful cars, parties until dawn, special catering arrangements at Southwood and an abundance of lovely females virtually living in the mess. Sqd/Ldr James Fisher began to wonder just where his squadron would fit in!

With the Battle of Britain over, G/Cpt Grice insisted that his station got back to some degree of discipline and smartness. With work proceeding on the reconstruction at a good pace, it was felt that in order to carry the war forward, old habits nurtured during the constant bomb attacks must go. One of the new routines adopted was the introduction of physical training. How well that went down with the men of 92 is not recorded! What is however recorded is the fact that for some time, the squadron had been without a commanding officer, although Brian Kingcome acted unofficially in this capacity. Now known as No 92 (East India) Squadron, the last week of October saw Sqd/Ldr Johnny Kent, AFC, DFC take up the vacant command. He found a squadron slack, undisciplined and very blatantly conceited. This did not last long as he summoned his officers and NCOs to his office and gave them the warning that if their conduct did not improve, the matter would be taken higher, even to 11 Group itself. Though they did not like it, 92 gradually improved over the weeks as the words sunk home.

November saw the number of sorties much lower as bad weather intervened. As the elusive '600' kill approached, everyone in all three squadrons wondered who would reach the magic figure. The last day of the month was cold with occasional rain and not really the ideal weather for flying. The two flight commanders of 74 Squadron, Mungo-Park and H.M. Stephen, were eager to ensure that their squadron got the infamous 600 and took off to go looking for the enemy despite the weather. As they roared down the runway, G/Cpt Grice remarked, 'Of all the bloody cheek,' and joined the procession heading towards the operations room, all eager to follow the sortie.

With the controller already advised, the news went to 11 Group operations room who vectored the two aircraft to a position above a Channel convoy. Sure enough, the ships enticed the enemy to send up eight Me 109s to attack. As the two pilots saw them, their shouts of 'Tally Ho' through the ops room radio brought a smile to all gathered there. Coming down on the 109s, Mungo-Park was the first to fire but the German pilot had seen him and pulled hard left. Stephen then got on his tail and as he did so he noticed that the other aircraft were all heading for home, leaving the lone 109 to fight it out. Mungo-Park again had him in his sights and this time hit the 109 causing the hood to fly off. It was, however, left to Stephen to finish him off as he fired from 20 yards out, leaving the enemy to dive through the cloud and crash near Dungeness. Oberleutnant Schmidt, unaware of his celebrity status, died 15 hours later and was buried with full military honours. Today he rests in the German Military Cemetery on Cannock Chase.

Biggin Hill bathed in the glory of being the first 600-kill station but not so Air Chief Marshal Sir Hugh Dowding, the architect of the Battle of Britain who had enabled Biggin Hill to cross this milestone. He had been relieved of his command and had been replaced at the top by Air Vice Marshal Trafford Leigh-Mallory, his opponent on the question of squadron tactics. Again, for many years after the war ended, argument on Dowding's cruel dismissal was to rage.

Although December was also to prove a quiet month, 66 Squadron undertook the first of Fighter Command's early offensive sweeps over Europe on the 20th. Known as 'Rhubarbs', these were low level strike operations carried out over occupied Europe. Now that the Battle was over, Fighter Command were impatient to carry the war back to Europe. The first of these sweeps was uneventful but later sorties were to prove successful for 66 Squadron.

As Christmas 1940 approached, awards were forthcoming for work carried out in October and November. 'Sailor' Malan got a DSO, as did H.M. Stephen. Mungo-Park got a DFC for his part in the 600th Hun and nine more DFCs and DFMs went to other pilots in 74 and 92 Squadrons.

Whilst Christmas was a period of limited celebration, it was also tinged with regret at the news that G/Cpt Grice was to be posted. For two years he had commanded the Bump and seen it through a very traumatic period. There was not one man who was not saddened by his going.

It was not until 27th December that operations could continue. On that day, two pilots of 92 went on a Rhubarb and although no enemy aircraft were encountered, they did shoot up a German staff car. It was, however, the waving of the French people in the fields that made them feel good as they flew low over the countryside.

The new year brought a change of units. 74 moved down to Manston on the Kent coast on 20th February as 92 returned to Biggin after a month at the same base, while 66 were posted to Exeter on the 24th after a rather uneventful period on the Bump. The month also saw the arrival of another auxiliary unit when No 609 (West Riding) Squadron brought their Spitfires across from Warmwell. G/Cpt F.O. Soden AFC, the new commanding officer at Biggin Hill, welcomed the newcomers and immediately put them on readiness for a 'Circus' sortie the next day. Another offensive operation, the Circus was a large fighter escort accompanying bombers in the hope that this would entice the Luftwaffe to appear. This period also saw the formation of the 'Big Wing', something that Leigh-Mallory together with Douglas Bader had been advocating for a long time. Two large wings were formed, the Biggin Wing led by newly promoted Wg/Cdr 'Sailor' Malan and comprising

Nos 92 and 609 Squadrons at Biggin and his beloved 74 Squadron, now at Gravesend, and the Tangmere Wing led by Bader.

During 1941 the nightly blitz continued. Whilst new aircraft types, specifically for night fighting, were in production, it sometimes fell to the day fighters to try their hands at doing battle by night. 609 were detailed for such operations in April 1941 which required them to fly down to the satellite airfield at West Malling in the evening, be at readiness all night then fly back to Biggin in the morning for breakfast and sleep. This continued for three or four nights but with little activity due to the weather conditions, they returned to normal operations.

May was a month of Rhubarbs and Circus sorties. 609 found success when they shot down several 109s during an air-sea rescue operation in the Channel. The eventual score was six destroyed and two probables for the loss of one Spitfire, Fl/Lt Churchim managing to land safely at Hawkinge.

Now known as 'Britain's Premier Fighter Station', Biggin Hill became the centre of attention. Much was said about the base in papers, magazines and in cinema newsreel programmes. During the filming of the epic war documentary, *The First of the Few*, the actor Leslie Howard became a familiar figure around the place as he researched material for his role as R.J. Mitchell, the designer of the Spitfire. One of the firmest favourites, however, was the Prime Minister who often dropped in on his way home to Chartwell near Westerham. He would spend time talking to anyone he saw regardless of rank or status.

As the year progressed, so the offensive operations became more intense. In May, the Biggin Wing destroyed 17 enemy aircraft with a further seven damaged, but sadly it was at the cost of twelve Spitfires lost and five pilots killed. G/Cpt Philip Barwell had replaced G/Cpt Soden as CO on the Bump and in June, a long heatwave arrived after a period of very unsettled weather. In addition to the usual offensive operations, a new type called a 'Roadsted' had been introduced. This consisted of fighter operations against shipping and 609 were to become very proficient in this new operation.

During June and July, the heat was on as operations increased against the enemy. Over these weeks the wing claimed 50 aircraft destroyed with 35 probables, a very impressive score. The end of July saw 609 take their Spitfire VBs over to Gravesend whilst 92 converted to the same mark of Spitfire at Biggin Hill. Back came No 72 (Basutoland) Squadron after nine months absence. It was as though they had never been away as they carried out 'Circus 81', the two wings combining their firepower to escort Blenheims going to bomb a power station. It was during this

Ground crew assist a pilot of 72 Squadron to make ready before an operation. (Central Press)

raid that one of the Blenheims dropped a long box by parachute. Whilst many were mystified as to its contents, when the raid was over and the fighters and bombers had returned to base, it became known that the box contained a pair of artificial legs for Douglas Bader who had recently become a prisoner of the Third Reich. Shot down over France, in his attempt to bale out from his blazing Spitfire he left his legs behind. On the instigation of the Luftwaffe fighter ace, Oberstleutnant Adolf Galland, it was arranged that a new pair be dropped over St Omer airfield during a routine bombing mission by the British. There was after all, chivalry amongst enemies!

It was now time for 'Sailor' Malan to relinquish command of the Biggin Wing although he protested strongly when told to take a rest. His place as leader of the wing was taken by Wg/Cdr M. Robinson. Another change was that, sadly, 92's days were numbered at Biggin after a very successful stay. They left their beloved Southwood to replace 609 Squadron at Gravesend. The latter flew back to Biggin Hill, glad to be home on the mother airfield. 72 were sent to Gravesend as well, as a new unit, No 401 (Ram) Squadron of the Royal Canadian Air

Force flew their Spitfire IIAs from Digby where they had formed from No 1 Squadron RCAF. Shortly after their arrival they converted to the Spitfire VB and were partnered with 609 Squadron.

The autumn brought very little change in the pattern of operations. It was around this period that the Luftwaffe brought the new Focke-Wulf 190 into service. With the prototype flying in June 1939, the first aircraft were delivered to a Jagdgeschwader at Le Bourget in May 1941. Two months later, FW 190s appeared in action with JG26, the famed Luftwaffe unit commanded by Adolf Galland. Based on the Channel coast, they were to give the ailing Luftwaffe a new lease of life against the Spitfire.

It fell to Sqd/Ldr Gilroy, the officer commanding 609 Squadron, to first encounter the type whilst flying a Circus operation. The Luftwaffe pilots declined to fight on this occasion but on 21st October, 609 suffered two pilots lost whilst flying a 'Rodeo', the name given to a fighter sweep over enemy territory looking for targets of opportunity. Strangely it was not the FW 190s that shot them down but the more familiar 109s. It was a sad note on which to leave Biggin but 609 departed to Digby on 19th November 1941. Their place was taken by No 124 (Baroda) Squadron who took over the Spitfire VBs of 609 on their arrival from Castletown where they had reformed in May 1941. Commanded by Sqd/Ldr Duke-Wooley, it was a very cosmopolitan squadron

Spitfire VBs of 72 Squadron at Biggin Hill in August 1941. (IWM)

124 Squadron, at Biggin Hill from November 1941 to May 1942. (IWM)

consisting of pilots from Belgium, Czechoslovakia, France, Norway, Australia and Canada as well as Britain.

With the squadron settled in, they began convoy patrols though these were very few due to the atrocious weather in December. Christmas was celebrated and everyone looked forward to a year of further success. However, Biggin Hill, Fighter Command, Coastal Command and the Navy were all to go through a very depressing period before the light began to shine at the end of the tunnel.

In February 1941, the fast, heavy gunned 30,000 ton German battle cruisers *Scharnhorst* and *Gneisenau* had seemingly disappeared from sight after sinking more than 100,000 tons of Allied shipping. Reconnaissance sorties failed to reveal their whereabouts until a French agent reported to London that the ships were in Brest. For some time, the Admiralty had convened an operation code-named Channel Stop. This was intended to stop German shipping from passing through the English Channel but with the news that the German ships were at Brest and preparing for a breakout, the operation was upgraded to Operation Fuller. It further became known that Hitler had ordered the two ships to return to Germany by the quickest possible route, ie, a dash through the English Channel.

The full story is told in the chapter on Manston, but Biggin Hill became involved when at 10.10 pm on 12th February two Spitfires from Kenley spotted the German armada beneath them. Immediately 250 aircraft of Bomber Command were made ready. In addition, MTBs from Dover were briefed to attack plus six torpedo-carrying Fairey Swordfish at Manston. Biggin Hill and Hornchurch squadrons were ordered by 11 Group to provide cover but at the Bump, neither 401 nor 124 Squadrons were even at readiness. Consequently, the controller advised Manston that the Swordfish escort would be late at the rendezvous point. Lt/Cdr Eugene Esmonde, leading the Swordfish attack, decided to go ahead and was airborne by 12.15 pm. Just in time, 72 Squadron from Gravesend arrived to provide some cover whilst the Biggin squadrons, airborne at 12.25 pm, decided to head for the Channel in the hope of finding the Swordfish over the water. Somehow they missed them and flew back to Manston only to find that the Swordfish were already going in to attack. It was like lambs to the slaughter as one by one, the flimsy aircraft fell victims to the terrible firepower the ships were unleashing. Most of the Swordfish were shot from the sky, including Eugene Esmonde who received a posthumous VC for his gallantry.

By now the Biggin squadrons had found the fleet and went straight into battle. Six 109s were shot down together with one 190 before, with fuel running low, all three squadrons were recalled. Despite further attacks by torpedo-carrying Beauforts and Wellington bombers, the German ships survived the dash through the Channel.

All of this gave way to a depressing time at Biggin. The weather both here and on the continent had prevented operations from continuing. In December 1941, Jamie Rankin left his position as wing leader and was replaced by Stanford-Tuck, an old friend of Biggin Hill. When it was possible, the wing found success although on one Rhubarb operation, Stanford-Tuck's aircraft was hit in the fuselage and engine by a series of vicious Bofors gun attacks. Baling out safely, he too became a guest of the Third Reich.

As the spring weather improved so did the opportunities for offensive operations. The war in general was not completely going the way of the Allies with several high points being claimed by Germany. However, an acute sense of optimism was beginning to prevail as the war continued to be carried back to the enemy.

No change in squadrons took place on the Bump until 3rd May 1942 when the first American accents were heard in the operations room. Flying in from Kirton-in-Lindsey and collecting the detachment that

Formed from US volunteers, 133 'Eagle' Squadron were based at Biggin Hill in 1942. (J. D. Rawlings)

had been operating from West Malling, the satellite airfield, the Third Eagle Squadron, No 133 took over the dispersal hut of No 124 who had moved to Gravesend. The Americans flew the VB mark of Spitfire and were glad to be at Biggin which they classed as the 'big time'. Making themselves quickly at home, they frequented the Queen's Head at Downe to get the taste of the English beer of which they had heard so much. It was soon to become their unofficial 'off duty headquarters'.

Four days after their arrival they joined the Biggin Wing in escorting six Bostons on an uneventful bombing mission. Success came their way on 17th May when 'Red' McColpin shot down one 109 with two other pilots claiming probables. The next two months saw an improvement in the success rate for Fighter Command. G/Cpt Dickie Barwell celebrated his first anniversary as CO of Biggin Hill in June, little knowing that he would soon lose his life in the most sad and depressing manner.

For some months a lone German reconnaissance aircraft had been plotted by the radar stations flying at a great height, beyond the range of the mark of Spitfire that the wing were flying. In June, Supermarine had produced the Spitfire VI and fitted the Merlin 47 engine into it. This

G/Cpt Dickie Barwell, CO, welcomes the Duke of Kent to Biggin Hill in 1942. Both were killed later that summer. (IWM)

high-powered engine plus the addition of a pressurised cabin gave the VI a far higher ceiling. Biggin Hill in June had received several of the new type and the temptation of the lone German proved too much for Dickie Barwell. On the evening of 1st July, together with Sqd/Ldr Bobbie Oxspring of 72 Squadron, he took the new aircraft intent on catching the Hun. Vectored to Beachy Head, they saw two other Spitfires approaching and unknown to Barwell and Oxspring, they too were bound on the same mission. Coming from Tangmere, the two Spitfires saw the unfamiliar shape of the new aircraft and immediately opened fire. In seconds, Dickie Barwell's aircraft was in flames and he fell into the Channel. The duty controller at Biggin had the sad task of informing Tangmere, 'I rather think your boys have shot down our station commander.' Despite a search for many hours, his body was never found. His death shocked everyone on the Bump and it took a long time for them to rally round.

Once again it was a time for change as 72 Squadron moved down to Lympne near Ashford on 30th June 1942, followed by 133 a few hours later. On arrival at the new airfield, the aircraft of both squadrons had broad white stripes painted on the cowlings and tailplanes. This was in readiness for a planned assault on the French coast at Dieppe but at the last minute the operation was cancelled. No 19 Squadron replaced them at Biggin but stayed only three weeks before departing to Perranporth. No 72 Squadron flew back to Biggin and re-equipped with the newer, faster Spitfire IX before handing them over to 401 Squadron – 72 were posted to Morpeth whilst 401 came back to Biggin from Gravesend to join 133 who had also returned from Lympne. It was a period of rapid changes.

With the Americans entering the war in late 1941, it was only a short time before they came to Britain. The 307th Pursuit (31st Fighter Group) had crossed the Atlantic and had been in training at Atcham flying Spitfires. Considered operational, they now came to Biggin to join 401 and 133 Squadrons. This was just in time as the cancelled Dieppe operation of June was on once again and, code-named Jubilee, was set for 19th August 1942.

In preparation, Nos 401 and 133 moved down once again to Lympne and were replaced by Nos 222 (Natal) and 602 (City of Glasgow) Squadrons, the latter being an auxiliary unit. On the eve of Jubilee, the station was closed to all as a security cordon was thrown around the entire area. Briefings were held behind locked doors guarded by armed personnel. Shortly before dawn on the 19th, 6,000 troops, mostly Canadian, attempted to get a foothold on French soil. At the same time the Biggin Wing comprising 133, 222, 401 and 602 Squadrons together with the 307th Pursuit were all getting airborne to form up over Lympne. Flying over the Channel they saw a black ominous cloud, thick and heavy, lying over the town of Dieppe.

Leigh-Mallory had 56 fighter squadrons at his disposal to cover the landings and it was hoped that the Luftwaffe would put 500 aircraft into the air to thwart the attempt. The Biggin Wing were to help maintain a fighter umbrella over Dieppe. The initial sorties produced just a handful of enemy aircraft but the second sortie of the day, at 10.15 am, saw the sky dark with Messerschmitts and Focke Wulfs together with Junkers and Dornier bombers. 602 led by Pete Brothers charged a bunch of Dornier bombers. Ten minutes later they could claim three destroyed, nine damaged and two probables. All the other units in the wing found success and a third sortie just after midday proved equally profitable. However, although it was triumph in the air with five enemy aircraft destroyed, seven probables and 29 damaged, all for the loss of six Spitfires, on the ground it was a different story. Of the 6,000 men, tough British and Canadian troops, only a third were to survive.

The 307th moved down to Merston in the Tangmere sector in September and the Eagle Squadrons, including No 133, became part of the US Army Air Force in the UK. No 340 (Ile de France) Squadron, a Free French unit, moved in from Hornchurch and were later joined by No 611 (West Lancashire) Squadron who came over from Redhill in Surrey. Both units flew Spitfires and were soon part of the forward planning for Operation Torch, the Allied invasion of French North Africa. On 12th November 1942, Rommel retreated from El Alamein and thus another victory was scored for the Allies. The old year was seen out with a sense of victory in the not too distant future.

The new year brought several changes to the Bump. 'Sailor' Malan returned to his old base as station commander. Whether or not the news of his return had reached the Luftwaffe High Command will never be known but by coincidence, the enemy returned to bomb Biggin Hill for the first time in two years. A cloudy 20th January gave way to sunshine and broken cloud around lunchtime. The mess was full when the tannoy blared out, 'All available aircraft scramble and protect base. Bandits approaching from the south east.' In a rush, all the pilots including 'Sailor', made for the door and the waiting Spitfires. 'Bloody cheek,' he retorted as he led the aircraft into the air. They were barely airborne when several FW 190s came streaking across the airfield. Carrying bombs, they overshot due to the pilots' alarm at seeing the Spitfires climbing and sadly dropped their bombs on Bromley, killing

Sqd/Ldr Jack Charles, 'Rene' Mouchotte, 'Sailor' Malan and Al Deere, Biggin Hill 1942.

four teachers and 45 children in a school. Swinging round, they made a dash for the Channel but the Biggin boys were waiting over Beachy Head. Seven of the 190s were shot down and all the Biggin aircraft returned safely. 'Just like old times,' remarked 'Sailor'!

Early 1943 was a period of Rodeos, Rhubarbs and Circuses. No 1 Squadron brought the first Hawker Typhoons to fly from the Bump when they arrived on 9th February from Acklington. They departed to Lympne on 15th March when their place was taken by No 341 (GC III/2 Alsace) Squadron, the second Free French fighter unit to form. Its leader, 'Rene', Commandant Mouchotte, had but one ambition – to make the Alsace Squadron the most famous in Fighter Command. It certainly was to rank amongst the top scoring units but sadly he was never to see his ambition come true.

Biggin Hill was fast approaching its thousandth victory. Expectation gripped everyone on the base and even the newspapers and radio sent their journalists to cover the event. On 7th May, the total stood at 995. Pilots due for leave refused to go lest they missed the opportunity of shooting down the magic 1,000th and collecting around £300 from a sweepstake being run on the station. Every sortie was filled with

Sqd/Ldr Jack Charles celebrates the 1,000th victory for Biggin Hill with fellow pilots of 611 Squadron and, below, the invitation to the party celebrating the 1,000th kill. (Kent Messenger: G. Wallace)

Group Captain A. G. Malan, D.S.O., D.F.C.,
and the Officers of the Biggin Hill Sector
request the pleasure of the Company of

Flight Lieutenant Nolany. and Lady

to a Dance at Grosvenor House, Park Lane, London, W. 1.,
on Wednesday, the 9th of June, 1943,
to commemorate the shooting down of the 1,000th Hun Aircraft
by Pilots of the Sector.

9 p.m. - 3 a.m.

This invitation must be produced to gain admission.

Biggin Hill - Gravesend - West Malling - Hawkinge - Lympne.

219

expectation. The 15th May 1943 dawned fine but not until 4.20 pm did Al Deere, the new Wing Commander Flying, announce a sortie. Making rendezvous with a formation of Bostons, the wing headed for Caen.

Back at Biggin, the non-duty personnel had all packed into the operations room for it was expected that this Circus would bring a result. As hoped, several FW 190s attacked the formation and with 341 Squadron keeping top cover, Sqd/Ldr Charles took 611 down to attack. He scored the 999th kill as a 190 exploded in front of him and he half rolled his Spitfire to bring another aircraft within his sights. As he fired, he had the satisfaction of seeing it dive to its death but at the same time, Commandant Mouchotte, 3,000 feet above, saw a lone 190 and shot it down. Biggin Hill's total had reached 1,001 but just who was the victor? At the de-briefing, both pilots thought that the other had shot down the 1,000th Hun and gave each other the credit. It was a difficult decision and in the end both pilots shared the prize.

High summer saw the wing in action daily. No 485 Squadron, a New Zealand squadron, had flown into the Bump on 1st July and departed to Hornchurch on 18th October 1943. They had replaced No 611 who left to go to Matlask. Sadly the popular Commandant of 341, 'Rene' Mouchotte, lost his life escorting a formation of B 17s in August. His loss shook everyone and 'Sailor' Malan spoke for the base as a whole when he said: 'He was a leader, a fighter and a gentleman. We shall miss him.' His name, however, was not and never will be forgotten. The padre, Sqd/Ldr Cecil King, had proposed that a chapel be consecrated on the station and, in memory of the many pilots killed whilst flying from Biggin, that their names be emblazoned in gold within. It was named St George's Chapel and dedicated on Sunday, 19th September 1943. (Today's St George's Chapel was built in 1951 but it still contains much of the furniture and the Book of Remembrance of the old one, which was destroyed in a fire.)

In autumn 1943, the plans for Operation Overlord were taking shape. This was the Allied invasion of Western Europe, D-Day, and was planned for 5th June 1944. In the event the weather proved too much on this particular day and the invasion was postponed for 24 hours. Sadly, Biggin Hill was not directly included in the plans for the operation.

The new year of 1944 brought the airfield under the umbrella of the 2nd Tactical Air Force. The end of 1943 had seen the Free French and the New Zealand squadrons posted to Perranporth and Hornchurch respectively in preparation for D-Day whilst the airfield became No 126 Airfield of the 17th (Fighter) Wing of the RCAF controlled by 83 Group of the 2nd TAF. Biggin became an all-Canadian station as Nos 401

(Ram), 411 (Grizzly Bear) and 412 (Falcon) Squadrons arrived. Equipped with the Spitfire VB, they soon converted to the Mark IX. The wing carried out sweeps and escort duties for the ever increasing bomber attacks on enemy positions prior to D-Day. As the run-up to the landings approached, the wing moved down to Tangmere and for the first time in its entire history, the Bump was left without any aircraft. It was downgraded to a sector station in No 24 (Base Defence) Wing of the No 85 (Base) Group of the Allied Expeditionary Force. Although this title was again changed a month later, no squadrons or aircraft were forthcoming for this once glorious fighter station had now become the heart of the balloon barrage in a fight to overcome Hitler's revenge weapon, the V1 or Doodlebug.

The first V1 to be launched against London fell at Swanscombe near Gravesend at 4.18 am on 13th June 1944. Biggin Hill, now No 22 Balloon Centre, became the home of Nos 945/7 Squadrons later joined by Nos 953 and 958. By June, 344 balloons were sited around the area manned by 519 airmen and 177 Waafs. The assault on London continued throughout July and August, many of the robots falling foul of the Biggin balloons. Just one landed on the airfield despite the fact that 2,400 got through to their target. It exploded on top of a Nissen hut at 5.30 am on 1st July killing the three occupants. By 5th September 1944 the campaign dwindled out as the Allies overran the launch sites. A resurgence of operations came the same month when No 340 (GC IV/2 Ile de France) returned for a brief stay with Spitfires. When they left in December, the base hosted a heavy transport squadron of the RCAF. With the advance of the Allies into Germany, Biggin Hill was just too far from the battle front to be of tactical use.

Victory in 1945 brought a little use of the airfield again but it was not until August 1946 that it reverted back to Fighter Command. Peacetime saw two auxiliary squadrons based there, both flying Spitfires until the new jet powered Gloster Meteor arrived. Nos 600 (City of London) and 615 (County of Surrey) carried on the traditions set by the wartime auxiliary units. They were joined by a regular squadron, No 41, to bring Biggin Hill up to full operational status. It remained this way until, with the disbandment of all the auxiliary units in 1957 and the posting of 41 Squadron to Coltishall in 1958, the airfield was placed under Care and Maintenance. It was later to become the Officer and Aircrew Selection Centre but this too moved to Cranwell in 1995. The base closed as a military airfield shortly after but the civilian use increased and today the airport is truly international.

St George's Chapel, flanked by a Hurricane and Spitfire, is today the only visible reminder of the airfield's past history. The annual Air Fair and the recently re-introduced Battle of Britain Airshow in September bring thousands of visitors to 'Biggin on the Bump'. They surely must reflect at sometime on the great historical significance of this world famous wartime airfield.

3
DETLING

A former First World War airfield, Detling was reopened in 1938 and greatly expanded as the threat of another war loomed. A single hangar was constructed together with buildings to be used as technical and domestic accommodation. It was to remain a grass airfield, extended to a 4,200 foot NE/SW landing run or grass runway. With work completed it opened on 14th September 1938 as part of No 6 (Auxiliary) Group of Bomber Command allowing No 500 (County of Kent) Squadron of the Royal Auxiliary Air Force to bring their Hawker Hinds up from Manston. Fl/Lt A.C. Bolton MC brought the advance party to prepare for the arrival of the rest of the squadron and found that Detling, though subject to hill fog, had reasonably good flying dimensions. The move from Manston was completed in twelve hours for, with the deterioration in the relations between Great Britain and Germany, war looked even more likely.

In 1939 the squadron took on the role of a general reconnaissance unit. Detling was handed over to No 16 (GR) Group of Coastal Command and on 19th March 1939, 500 Squadron converted to the Avro Anson, a new low-winged, twin-engined aircraft which was a development of the civilian Avro 652.

Maidstone, the county town of Kent, marked the occasion in May by giving 500 Squadron the Freedom of the Town. The theme of co-operation between town and squadron continued two weeks later when over 15,000 people attended the annual Empire Air Day flying display. The pilots excitedly showed off the new Ansons little knowing

'Up front' in a 500 Squadron Avro Anson at Detling, 1939. (Kent Messenger)

that by the end of the year, they would be engaged in fighting a war.

On 7th August the squadron attended its last peacetime camp at Warmwell airfield in Dorset. They returned to Detling on 13th August and on the 25th came the signal that everyone had been expecting, embodiment in the RAF proper and active service. As German troops prepared to invade Poland, the peacetime operations book of 500 Squadron closed and the war edition was opened.

The main task of 500 Squadron during these early months of war was reconnaissance operations over the Channel and in the Dover Straits, together with convoy escort duties. The Ansons had adopted a very warlike appearance with fuselages camouflaged to blend in with the sea. The commanding officer, Sqd/Ldr LeMay had felt that with just one .303 gun firing forward and another in a turret, the aircraft was under-armed. Upon his instructions, two additional machine guns were fitted to fire through the side windows and his own aircraft had a 20 mm cannon fitted to fire through the bottom of the fuselage. It fell to the armament manufacturers, Tilling-Stevens of Maidstone, to manufacture and perfect a suitable gun mounting after a block and pin design by the squadron armament section had proved a little precarious.

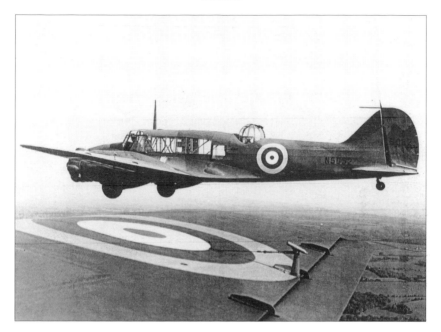

500 Squadron airborne from Detling. (R. Young)

Called 'Bristling Porcupines', it was reckoned that when the cannon was fired through the floor, the Anson gained another 100 feet in height!

500 largely had to work under orders from the Admiralty as so many operations were based on maritime exigencies. This led to difficulties particularly for the operation controllers and the air crews. The naval mind, used to manipulating vessels with weeks of operation, never seemed to fully comprehend that aircraft, with their limited fuel supply, had only one way to go when that ran out. Down! Several crews were ultimately lost trying to regain base after staying out longer on patrol over a convoy and thus running out of fuel. Flt/Sgt John Thompson of 500 recalls early days at Detling.

'The poor air crews had to contend with the darkness and the blackout which blotted out many landmarks and of course, the fog which encompassed Detling at frequent intervals. Sometimes crews were unable to locate the field quickly enough when their fuel was low. They either crashed or force landed in the surrounding territory.

'A spare Anson perspex rear turret was mounted on top of the camp water tower and a poor unfortunate "erk" was posted on top, complete with a pair of binoculars and a field telephone to inform the operations room when he could hear aircraft engines within the vicinity. It was also his responsibility to warn of approaching raiders and to give the "Aerodrome raid imminent" signal. On receipt of this, and only then, personnel were allowed to cease work and take to the shelters. All of this was fine in theory but come the practice, the poor airman could not get down from the water tower quick enough for sitting up there all exposed and alone, he was a sitting target for any enemy aircraft.

'During this phoney period, always present was the threat of invasion and attack by paratroopers in the guise of "nuns". My flight commander, a shy diffident man but a very good officer and pilot, was the proud possessor of a vintage De Dion Bouton car and also a very smart Bentley. At his instigation, we fabricated and welded up a couple of light metal mountings to take a Vickers "K" machine. On an occasional quiet evening, the flight commander would approach me and suggest it might be a good idea to go hunting for parachutists. Nothing loath, we would pile four or five lads aboard and with the guns mounted and armed, off we would go on our intrepid patrol. Diligently we would search in all the bars of the Black Horse and the White Horse at Bearsted and finally the Cock Horse at Detling with meagre success. Forays north to the Wheatsheaf and the Three Squirrels were considered too reckless as these areas were the haunts of the ruffian 'B' flight personnel and they couldn't be relied upon to observe the tenets of the Hague Convention!'

The war was only two days old when 500 Squadron made their mark upon the history books. Anson 5066 was on patrol together with 5051 in the Channel approaches. Piloting the former aircraft was Sqd/Ldr Crockart with F/O Keppel, Corporal Wanstall and AC2 Coomber as crew. The pilot of 5051 was F/O Green with F/O Maby, LAC Walton and AC2 Rodgers as his crew.Coming down just below the fleecy cloud, Keppel noticed an enemy submarine, apparently stationary and on the surface. Wheeling round and seeing that the submarine was about to dive, Crockart dived and dropped his bombs in the vicinity of the vessel. By the time the Anson had turned round for a machine gun run, the submarine was submerged. Anson 5051 began to position for a run-in but it was too late, no sign could be seen of the enemy. Both aircraft patrolled the area for a time but no wreckage or oil were observed. Running low on fuel, both aircraft returned safely to Detling, achieving the honour of being the crews to make the first air attack of the war.

Later in the month, 500 were joined by a detachment of No 48 Squadron also flying the Anson. With the main squadron based at Thorney Island, further detachments of two or three aircraft were sent

Fl/Lt Baxter of 500 Squadron in the Detling mess. (W. Keppel)

to Bircham Newton, Guernsey and Carew Cheriton.

September moved into October and with the weather at its worst, operations were hampered and resulted in several fatal crashes. Anson N.5233 was returning from a patrol after escorting a convoy through the Channel. Over Benenden, on the approach to Detling, it developed engine trouble and began to lose height quickly. The order was given to abandon the aircraft and the pilot, F/O D.G. Maby attempted to gain a little more height. Managing to reach the crucial level, LAC Mesent baled out to safety. Sadly, no more of the crew had the opportunity to jump and F/O Maby, P/O A.M. Patterson and Corporal J.F. Drew perished in the crash, the first fatalities of the war for 500 and for Detling. In December, a crewman died from his injuries when another Anson crashed near the airfield and a further two incidents connected with patrols in the dreadful weather saw more deaths when aircraft could not find the airfield visually and ran out of fuel. It must be remembered that at this time no form of radar was in operation, the only aid to finding their way home was by means of a DF or direction finding instrument which at times was wholly unreliable.

The new year saw 500 covering further convoy movements, reconnaissance of enemy positions and escorting boats from France across the Channel. With an improvement in the weather, the squadron were able to fly 1,386 hours in April, this amount rapidly increasing as the Dunkirk evacuation approached.

The month of May 1940 was not good for Great Britain. With the Norwegians surrendering to the Germans on the 1st, the enemy turned its attentions to Holland, Belgium and Luxembourg. On the 15th, Holland capitulated and the German Army began its assault on France. By the 23rd they had reached the harbour port of Boulogne. For the British Expeditionary Force, fighting alongside the French Army, it meant that they were surrounded by enemy forces. However, instead of the ignominious surrender hoped for by the Germans, they were to be plucked from the hands of capture by evacuation.

Operation Dynamo, the evacuation of the Allied troops, began on 25th May. In preparation, a detachment of No 4 Squadron equipped with Westland Lysanders arrived at Detling together with various naval units. No 825 flew their Fairey Swordfish in from Worthy Down on 18th May followed by the Fairey Albacore torpedo bombers of No 826 Squadron who came down from Bircham Newton. All three squadrons immediately commenced anti-submarine patrols, night reconnaissance and E-boat attacks connected with the Dunkirk landings. Still more FAA units arrived during May when the Blackburn

An everyday scene in the early stages of the Battle of Britain. An Avro Anson of Coastal Command patrols over a Channel convoy. (IWM)

Skuas of No 801 Squadron came in from Sealand followed by the Blackburn Rocs of No 806 also from Worthy Down. Detling was becoming very busy as further units connected with the evacuation arrived in the form of Bristol Blenheims of Nos 235 and 254 Squadrons. These were acting in the role of bombers attacking the German troops that were rapidly advancing on Dunkirk.

One of the Skuas based at Detling over this period was part of No 2 Ack-Ack Co-Operation Unit and was flown by P/O D.H. Clarke. His orders were to patrol each night west of Dunkirk and drop powerful flares to light up any units of the German navy who might attempt to interfere with the evacuation. After a period of sleep following his patrol, he would assist the ground crews in arming the Swordfish that were going on a fighter patrol over the beaches. It was hoped that the Swordfish would fool the Germans into thinking that it was a Gladiator biplane fighter. Late one morning they took off together with a force of 37 Rocs and Skuas. P/O Clarke watched their return from Dunkirk shortly after lunch.

'There were not many of the little fighters left, I counted six. One of them belly-flopped on the grass and I went across to see what had happened. The aircraft was a complete write-off. Bullets and cannon shells had ripped the fuselage from end to end, the rear cockpit was sprayed with blood. The front cockpit was worse. Two bullet holes through the back of the pilot's seat showed where he had been hit and his parachute, still in position was saturated in blood. The instrument panel was shattered and on the floor was the remains of a foot.'

Of the original force of fighters, nine came back and five were written off on inspection. The remaining four aircraft were airborne within the hour. They looked very pathetic limping back to Dunkirk all alone.

The struggle carried on for five days, every one seeing more and more troops being brought back home. As aircraft from Detling flew over the Channel they could see below ships and boats of all sizes and

The fitting shop of 500 Squadron at Detling, 1940. (Kent Messenger)

shapes, rising up and down in the swell as they continued to rescue the BEF from the jaws of their enemies. Each evening the Detling mess was a little less full as aircraft failed to return from patrols. By 31st May 1940, Dynamo was over.

Before the month of May was out however, an incident at Detling earned a Waaf the first George Cross to be won by a woman. During the afternoon of the 30th, several crews had attended a briefing for an operation to be carried out later that night. Codenamed Dundee, it was to be an attack on a gathering of enemy ships and barges near Boulogne. One of the designated Ansons was MK-W, serial no R3389, crewed by P/O Bond as pilot with F/O Chambers, Corporal Petts and LAC Smith.

The flight across the Channel was uneventful and with good visibility over the target area, it appeared as though all was well. Turning to drop his bombs after the other Ansons, P/O Bond approached the target at low level and prepared to release his bomb load. With a shout of 'now' from the pilot, Cpl Petts pressed the bomb release but nothing happened. A second attempt produced no result either and Bond, by now low on fuel, had no alternative but to abandon the attack and return to Detling, praying that a soft landing would not release the bombs. Leaving the French coast behind, the Anson was about half-way across the Channel when the port engine began to falter. Realising that the problem was fuel starvation, Bond coaxed the aircraft along gently as the bad weather began to close in again. Losing height gradually on one engine, the Anson crossed the English coastline at Dover and through the patchy cloud, the crew looked for the lights of Detling. Switching on the DF set they found that they were just a few miles from the airfield.

With a great deal of skill, the pilot put the Anson down on the grass runway as flames began to lick around the engine exhausts. Unfortunately it was a fairly heavy landing and as soon as it touched the grass, the aircraft began to crab sideways causing the undercarriage leg to break and the fuselage to come into contact with the grass. With the flames spreading along the port wing rather rapidly, the Anson slithered to a halt in a cloud of dust and smoke.

To Corporal Daphne Pearson, lying on her bunk in the Waaf quarters, it was not unusual to hear the Ansons splutter a bit when returning from a raid. 'We always had to be ready as there were many crashes among our own aircraft,' she recalled. On this particular evening however, she heard the crash and realised that it was a major accident.

The medical sections Corporal quickly put on her fisherman's jersey, pulled on slacks and Wellington boots and, seizing her tin hat, ran out

Section Officer Daphne Pearson, awarded the George Cross whilst at Detling. (IWM)

of the building and across the field. Running towards the stricken Anson, she scrambled over a hedge, fell down an incline full of nettles until, nearly at the burning wreckage, she saw three men staggering towards her. With the ambulance now in attendance, she realised that the fourth man must still be in the aircraft and without any thought for her own safety, she ran towards the burning fuselage. P/O Bond could be seen slumped over the control column obviously having been knocked unconscious.

Pulling the side door open, she released his straps and pulled him from his seat, dragging him clear of the aircraft. As she was bending over him to free him from his parachute he regained consciousness momentarily and murmured something about the bombs still on board. She immediately realised that at any moment the aircraft would explode and with this thought, Daphne began to pull the wounded pilot towards the incline that she had recently fallen into. Placing her tin hat on his head, she had barely reached the end when the 120 lb bombs aboard the Anson exploded. Throwing herself on top of the pilot, Daphne felt as though a giant hand was trying to lift her up into the air as the shock wave hit them. But for the ground around them, the splinters of metal would have killed them both.

Daphne saw that P/O Bond had a lot of blood around his mouth and a tooth protruding from his upper jaw. In her own words: 'I reassured him about his face, pulled the broken tooth out and was just about to attend to his other injuries when the ambulance arrived.' Tidying him up as best as she could, Daphne helped place the injured pilot into the ambulance and only when she had assured herself that no more assistance could be given, did she leave the scene. All this had been done entirely without thought for her own safety.

In June 1940, Daphne Pearson received her commission and the following month the *London Gazette* announced that Corporal (now Assistant Section Officer) Pearson had been awarded the medal that ranked next to the Victoria Cross, the Medal of the Military Division of the British Empire for Gallantry, the EGM. On a hot day in August, she went to Buckingham Palace for the investiture and ended up fetching water and caring for all of the men who had fainted in the extreme heat that August. In 1941, she went back to the Palace for a second investiture to exchange her Gallantry Medal for the George Cross.

The 1st June arrived in dramatic fashion when Anson MK-V piloted by P/O P. Peters was attacked by nine Me 109s whilst on a Channel convoy escort patrol, with the co-pilot, Sgt D. Spencer and LAC Pepper manning the side guns. The 109s over estimated the speed of the Anson and whilst diving to attack, overshot the aircraft allowing P/O Peters to fire the front gun at the enemy. To his amazement and joy, he saw a 109 dive into the sea whilst LAC Smith, manning the rear turret, got another. Leaving the area rather rapidly, Peters set a course for Detling. The news of his success had gone ahead of his landing and upon arrival at the airfield he was welcomed by loud cheers and applause. When the ground crew inspected the aircraft, one bullet hole was found in the front section but no bullet. When Peters had his parachute repacked some time later, an intruder was found in the pack. One German bullet!

Another morale booster came on 24th June when Anson MK-N was on patrol. Fifteen minutes into the duty, several 109s attacked without once hitting the aircraft. Sgt Prentice, however, was able to send several salvoes into the belly of a 109 and had the satisfaction of seeing it crash into the sea.

July, however, was to prove a depressing month for 500 and for Detling airfield. On the evening of the 11th, three aircraft were detailed for a night patrol. It was a particularly foul night as the aircraft moved from the dispersals to the grass runway. Two of the Ansons successfully took off but the third, MK-F piloted by Sgt Wilson with Sgt Shier, Sgt O'Kelly and Sgt Worton as crew, crashed just as it became airborne. The aircraft came down in some woods, known locally as Civily Woods, about half a mile from the airfield. Tragically all of the crew perished in the crash, the bodies not being recovered until the next morning.

The next night was again a bad one when Anson MK-D failed to return to base from a fight in which three Heinkels attacked the convoy. In the same operation however, Anson 'L' flown by P/O Pain with F/O Jay, P/O Bliss and Sgt Oakwell as crew, sent one of the Heinkels into the Channel. The squadron diary for the operation gives an account in very dispassionate terms. 'Aircraft joined convoy of 21 MV [motor vessels] and 2 DR [destroyers] at LSWT 1757 at 07.40 hrs. At 08.40 hrs, convoy was attacked by three Heinkels 111K. Anson climbed to intercept and found the enemy at 6,000 feet. Anson shot down one Heinkel. Spitfires then appeared and shot down several more.'

July also saw the arrival of Wg/Cdr C.H. Turner to command 500 Squadron. The task was still convoy patrols and bombing of enemy-held harbours and with the departure of the FAA Squadrons shortly after the Dunkirk operation, they were now joined by the Blenheims of No 53 Squadron who arrived from Gatwick. They were also tasked with reconnaissance and bombing operations.

July rolled on and high summer was fast approaching. For some time it had been known that 'the Battle of Britain' was about to begin. Detling was not a fighter airfield and was therefore supposed to be of little interest to the Luftwaffe. The next month was to prove that this was totally wrong.

August arrived bringing with it a heat wave. The Detling squadrons were still carrying out the arduous duties of protecting the Channel convoys, mine spotting and bombing enemy-held harbours. On Monday, 12th August, the official grouse shooting season opened in Scotland as it had done for centuries. At Detling, the diarist recorded that Tuesday, 13th August 1940 was the day that the airfield was bombed beyond recognition.

The airfield had been relatively quiet all day. Several air raid

A He 111 wallows in the Channel after being shot down by an Anson from Detling July 1940. (C. D. Pain)

warnings had sounded in Maidstone but none lasted long and no enemy aircraft were seen in the vicinity. At 15.53 hours, the airfield was placed on an 'air raid yellow' warning, meaning that enemy aircraft were supposed to be in the area. This was upgraded at 16.00 hours to 'air raid red' indicating that aircraft had been located in the area. At 16.05 hours, Detling was attacked without any upgrading of the air raid signal. Shrieking from the cloud, 86 Junkers 87 Stuka divebombers of Lehrgeschwader 1 operating from Tramecourt in France and commanded by Hauptmann Von Brauchitsch dropped their first bombs, just as many of the airmen and women were making their way to the mess for tea. With no opposition, the accuracy of the raid was very good and in seconds the runway was hit, the hangar was hit and worst of all, the semi-sunk operations room received a direct hit. As it disappeared in one large explosion, the station commander, G/Cpt Edward Davis, a former tennis champion, fell dead with a piece of jagged concrete driven straight into his skull. Several shelters were hit with many dead and injured. Twenty two aircraft were destroyed in the hangar together with fuel bowsers and other forms of mechanical transport.

As the Stukas spread death and devastation at Detling, the local population wondered just what had hit them. Casualty Clearing Officer Wallace Beale, a Maidstone undertaker, sped to the shattered airfield together with local units of the Civil Defence. The scene they found would have made many a weaker man faint. Of the 67 people killed, many needed only the five foot coffins reserved for unidentified remains. A further 94 were injured and many of them could not be treated in the station sick bay, so serious were the injuries. A fleet of ambulances arrived to take them to Preston Hall hospital and further afield. Several of the machine gun posts situated around the perimeter of the airfield had been badly hit and it was not known until later in the evening that they also contained dead and injured.

It was a case of the airfield being caught off guard. With the warning coming too late, many were unable to make the shelters and died or were injured where they stood. In spite of the hit on the ops block, the airwomen went on plotting in another building. Corporal Josie Robins was awarded the Military Medal for her courage whilst under fire. She was in a shelter when it received a near hit. A number of men were killed and two seriously wounded, yet through the dust, fumes and rubble, Cpl Robins administered first aid before fetching stretchers and remaining with the wounded until they were evacuated. The citation of 20th December 1940 stated that she displayed courage and coolness of a very high order in a position of extreme danger. Another Military Medal was awarded to Sergeant Youle, also a Waaf, as a result of her courage in the same attack. She was on duty in the station telephone exchange when it received a direct hit. Her staff were subjected to a rain of debris and splinters and to the noise of exploding bombs. It was solely due to the cool bravery and the superb example set by Sgt Youle that the telephone operators carried on their task with calmness and complete efficiency at a most dangerous time.

The taxiways and dispersal points around the perimeter were badly bombed as well as the entire grass landing area. One machine gun post and two anti-aircraft sites suffered direct hits, killing all the army personnel manning them. One gunner situated in a similar post was heard to say that he had preferred it at Dunkirk!

By early evening, all available personnel were put to filling in the craters on the landing area and later that night, sufficient areas had been filled in to allow the Ansons to take off on operations. A mass funeral was held at Maidstone Cemetery for the majority of the dead, a harrowing experience for all those who attended and took part.

With the airfield a shambles, many personnel now lived off site. The

80

The funeral of the Detling victims killed in the 13th August raid, at Sutton Road cemetery, Maidstone. (Kent Messenger)

Waafs were billeted in a large house on the Sittingbourne Road called Woodlands, whilst the airmen were accommodated in several large houses in the area. Despite the devastation however, all essential services were back in operation by the afternoon of the 14th. The raid, though crippling, had little effect on Fighter Command. German intelligence had deemed the airfield to be a fighter base and gloated over the fact that the Stukas had very nearly decimated it.

Despite the fine weather, the next few weeks saw no attacks on Detling, allowing repair work to carry on. With the departure of all the FAA squadrons, the field was left to the Ansons and Blenheims. With the Battle of Britain still raging overhead, the aircraft continued to fly out of Detling at low level and head for the Channel to take up their positions over the convoys. Most of the Ansons of 500 had now been fitted with a 20 mm cannon secured to a new and stronger mounting supplied by the British Cannon Manufacturing Company. This made the Ansons of 500 the only aircraft in the world to fly with a free-mounted cannon in addition to their normal gun complement. As a relief from flying constant convoy patrols, the squadron was also tasked with flying over London and reporting on the effectiveness of the blackout. From the air it was perfectly easy to see just where light was

81

coming from. This work, however, did entail each crew writing a report on what they saw and sending it to the Air Ministry. For this reason alone, it was not a popular operation!

As the end of August approached, enemy aircraft once again began to fly around the airfield. On the 30th, Detling, by now nearly back to normal, suffered another raid. The day had begun with a renewal of the attacks upon Channel shipping. In the morning and afternoon, many of the major fighter airfields in Kent were bombed but the worst crisis was when the radar stations of Dover, Pevensey, Rye, Foreness, Fairlight, Whitstable and Beachy Head were all put out of action due to a mains electricity failure. Now it was left to the sharp eyes of the Observer Corps to give an early warning. This they did in the late afternoon when they plotted a large force of enemy bombers making for Detling.

This time the airfield was warned in time allowing many non-essential personnel to take to the shelters. As the sirens began to sound in Maidstone, Captain Eschwege and the Me 109s of JG 52 based at Coquelles arrived over the airfield. Together with the Me 110s of ZG 26, they commenced to bomb and machine gun Detling. Dropping high explosive and delayed action bombs, the Messerschmitts set a fuel dump on fire, badly damaged the runway once again and demolished further buildings, one of them containing a 53 Squadron Blenheim. The main electricity cable was cut by a single bomb and this in turn rendered the airfield non-operational for 15 hours.

The next day, the 31st, a force of 100 bombers made for the Coastal Command airfield at Eastchurch, just a short distance away from Detling. On their way home, the fighter escort subjected the airfield to a machine gun attack but no bombs. Some slight damage occurred. Sunday 1st September dawned fine and warm as 120 enemy aircraft crossed the English coastline and split into several formations. One attacked Detling at around 11.30 am and a second attack of the day came at 4.30 pm when 50 bombers dropped high explosive bombs. Most of the temporary hangars put up for maintenance work were wrecked but they contained no aircraft, these were now dispersed in the woods around the airfield. Yet again, the runway suffered and further buildings were destroyed as the airfield once more became non-operational.

During the following night, whilst clearance was continuing, several lone raiders attacked. These were mainly nuisance raids and did little damage apart from hindering the reconstruction work. September promised further fine weather indicating that there would be no easing of maritime operations. It was still a very dangerous sky for the Ansons as Fl/Lt Richard Rodgers remembers.

'We carried on with our Channel patrols throughout September. On the 24th we took off at 10.55 in Anson N5355 flown by F/O Armstrong for our usual search in the Straits. On that I was detailed for both gunnery and wireless. F/O Armstrong spotted a single-engined Henschell spotter plane about half-way across the Channel heading for the French coast. We went straight in to attack using the fixed Browning front gun in the nose. It was a decoy for immediately we were sprung upon by three 109 fighters diving down at us from out of the sun. We turned for home at sea level. I fired continually from the rear turret and had the satisfaction of seeing the leading fighter turn away after his attack with intermittent puffs of smoke issuing from under his engine. The other two pounded us pretty much as we fish-tailed and weaved about but they broke off the attack when we crossed the Kent coast.

'I was called forward urgently by F/O Armstrong and was very much taken aback when I saw the mess in the cabin. The wireless equipment was completely shattered and had I been sitting there, as usually I did, I would have been blown to pieces. There were a lot of holes in the fuselage, some broken windows and torn fabric. I went up beside F/O Armstrong, who was looking very pale. He shouted in my ear that he had been hit in the legs and asked me to stay with him. There was blood from his wounds seeping through his flying clothing and some also on the floor near the rudder pedals. I will never know how he managed to pilot the aircraft but I map-read for him and eventually we arrived back over Detling and fired off a succession of red Verey cartridges. I saw the ambulance and fire tender move out below and position themselves in readiness. We came in on a steady, fairly flat approach and landed in a slightly uphill direction. Near the end of the landing run the aircraft turned into a gentle ground loop as F/O Armstrong was unable to correct the swing due to his injuries. We quickly got him out and into the waiting ambulance which took him straight into the Rochester/Chatham hospital. It was a bad feeling to have death so near to you.'

On 5th September 1940, the Luftwaffe landed at Detling. It was not the much prophesied paratroop landing but more a case of being lost. The aircraft was a Me 109 flown by Oberleutnant Carl-Heinz Metz. Hearing the sound of an aircraft approaching, the duty watch at Detling sounded the siren. Looking to the north of the airfield, a single aircraft was seen to lower its undercarriage. The siren stopped and to the amazement of all the duty personnel, an enemy aircraft did one circuit and landed. The fire tender and guard truck raced to intercept the 109 but the pilot brought the aircraft to a perfect landing. Standing up in the cockpit, Carl-Heinz Metz raised his hands above his head and gracefully surrendered. He had realised he was hopelessly lost and short of fuel when he sighted the airfield a few miles away. Rather than face a wet crash-landing in the Channel, he lowered his wheels and landed. He was later transferred to a prison camp and the intact aircraft was flown to Farnborough for evaluation.

After a fairly hectic period at Detling, 53 Squadron took their Blenheims to Thorney Island on 24th November 1940. As the rebuilding programme gathered momentum, new Blister hangars began to appear in the dispersal areas. Even this small crumb of comfort did nothing to appease the poor ground crews who since the bombing, had to service the aircraft outside in all weathers. The Blister hangars, open to the elements at each end, were just as draughty.

The frost and snow ensured a quiet Christmas for Detling as it prepared to enter a new stage of its life. The postponement of Operation Sealion, the proposed invasion of England on 17th September, did nothing to lessen the amount of convoy patrols in the Channel. Again, despite the fact that by now Hitler had ordered that the attacks on the airfields stop at the expense of crippling London in the hope that it would bring England to her knees, Coastal Command and 500 Squadron in particular were still facing a difficult task.

Despite all of this, the new year opened with the *London Gazette* announcing that ten members of the squadron had received mentions in despatches. Tragically, three of them had been killed before they knew of their awards. With the Battle of Britain resulting in a victory for Fighter Command, life at Detling had become more stable. 'A' Flight of 500 had been sent on detachment to Bircham Newton in Norfolk and were engaged in similar work but this time over the North Sea. In March Wg/Cdr Turner left the squadron and was replaced by Wg/Cdr M.Q. Chandler. He brought the news that the squadron was in line for a change of aircraft and with the return of 'A' Flight to Detling, they did convert to the Blenheim after temporarily ceasing operations at midnight on 7th April 1941.

The conversion went very smoothly and within a few weeks they had settled into an operational routine. This, however, was not to last as rumours began to abound that 500 were to leave Detling. On 15th May, the rumours became fact when it was announced that the entire squadron was to go to Bircham Newton. For nearly three years, Detling had been home to 500. It had shared in their joy and sorrow. It had seen their triumphs and their despairs. Now it was time to move on as Detling was earmarked to become an army co-operation airfield and then a fighter base.

With the departure of the Ansons, Detling was left to get on with its reconstruction until 4th August 1941 when No 26 Squadron brought their Curtiss Tomahawks over from Gatwick. Although labelled a fighter by the Americans, all home-based aircraft operated as low level reconnaissance platforms. They stayed for four days carrying out several sorties before moving back to Gatwick, leaving Detling without any squadrons.

Aircraft still flew in and out but it was not until 10th February 1942 that a resident squadron arrived in the shape of No 280 Air Sea Rescue. Having been formed at Thorney Island in late December 1941, it was intended to equip the squadron with Hudsons but when these became required for other units, it was the faithful Anson that again flew into Detling. With the motto of 'We Shall Be There', 280 carried out rescue operations before transferring to Langham on 31st July 1942.

Although still a small grass airfield, Detling was often used in an emergency for heavy four-engined bombers returning from missions over enemy territory. When these incidents occurred, it took all the skill of the pilots, both British and American, to land safely within the confines of the airfield.

Detling changed from Coastal Command to Army Co-operation Command during 1942 allowing No 239 Squadron to bring the first Mustang 1s to fly from the base on 19th May. Unlike other American fighters supplied to the RAF, the Mustang was not merely a British version of an existing American type. It was designed from the outset as an RAF aircraft and although handicapped at high altitudes by the lack of power emanating from the Allison engine, it proved successful as an armed tactical reconnaissance aircraft. Later marks were to prove more successful. Once again, it was a quick turn-round as the squadron left for Gatwick on 31st May 1942.

As we have seen during the Battle of Britain, defence of Detling and all the other airfields was left to ground personnel of the RAF and the army. In 1942, airfield security was firmly placed in the hands of the newly formed RAF Regiment. No 2368 Squadron was formed at Detling in March 1942 and four weeks later had the honour of carrying out guard duty at Buckingham Palace, the first Regiment squadron to do so. Summer 1942 also saw the finish of the rebuilding programme as the new station chapel was dedicated by the Archbishop of Canterbury.

As the war began to be carried back to Europe, Detling became a

Fighter Command airfield, though still entirely grass. No 26 Squadron brought their Mustang 1s in from Gatwick for the last of the army co-operation duties to be flown from the airfield. They departed to Stoney Cross on 1st March 1943. Two weeks later with its new status as a fighter airfield, Detling saw the formation of No 318 (Danzig) Squadron, an all Polish unit. It was formed as a tactical reconnaissance unit and received Hurricanes for training purposes, the first true fighter to use Detling. With their arrival, language became a problem between the pilots and the operations room controllers. Whilst some of the Polish pilots spoke very broken English, others spoke very little at all. It was decided to hold classes for basic English in the air, something that did not prove a great success. It was found that when calm, the pilots did use what English they had learnt. However, in moments of intense excitement and battle, they would revert back to their own tongue. Despite protests from the controllers, once this happened it took a long time for them to come back to English! Training continued until August 1943 when the squadron left for the Middle East.

In 1940, the army had taken over eight Plus D (90 hp Cirrus Minor) light planes for experiments with a new type of artillery spotting work, later to be known as Air Observation Post duties. The success of the trials resulted in the production of the Taylorcraft Auster, the third version of which came to Detling in the form of No 655 Squadron. They carried out training exercises with the local searchlight and ack-ack units before being posted to North Africa in August.

The Mustangs of No 26 returned on 22nd June 1943 for a period of further training until 11th July when they left for Martlesham Heath, leaving Detling rather quiet, for a period at any rate. The peace did not last long for in October it once again became a front line airfield.

With the improvement in the fortunes of war, the era of the big wing arrived. No longer was it to be the task of the fighter to be on the defensive for in future, two or more squadrons would fly together and roam across enemy territory in the hope of enticing the enemy aircraft up and causing as much damage as possible to them and any ground installations. The wings were led by a Wing Commander of some standing and the operations could be escorting bombers or just flying in enemy airspace looking for targets of opportunity. Detling became the base for No 125 Airfield which included No 132 (City of Bombay) Squadron who flew the Spitfire IXB, No 184 flying the Hurricane IV and No 602 (City of Glasgow) also flying the Spitfire IXB. Arriving from Newchurch on 12th October 1943, the wing was commanded by Wg/Cdr R.D. Yule, DSO, DFC and Bar. Many of their operations were to act as escort to the ever increasing number of American bombers that were bombing German targets on the ground.

Later in the year, Noball sites, the name given to the V1 rocket launch pads, came under heavy attack. It had been known for some time that the enemy had invented a robot bomb and photo reconnaissance aircraft had brought back evidence of this.

At this particular time, No 184 Squadron were still flying the tank busting Hurricane IV. With their four 60 lb rockets attached to the wings, they were no match in speed for the Me 109 or the FW 190. On 8th December 1943, eight aircraft from 184 had just crossed the French coast enroute to bombing a Noball site when ten 109s attacked them. The Hurricanes, with the extra weight of the rockets, never stood a chance and sadly, six were lost whilst the other two crashed on landing. Such a disaster ensured that whilst 184 were still flying the Hurricane, the Spitfires of the other two squadrons would act as escorts. A typical operation is recorded by one of the pilots of 602 Squadron, Pierre Closterman, on 15th December 1943.

'There was mist and damp and the clouds scraped the tree-tops. At least we would get some rest that day. Sitting in front of bacon and eggs and several slices of toast done to a turn and dripping with butter, I was having breakfast in the mess at the same time arranging the programme for the day. Suddenly the tannoy blasted, "Will the following pilots of 602 report to intelligence immediately." Seething, I heard my name among the eight called.

'At 09.40 hours, the Spitfires took off and plunged in the mist towards Dungeness. In mid-Channel, visibility improved and the ceiling rose to 1,000 feet. We followed the course of the Somme as far as Abbeville and all was quiet. No flak, everything seemed deserted and asleep. Suddenly the ball began. From each bank light flak opened fire. The air filled at once with long incandescent trails, red and green 20 mm tracers criss-crossed each other painting quite a picture. Turning 90 degrees left, we caught sight of three 109s under camouflage nets in the corner of a field. Going in after each other, we gave them hell and finished by shooting up the control tower. Drenched with sweat, we turned for home and landed at Detling in pouring rain and dense fog. Home sweet home!'

No 125 Airfield transferred to the 2nd Tactical Air Force on 15th November 1943. This force had been established to replace Army Co-Operation Command on 1st June 1943. It absorbed part of Fighter Command which was itself renamed Air Defence of Great Britain, a title that it kept until 15th October when it reverted to its former name. In the months that followed, 2 TAF would grow to an air armada of more than 5,000 operational aircraft.

A new squadron formed at Detling on 1st December 1943 in the shape of No 567. This was formed from No 1624 Flight which was used for anti-aircraft co-operation duties in the south east of England. It used a variety of aircraft including Martinets for target-towing, Hurricanes for simulated attacks and Oxfords for gunlaying and searchlight practice. With a detachment at Eastchurch, the unit gave sterling service until it went to Hornchurch in Essex on 14th November 1944.

The Detling wing were now doing daily battle with the FW 190s. When they were not on escort duties the Spitfires patrolled and roamed across areas of France where they knew the enemy aircraft were likely to be. Though the wing had a lot of success they also lost valuable pilots and aircraft. A typically bad sortie was the one flown on 21st December when the wing was bounced by 30 FW 190s. In the battle, two pilots of 602 were lost together with three from 132. All for shooting down two 190s.

The new year saw the same pattern of operations continue but it was all change for two squadrons in January, when 132 went to Castletown on the 17th and 602 moved to Skaebrae at the same time. No 184 were to move to Odiham on 6th March and convert to the Typhoon 1B whilst No 118 with the Spitfire VI arrived at Detling on 20th January with No 453 with the Spitfire VC beating them by one day. Both squadrons flew similar operations with the 2nd TAF before moving on in March. Glad to be back, Nos 132 and 602 returned and began to prepare for Operation Overlord, the Allied invasion of France. It was a period of rapid change at Detling.

Shortly after their arrival, the Spitfires were fitted with bomb racks in order to carry on attacks on Noball sites. These launch pads took roughly four to five months to build together with a below ground air raid shelter for the engineers and controllers. With the majority of the concrete not exceeding two inches in thickness, the rockets and bombs were able to penetrate much of it. The main difficulty at this time for Noball operations was the accuracy of the attacks by the squadrons.

Nos 132 and 602 were not to take part in the D-Day landings from Detling for they were posted to Ford on 18th April 1944. One month later, a Spitfire wing consisting of Nos 80, 229 and 274 Squadrons arrived to carry on the offensive. Arriving on 19th May and led by Wg/Cdr E.P. 'Hawkeye' Wells DSO, DFC, all the units flew the Spitfire IX and had moved over from Hornchurch. Wg/Cdr Mike Crossley, he of Biggin Hill fame, arrived to command Detling at a time when the airfield was approaching its busiest period since 1940.

Spitfires of 132 (Bombay) Squadron at Detling in 1944. (IWM)

The wing were briefed to clear the forward areas in support of the Allied landings and to attack trains, lorries and anything else that moved in enemy territory. In addition, attacks carried on against the Noball sites.

Originally planned for 5th June, bad weather postponed the invasion for 24 hours. In the early hours of the 6th, Allied naval forces landed troops on the French coast between Cherbourg and Le Havre. The Detling wing were still tasked with clearing the forward areas and as they flew over the Channel, could see the myriads of naval vessels making their way across the water.

With D-Day a success, the wing moved out on 24th June to Merston in Sussex. The threat of the V1 campaign took over as more and more 'Doodlebugs' were launched against London. One method of bringing them down before they reached their target was by shooting them out of the sky. For this very dangerous work, codenamed 'Diver', Nos 1 and 165 (Ceylon) Squadrons arrived from Harrowbeer on 22nd June. Flying the Spitfire IXB, they commenced anti-diver patrols against a target that, because of its size and speed, made it difficult to hit. It was normal for the fighters to attack from the rear when about 300 yards away. One obvious danger was that the V1 would explode in their face damaging their own aircraft. A later technique was that of the fighter flying alongside the V1, allowing the closeness of the two wings to upset the airflow, causing the V1 to tilt and fly into the ground.

The Detling wing joined the other anti-diver squadrons in maintaining daylight patrols in three areas stretching roughly from Dover to Beachy Head, Dover to Newhaven and Haywards Heath to Ashford. They flew at around 12,000 feet in lanes of three, aided by other squadrons when the V1 attacks began.

No 1 were the first to score when they shot down one on 24th June. The rest of the month saw success for both squadrons until they were posted to Lympne, nearer the coast, on 11th July 1944. In their place came Nos 118, 124 (Baroda) and 504 (County of Nottingham) Squadrons to carry out further Ramrod and bomber escort duties. They too stayed but a brief time, moving out on 9th August to allow Nos 1 and 165 to return. Detling was again back to anti-diver operations.

Daily the V1s flew over or close to the airfield. The official German aiming point was the Tower of London but many fell short of this due to engine failure, being shot down by fighters or the ack-ack barrage or catching balloon cables. By 29th June, local defences included 680 balloons, 376 heavy anti-aircraft guns and 522 light anti-aircraft guns sited along the ridge of the North Downs. Early warning of the V1s came from the radar stations at West Hythe, Swingate, Fairlight and Beachy Head. Plotted as they left the French coast, it enabled the fighters to be airborne in plenty of time in the hope of catching them crossing the Channel, thus saving lives on the ground.

The wing remained at Detling until 15th December. When the V1 attacks got fewer, due to the sites being overrun by the advancing Allies, they continued the escort duties. Participation in a large operation took place on 17th September when they escorted the airborne troops taking part in Operation Market, the plan to secure the Rhine bridgehead at Arnhem. For the next nine days they flew escort duties to some 4,000 aircraft and 500 gliders taking the 'paras' to begin the assault. No enemy aircraft were encountered but opportunities presented themselves for some ground attack work. With the end of the operation, it was back to Ramrods until 15th December when they departed the airfield.

Detling's war was fast approaching its end when it was placed under Care and Maintenance on 18th December 1944. With heavier and more powerful aircraft entering service, a grass airfield was not really suitable for such operations. Although war was to rage for a further seven months, Detling was only used as a demonstration and instructional unit for No 1336 Wing of the RAF Regiment. In October

1945, the station became part of No 60 Group with No 75 Signals Wing moving in until 1946. Once again it was placed under Care and Maintenance and No 141 Gliding School who had formed in 1946 were replaced by No 168 GS, this later becoming the Home Command Gliding Instructors School. They stayed until 1955 when No 1903 (AOP) Flight moved in with Austers to remain for a year. When they moved to Feltwell in Norfolk, Detling finally closed on 1st April 1956.

Civilian gliders in the form of the Kent Gliding Club used the field until they found a permanent site at Challock leaving the grass airfield to a very uncertain future. Much of the land was returned to its original owners but the Kent County Council purchased an area of the airfield to use as the County Showground, an event held yearly that attracts thousands of visitors. A civilian VOR airway beacon was placed on part of the landing area to aid the many civil aircraft flying overhead, perhaps a fitting tribute to an airfield that had contributed so much to the war effort.

Today the one Bellman hangar is still standing albeit now clad over for protection and the operations block, which was built towards the latter part of the war, is in use though as a refrigeration unit! Detling is giving up some of its secrets even today for 1993 saw much of the area evacuated when a Bomb Disposal team arrived to deal with a cluster of pipe mines that had been laid in the grass during 1940 in case of an aerial invasion. The Pickett-Hamilton Retractable gun turrets that were placed along the landing area are still in place though very badly flooded, something to which they were prone too during the war. Though sheep now graze on most of the site, for the avid historian there is still much to see.

In 1998 a memorial was erected and dedicated to all the squadrons that served at the airfield. It was provided from public funds by a group which included yours truly and four local Detling people. The day was further celebrated by a flypast of the Swordfish from the Royal Naval Flight and a Hurricane from the Battle of Britain Memorial Flight. This is the final chapter in the history of RAF Detling.

4
EASTCHURCH

Born in the earliest days of flying, the name Eastchurch is synonymous with the first experimental flying in the UK together with the birth of the Royal Aero Club. Illustrious people such as the Hon C.S. Rolls, Lord Brabazon and Francis McClean were initiated to the joys of flying at Eastchurch and it was here that the famous aircraft manufacturing company of Short Brothers first came to prominence.

It was the Admiralty that established flying on the island and which by 1912 had greatly expanded the site. During the First World War it was a Royal Naval Air Station but with the cessation of hostilities, flying activity on the station slowly faded. It became the Armament and Gunnery School in 1922 with various squadrons and units spending time there. As the clouds gathered for the second conflict, a Station Headquarters was established on the site as the School moved over to Manby allowing No 21 Squadron to bring their Hawker Hinds up from Lympne on 15th August 1938 and rapidly convert to the Blenheim I. Two weeks later No 48 flew their Avro Ansons in from nearby Manston and Eastchurch was transferred to No 16 Group, Coastal Command. The Munich crisis of September 1938 brought the airfield and its units onto a full war footing but when the country was told 'it was peace in our time', the emergency was relaxed a little.

The easing of the tension was a welcome relief to Coastal Command who at this time were in some difficulty. With ten squadrons of Ansons, one of Hudsons, two of Sunderlands and even older aircraft such as the Stranraer and London, the command was in a poor state. This was to improve rapidly by September 1940 but at the opening stages of the war, Eastchurch together with other Coastal Command stations was not really equipped for a full scale conflict.

Before this happened however, No 21 Squadron moved to Watton in Norfolk on 2nd March 1939 with 48 Squadron going to Thorney Island in August. Two days before war broke out, Eastchurch was reduced to Care and Maintenance.

Hurricane Is of 87 (United Provinces) Squadron at Eastchurch on a morale boosting visit in 1939. The 1939 camouflage had the portside underwings painted black and the starboard underwings painted white. The RAF roundels were outlined in yellow. (R. G. Moss)

With the phoney war period at this time, its closure did not affect Britain's air supremacy at all. It was only to last until December when the airfield became the Polish Training Centre. As the first batch of bewildered and bedraggled Poles arrived, the task of recuperation and the allocation of work began. The cruel winter of 1939/40 did not have the same effect on them as it did the station airmen at Eastchurch. They were somehow hardened to the frost and snow whilst the English huddled around the stoves as much as possible. As if to enlarge upon this fact, by March 1940, 1,300 Polish airmen were billeted on the camp. As the period of the Dunkirk evacuation approached and although Eastchurch was not involved in Operation Dynamo, the training centre was moved to Blackpool in May as the airfield entered a new stage of its career.

59 Squadron had been flying out of the French airfields of Crecy-on-Ponthiem and Poix as part of the British help to France. With the rapid advance of the Germans into Holland, Belgium and then France, they had returned to Lympne on 20th May 1940. On the 31st, the Blenheim IVs flew into Eastchurch and commenced reconnaissance flights over

their old territory. With detachments still at Boos and Dreux, 59 were joined by 53 Squadron in June but by the 13th of the month, both had left.

On the outbreak of war, an Advanced Air Striking Force was sent to France in the hope that their presence would halt the German advance. It was the Fairey Battle light bomber that spearheaded the force and it was a Battle gunner that claimed the first German aircraft to be shot down during the war in the west. With the German attacks on the Low Countries, the aircraft were sent into action and encountered heavy losses. On 10th May 1940, the Fairey Battles of No 12 Squadron attacked the Maastricht bridges with disastrous results. F/O D.E. Garland and Sgt T. Gray were killed, but each man's bravery whilst under extreme fire was recognised by a posthumous Victoria Cross.

Returning to the UK in June, No 12 arrived at Eastchurch on 12th August, still equipped with Battles, and commenced night attacks on enemy invasion craft in the French Channel Ports. They were joined by No 142 Squadron again equipped with Battles who were performing similar operations. In addition to the light bomber squadrons, a detachment from No 19 Squadron flying the Spitfire IB had arrived from Fowlmere on 24th July 1940 and No 266 (Rhodesia) Squadron had flown their Spitfire Is in for two days on 12th August. With Eastchurch visibly overcrowded, the Luftwaffe Intelligence Service decreed the airfield a fighter base and promptly attacked it.

The raid came on the opening of Eagle Day, 13th August. Early that morning as the mist cleared, Luftflotten 2 and 3 were eager and ready to go. At Epinoy, Arras and Cambrai, the Do17s of Kampfgeschwader 2 under the command of Oberst Johannes Fink, were already bombed and fuelled up. As they got airborne and circled Arras waiting for their escort of Me 110s, Fink thought about the earlier briefing that had told him that it was just a matter of time before the English capitulated. The arrival of the escort brought his mind back to reality but he was puzzled by the antics of the 110s who appeared to be flying all around his bombers in a series of unusual manoeuvres. Shrugging it off as boyish, excitable behaviour, Fink set course for his target, Eastchurch airfield.

The true circumstances of the escorting 110s strange behaviour did not come to light until much later. With a change in the weather forecast to cloudy conditions, the start of Eagle Day was postponed by Goering's headquarters until later in the day when it was said conditions would improve. The postponement message, however, only reached the fighter escort and not Fink and his force of bombers due to a faulty radio in his aircraft. The antics of the escorts were their way of trying to inform him the early raids were cancelled.

So KG2 moved out over the Channel minus its fighter escort. Fleecy cloud did in fact cover them across the water but as the armada crossed over Margate, it began to thin a little. Over Faversham and flying at 10,000 feet, his target was plainly visible. Eighty four bombers spread out over the sky began to jostle for a bomb run position. Eastchurch seemed asleep with the rows of aircraft sitting neatly in lines on the grass. Fink smiled to himself and thought if every raid was to be as easy as this, the battle would be over in a month or less.

G/Cpt Frank Hopps, the CO of Eastchurch, had no prior warning of the raid. It was only when he took a call from HQ Coastal Command at 6.30 am that he realised his airfield was in danger. The warning came too late for as he put the telephone down and turned to pull on his flying boots, the first bombs were dropping. Throwing himself into the nearest trench, he watched the devastation of his airfield in utter amazement.

The noise was deafening as bomb after bomb rained down. Fires sprang up everywhere and the entire area was enveloped in thick, acrid black smoke. The operations room received a direct hit, cutting off all telephone lines with the outside world. The neat rows of aircraft that Fink had seen on his approach had gone and in their place were burning hulks with ammunition exploding everywhere and adding to the general carnage. With no real emergency plan in operation, the airmen

A Do 17 shot down during the attack on Eastchurch on 13th August 1940. It force-landed at Stodmarsh. (MAP)

were lost and bewildered, not knowing whether they should stay where they were or rush out to shelters and trenches. Some that did go outside did not make it to cover as the splinters of metal from the exploding bombs tore through anything in its way including human flesh. In one loud explosion above all others, the fuel dump went up in flames as Eastchurch shook and quivered under the assault.

Above the airfield the Luftwaffe did not have it all their own way despite the destruction they were causing on the ground. Already as they approached Eastchurch, the Spitfires of 74 Squadron from Hornchurch had broken the armada up. Even so, 50 of Fink's aircraft had made the airfield but after dropping their bombs ran into trouble as they turned for home. 111 Squadron from Croydon were waiting for them, their Hurricanes poised to avenge the desecration of Eastchurch. And this they did with no fewer than five Do 17s shot down and six damaged.

Back on the ground, people were emerging from cover to survey the damage. They could not believe their eyes at the carnage as the fires still raged. Five Blenheims were total wrecks together with all six Spitfires of No 266 Squadron. Twelve people were dead with a further 26 badly injured. Of the buildings, the ops room had received a direct hit, the NCOs' mess had caught another and some of the technical buildings were in flames. As night fell on Eastchurch, the fire tenders and ambulances were still fighting the fires and recovering the dead and injured. Most were taken to the Sheppey hospital but when this became full, they had to endure a journey to Sittingbourne. The airfield was rendered unserviceable but due to the efforts of everyone including the local GPO engineers, it was back on air within ten hours. The remaining aircraft were dispersed at various points around the field. Had this been done originally, the loss of aircraft may not have been so great. Later that evening, the figures for the day came through from HQ Fighter Command. No 11 Group had lost 13 aircraft over 700 sorties but 35 enemy aircraft had failed to return home. Most were littering the lush Kent countryside.

Slowly the base returned to normality as the two resident squadrons continued their reconnaissance and bombing duties. The devastation did little to hinder Fighter Command for Eastchurch was not a fighter base. Obviously the German High Command still considered it so for the next raid on 15th August undid much of the work done in clearing up. It came at around 3.30 pm when several enemy aircraft detached from a large force raiding nearby Rochester and dropped a number of high explosive bombs. Since the raid on 13th August, many personnel had moved off the airfield to a requisitioned house at Warden Bay whilst the sick quarters was moved into Eastchurch village. Hence the latest raid did not cause any loss of life, but it certainly made another mess of the airfield. Five days later the Luftwaffe returned, still convinced that Eastchurch was a fighter base. On this occasion very little damage was done as the bombs fell around the perimeter.

The airfield was subjected to several night raids, one of them coming on the night of 30th/31st August. From 8.30 pm, raiders were coming in and aiming for the Midlands with Liverpool as the main target. Several single aircraft detached from the main force and bombed airfields in the South East including Eastchurch. Again, very little damage was done.

September saw the Luftwaffe continuing its timetable of bombing Kent airfields and on two consecutive days there were raids on Eastchurch, the worst being on Monday, 2nd September. With morning breaking fine and warm with early morning mist, the Luftwaffe stepped up the tempo in a last all out effort to bring Fighter Command to its knees. Eastchurch was not on the list until the afternoon when around 3.15 pm, the Chain Home radars picked up signs of a large force assembling over Calais; 250 bombers then crossed the Channel and spread out over Kent. Around 3.50 pm, several Do 17s came in low over the Isle of Sheppey and dropped many bombs. One bomb hit the ammunition dump whilst others demolished the Naafi and administration buildings. Once again, black smoke and flames leapt into the air as the water and sewerage mains were fractured. One direct hit on a hangar caused the loss of six aircraft, this particular bomb killing four airmen inside and wounding a further twelve. Once again, Eastchurch was out of contact with the outside world for several hours.

The results of the bombing forced Nos 12 and 142 Squadrons to move over to Binbrook leaving the airfield virtually abandoned except for the station permanent staff. Although it was to remain in Coastal Command until June 1941, very little use was made of its facilities, though it was once again made serviceable. Transfer to Technical Training Command came in June 1941 and saw the arrival of the RAF Artillery School, forerunner of the RAF Regiment. Spitfires returned to Eastchurch on 30th June 1942 when No 124 (Baroda) Squadron came in from Gravesend. They used the base as a forward operating airfield and commenced Ramrod operations. Leaving one month later and going back to Gravesend, they were replaced on 3rd July by No 401 (Ram) Squadron of the RCAF. Their Spitfire VBs were also used on Ramrod operations in addition to pure fighter sweeps. On 25th July they moved to Martlesham Heath and converted to the Spitfire IX.

As Tuesday 18th August 1942 dawned in the French town of Dieppe, very little difference was felt by the local residents. With the German occupation of their country, they had adapted to take life as it came. Little did they know that on the other side of the Channel, an operation had been planned for the 19th involving their town that was intended to shorten the war by years. As it turned out, it proved to be a total disaster in which the Canadian Army saw many of their troops taken prisoners of war. This was Operation Jubilee, the ill-fated invasion of Dieppe. Eastchurch was to play a major role in keeping the enemy aircraft at bay during and after the landings.

By early August, it had been decided to base 'lodger' squadrons at the airfield, the intention being that the base would remain under the control of Technical Training Command but squadrons would be using the airfield for short periods. In came No 65 (East India) Squadron on 14th August followed by No 165 (Ceylon) Squadron a day later, both flying Spitfire VBs. The latter had only formed in April 1942 and although scrambled many times from their base at Ayr, saw no action until they arrived at Eastchurch. For three days, both units carried out several sorties until the day of Operation Jubilee, 19th August.

From early morning, both squadrons were at full readiness but it was 65 that were first airborne at 03.30 am when they acted as escort to

Air cadets assisting in the start-up of a 65 Squadron Spitfire at Eastchurch in 1942. (J. D. Rawlings)

bombers attacking forward targets prior to the landings, in this ill-fated invasion of Dieppe. This sortie was uneventful and all aircraft returned safely to Eastchurch. Up to 9 am the RAF had the sky to themselves with no German aircraft apparent. The second sortie of the day was not quite so easy as the Luftwaffe took to the skies. Flying top cover to a formation of Bostons, 65 shot down two Do 217s. Success also came the way of 165 Squadron whose role was to provide cover for ships of the Royal Navy carrying the Canadian troops. During several sorties, they shot down two Do 217s, damaging another and a Ju 88 in the process. Whilst both squadrons suffered no loss, it was obvious to the pilots that a tragedy was unfurling below. The presence of the RAF, however, over Dieppe ensured that from the air, no enemy bombing formations got through to add to the Canadians' plight. Any attacks on the landing troops were kept to single aircraft as squadrons of Spitfires and Bostons kept up the pressure all day long. By nightfall, almost 3,000 sorties had been flown by the RAF. Sadly, this success was not repeated on the ground as the withdrawal of the battered army began. Dieppe had been the failure prophesied by so many.

The Eastchurch squadrons had good reason to be proud of their achievements but with the crisis over, both left for Fighter Command bases. The station once again went into a state of Care and Maintenance.

No 72 Group Army Co-operation Command arrived on 12th October 1942 as the station transferred to Army Co-operation Command with the Technical Training Command remaining as a 'lodger' unit. Yet again, operational flying became very sparse, a situation that continued until 1943 when, during a large army co-operation exercise, several units spent time at Eastchurch. No 184 brought their Hurricane IIBs to the base in March and immediately sent a detachment to Zeals. The Hurricanes were used on anti-tank operations and were joined in April by the Spitfires of No 132 (Bombay) Squadron, both units combining shortly after to form No 122 Airfield. The wing commenced fighter sweeps over France yet again, but their time at Eastchurch was limited and by May, 122 Airfield had gone and the base had been transferred to No 54 Group.

From this time on, usage of Eastchurch as a flying field was severely curtailed. Instead it became a Combined Aircrew Reselection Centre. During October 1943, No 18 Armament Practice Camp was formed at the field with the unit being equipped with the Miles Master III, a two-seat advanced trainer. Target and drogue towing was provided by No 291 Squadron and No 567 Squadron, both units supplying detachments to Eastchurch. Further work was carried out on the reconstruction of

The memorial in Eastchurch village commemorating the first home of British aviation, since 1909. (R. J. Brooks)

the airfield after the 1940 raids when three Bellman hangars were erected to house the Masters together with Pierced Steel Planking being laid in the dispersal areas. This was how Eastchurch remained for the rest of 1943 and into 1944.

Being a grass airfield it was obviously restricted in its use but this did not stop heavy bombers landing in times of distress. Apart from this occasional excitement, Eastchurch remained an Armament Practice Camp for the rest of its war together with the aircrew centre still in situ. The APC moved to Fairwood Common in August 1944 although the base still provided lodger facilities for squadrons in training. The end of the war saw Eastchurch revert to Care and Maintenance on 1st September 1946, reducing to an inactive site in 1947. From this condition, it never recovered and lay decaying until June 1950 when the Air Ministry relinquished the field and the Home Office established an open prison on the airfield domestic site.

5
GRAVESEND

It was the National Aviation Day Tours of Sir Alan Cobham that first placed Gravesend Airport on the aviation map. When he visited for the first time on 16th April 1933, the prospect of a cheap flight ensured that the little airfield was packed to capacity.

Originally known as Gravesend-London (East), it acted as a diversion airfield for Croydon but its first real use came in 1933 when Edgar Percival, a disciple of Alan Cobham, established his manufacturing plant in the small hangar erected on the site. Having tasted success with a three-seat low wing monoplane which he flew from nearby West Malling, Percival went on to produce a beautiful range of aircraft known as the Gull and the Mew Gull. In all, 22 were built at Gravesend and were owned and flown by such illustrious aviators as Jean Batten, Amy Mollinson (nee Johnson) and Sir Charles Kingsford-Smith.

Edgar Percival remained at Gravesend until December 1936 when he moved his facility to Luton. The hangars were not left vacant for long as Essex Aero Ltd arrived. Their business was the overhaul and conversion of aircraft used for racing. With business thriving, Airports Ltd, already the owners of Gatwick, purchased Gravesend with the idea of making it a commercial success. They failed and offered the site to Gravesend Council to use as a municipal airport. Whilst the wrangling over price and contract details went on, the obvious rumblings from Germany stopped all further negotiations. The airfield was saved from a possibly ignominious end when the Air Ministry stepped in and

An aerial photo of Gravesend taken from 3,000 feet on 18th August 1942. The extension runway across Thong Lane can be seen centre left. (RAF Museum)

proposed that Gravesend become a training school under the plans for the expansion of the RAF.

With Airports Ltd being awarded a contract by the Air Ministry, No 20 Elementary and Reserve Flying Training School was formed at the airfield on 25th September 1937. By 1st October, a full complement of six Tiger Moths and six Hawker Harts had arrived and training began, not only for the RAF pilots but Fleet Air Arm as well. Accommodation was sparse for only the little clubhouse and the control tower were available as living quarters. These were indeed used for such a purpose together with some of the trainee pilots being billeted in local houses. Record breaking flights continued from the airfield, one of the most publicised being the Cape of Good Hope flight in the Percival Mew Gull G-AEXF flown by Alex Henshaw.

Although just a grass airfield and somewhat bumpy at that, 20 ERFTS used Gravesend for nearly two years. Daily the Tiger Moths and Harts would be seen around the area, the activity seeming to increase as war became more and more inevitable. By early 1939, however, plans were being formalised to requisition Gravesend Airport as a military base. When war broke out on 3rd September 1939, 20 ERFTS closed, Airports Ltd relinquished the lease and the Air Ministry took over fully as

102

Gravesend became a satellite airfield to Biggin Hill and came under the umbrella of No 11 Group Fighter Command. Despite the acquisition by the Air Ministry, Essex Aero continued to operate from the airfield and took on many military contracts including the manufacture of fuel tanks for Spitfires and other aircraft.

Although only allocated satellite status, it was decided that the airfield should have two decoy airfield sites. This was the ultimate deception plan to encourage the Luftwaffe to drop its bombs elsewhere. The sites chosen were usually well away from the airfield and in less populated areas of the county. For Gravesend, one site chosen was at Cliffe Marshes with the other being at Luddesdown. The former was planned to be a 'K' site with dummy aircraft and buildings whilst the latter was a 'QX' site equipped with the same but with the addition of fake Drem runway lighting. It was also planned that if the expected Luftwaffe attacks caused Gravesend to become unserviceable, the station would move over to Radlett in Hertfordshire.

So, Gravesend prepared to go to war. It was arranged that the old civil clubhouse would still be used for accommodation in addition to the use of the Laughing Waters (now called The Inn on the Lake) roadhouse in nearby Shorne. Several houses were requisitioned for ground crews whilst the officers were allowed to use Cobham Hall, the ancestral home of Lord Darnley.

The first few months of war saw very few movements as construction to a military standard continued. It fell to No 32 Squadron to make their mark on the airfield when they brought their Hurricane Is over from Biggin Hill on 3rd January 1940. After a very hard Christmas period with frost and snow being the norm, the phoney period of the war continued. 32 had moved over to Gravesend to allow the big reconstruction programme to continue at Biggin but the weather ensured that they flew very little. They stayed for three months before going down to Manston on 3rd March, being replaced on 10th May by No 56 (Punjab) Squadron from North Weald.

Operation Dynamo, the rescue of the beleaguered BEF from the beaches at Dunkirk, was an epic operation and involved almost every station and squadron in Fighter Command. Gravesend was not left out as No 610 (County of Chester) Squadron of the Royal Auxiliary Air Force arrived from Biggin Hill on 26th May 1940. Flying Spitfires, they provided top cover over the evacuation beaches and came into daily contact with the Me 109s. Sadly, in two dogfights, two Commanding Officers of 610 were shot down, Sqd/Ldr Franks and Sqd/Ldr Smith. For several days the squadron flew back and forth as Fighter Command struggled to keep the evacuation area free of enemy aircraft. On 27th May, 16 Hurricane and Spitfire squadrons made 287 sorties over northeast France destroying ten enemy aircraft but losing 14. Despite the bad weather from the 28th, 610 continued their patrols until the operation ended on 4th June. They then went back to anti-shipping operations until they returned to Biggin Hill on 2nd July.

The next day saw the arrival of the first twin engined aircraft to fly from Gravesend when the Bristol Blenheim 1Fs of No 604 (County of Middlesex) Squadron, Royal Auxiliary Air Force flew in. Converted from the bomber version of the aircraft by a kit manufactured by the Southern Railway Ashford factory, they were a stop-gap night fighter whilst awaiting the specially designed Bristol Beaufighter.

No 604 were briefed to carry out night patrols from Gravesend. Their Blenheims carried the first of the airborne radars which were later to help achieve such success for night fighters. However, these early marks were to prove very fickle and would contribute to a very frustrating time for 604 at Gravesend before they left for Middle Wallop on 26th July, leaving behind the Spitfires of No 72 (Basutoland) Squadron who had joined them for a week in June before departing for Acklington. By this time the first phase of the battle had begun. There had been sporadic attacks on convoys in the Channel but at this time, no attacks on the airfields of Fighter Command. As 604 departed they were replaced by a day fighter unit, No 501 (County of Gloucester) Squadron of the Royal Auxiliary Air Force. They flew the Hurricane I and had been in France attempting to stem the German advances. With the Dunkirk evacuation over, they had returned to England via the Channel Islands.

On 10th July, the Luftwaffe intensified its attacks on shipping and the ports but it was not until Saturday, 27th July that 501 tasted battle and a loss. With a little cloud in the Channel, the Luftwaffe carried out early attacks on a convoy off Swanage, one off Harwich and another entering the Thames Estuary. Dover was also a specific target and suffered badly in these early raids. 501 had to wait until 5 pm before being scrambled, in this case from Hawkinge, nearer the coast. As they raced to the defence of Dover, the Me 109s of Jagdgeschwader 52 flying from Coquelles were attacking shipping in the harbour. A dogfight developed in which F/O P.A.N. Cox in Hurricane P3808 was hit by gunfire from the 109 of F/W Fernsebwer. Failing to bale out, F/O Cox died as his aircraft dived into the Channel. It was a sad squadron that returned to Gravesend that evening.

Monday, 29th July saw further raids on Dover with the first raid

A pilot of 72 Squadron in his Spitfire at Gravesend in 1940. (Kent Messenger)

coming at 10.20 am. This time it was the Ju 87 Stuka divebombers that carried out the attacks. Together with other squadrons, 501 were scrambled several times, the only loss being a Hurricane at 7.45 pm when it was hit in the port mainplane. P/O Bland was however unhurt and managed to land his damaged aircraft back at base. Two days later the raids intensified on shipping and coastal towns. Fighter Command flew 395 sorties that day with 501 Squadron losing Hurricane P3646 at 7 pm in the evening. The pilot, P/O R.S. Don baled out and was admitted to Canterbury Hospital with injuries. Six enemy aircraft were shot down.

With Hawkinge being used as a forward airfield, it soon became apparent that in the battle to come, it would be one of the major targets of the Luftwaffe. Already it had seen some bombing as the enemy attacked Dover and Folkestone but with the coming of the second phase of the battle, it was to suffer tremendously. Until that time however, 501 were to be scrambled for much of their time from Hawkinge.

Early August saw the squadron in daily action. The day before 'Adler Tag', 12th August 1940, radar stations and coastal airfields were attacked, including Hawkinge. The field was so badly damaged that for a few days, 501 were forced to fly direct from Gravesend to the battle zone. They were flying from their home base when they suffered the worst losses so far in the battle.

Scrambled around 11.00 am in defence of two convoys codenamed 'Snail and Cable', plus the city of Portsmouth, Hurricane P3397 flown by Sqd/Ldr A.L. Holland was forced to land at Dover, whilst Hurricane P3803 and its pilot, F/O K. Lukaszewicz went missing at 12.55 pm off Ramsgate never to be found. In the afternoon sorties, Hurricane N2329 was damaged with Sgt J.H. Lacey managing to crashland whilst P2986 tipped onto its nose when landing at badly damaged Hawkinge. Only the skill of its pilot, Fl/Lt J.A. Gibson enabled the Hurricane to be repaired.

The same pilot was forced to bale out on Thursday, 15th August when flying Hurricane P3582. He was shot down by a Ju 87 and watched his aircraft bury itself into the soil at Alkham whilst he gently floated down. In the same engagement, two further Hurricanes were lost.

Sunday, 18th August 1940, forever known as the hardest day, was certainly that for 501. This was the day that the Luftwaffe in an all out effort attempted to destroy Fighter Command. Massed formations were over England from early morning with many Kent airfields being attacked. Though Gravesend was not on the hit list, 501 together with many other squadrons of Fighter Command suffered grievously.

With the first of the enemy formations crossing the coast at just after midday, the twelve Hurricanes of 501 were scrambled early to fly down to Hawkinge and await developments. They waited until lunchtime without being called whereupon they were detailed to fly back to Gravesend. All the pilots were dreaming of a rare afternoon off as they lifted from the Hawkinge grass. That was until the ground controller interrupted their thoughts telling them to climb to 20,000 feet and orbit over Canterbury. Cursing under their breath, the pilots altered course, gaining as much height as possible. It was none too soon as the Do 17s of Kampfgeschwader 76 and the Me 109s of Geschwader 26 approached. Still more enemy aircraft were behind them with the He 111s of Kampfgeschwader 1 escorted by a further Gruppe of 109s from Jagdgeschwader 51. With such a formidable force, a furious battle began over Kent.

First to be shot down was F/O F.R.L. Dafforn in Hurricane R4219. Baling out over Biggin Hill, he watched his aircraft crash at Cronks Farm, East Seal. Two more came down at 1.30 pm, P/O K.N.T. Lee being admitted to hospital with leg wounds whilst P/O E. Kozlowski crashed at Whitstable and was seriously injured. Within minutes, Sgt D.H.E. McKay baled out of his blazing Hurricane and although slightly burnt, he survived. Next to fall to the guns of Oblt G. Schoepfel of JG 26 was Hurricane P3208 in which sadly, P/O J.W. Bland was killed.

As 501 regrouped and flew back to Gravesend to refuel, it was a sad squadron that landed. Scrambled again at 5 pm, they suffered a further loss when Fl/Lt G.E.B. Stoney in Hurricane P2549 was also killed. By nightfall, as the squadron was stood down, the mess at Gravesend was strangely empty. The hardest day had turned into the saddest day for Gravesend.

Late August continued in a similar vein to the rest of the month with 501 achieving some success in shooting down the enemy but also being badly hit themselves. Three aircraft with one pilot killed were lost on Saturday, 24th August whilst the CO himself had a narrow escape from death on the 27th when his Hurricane was hit. Though badly damaged, Sqd/Ldr Hogan managed to land it back at Gravesend.

In September the Luftwaffe began to step up the tempo of attacks. With Fighter Command showing no signs of diminishing in defensive activity, the attacks on the airfields increased. Yet again Gravesend did not receive any raids, possibly due to its status as a satellite airfield. 501, however, once again found success and some loss during this period. Sadly, several pilots were killed. F/O A.T. Rose, P/O A.C. Adams, Sgt O.V. Houghton and Sgt G.W. Pearson all lost their lives before 501 departed to another fighter airfield, Kenley, after a rather depressing time at Gravesend.

They were replaced by No 66 Squadron, a Spitfire unit commanded by Sqd/Ldr R.H.A. Leigh. 66 had been the first regular squadron to receive Spitfires back in 1938 and was the first squadron to fly the type from Gravesend. They continued the daily interception patrols, falling foul of the Luftwaffe on Saturday, 14th September when P/O R.H. Robbins in Spitfire X4327 was shot down at 7 pm by an escort of 109s. P/O Robbins was seriously injured and taken to Leeds Castle Hospital. Twenty minutes later, Sgt P.H. Wilcocks was forced to land Spitfire N3029 with engine failure some distance from Gravesend. Whilst he was unhurt, his aircraft was a write-off. The squadron were to lose a further 20 aircraft with five pilots killed before moving over to West Malling on 30th October.

The early warning system was fully operational by the time the battle commenced, but it could not possibly tell just how many enemy aircraft were in a formation. Though its operators reported '50+ bandits

66 Squadron in the clubhouse at Gravesend, 1940.

A mishap for 66 Squadron at Gravesend, 1940. (Dizzy Allen)

approaching' etc, in order to get a more accurate figure it had become necessary to use the human eye. At Churchill's instigation, No 421 Flight formed at Gravesend for this purpose on 7th October 1940, from a nucleus of personnel from 66 Squadron. The flight was used to patrol the sky at high altitude over the Channel and radio back accurate figures. Initially equipped with Hurricanes, Spitfires were to follow shortly after the flight was formed. They did not operate from Gravesend for long, moving over to West Malling along with 66 Squadron.

Although 141 Squadron had suffered grievously on its first and last daylight encounter with the enemy (see Biggin and West Malling chapters), they had been relegated to night fighting duties since their rest period in Scotland. They came to Gravesend on 3rd November to continue in this role.

They were joined on 23rd November by the Hurricanes of No 85 Squadron, commanded by Sqd/Ldr Peter Townsend, he of royal fame. Both squadrons were operating by night but at this early stage of the war and with no airborne radar to assist 85 Squadron, they did not have the success of later night fighters. However, over the period 1940/41, the Defiant achieved the highest number of kills per interception of any night fighter of the period. Both squadrons remained at Gravesend over the Christmas and New Year of 1940/41 until 85 moved over to Debden on 1st January. By this time Gravesend had become a self accounting station and less of a satellite to Biggin Hill. A period of construction began in which further domestic and operational buildings were erected.

Another Defiant squadron replaced 85 in the form of No 264 (Madras Presidency) on 1st January. They only stayed for eleven days before crossing over to Biggin Hill leaving No 141 as the resident unit. It was owing much to the leadership of Sqd/Ldr E.C. Wolfe that 141 did achieve some success in shooting down the enemy at night. With the daylight raids petering out in November 1940 due to the losses of aircraft and crews in the Luftwaffe, plus the shortage of daylight hours, Goering had issued new orders for the attack on Britain to continue at night. Hurriedly equipping the Defiant with airborne radar had ensured that the Germans did not have it all their own way. 141 were to continue at Gravesend until 29th April 1941 when they moved to Ayr.

With the night fighters gone, daylight operations returned when No 74 (Trinidad) Squadron arrived from Manston with the Spitfire IIA on 30th April. Receiving the mark VB in May and led by Sqd/Ldr J.C. Mungo-Park, the unit began offensive operations over the coast of

264 (Madras Presidency) Squadron were based at Gravesend in December 1940 with the ill-fated Boulton Paul Defiant. (IWM)

France. With the war in the air turning from defensive to offensive, the era of the 'Ranger' and 'Rodeo' operations had arrived, both names being codewords for penetration flights over enemy territory.

From this period of April through to the end of the year, Gravesend saw a rapid change in Spitfire squadrons. When 74 left on 8th July 1941, they were followed by No 72 (Basutoland) who flew in a day later until the 26th of the month; 609 (West Riding) Squadron of the Royal Auxiliary Air Force came on 26th July and left on 24th September; 92 (East India) arrived on 24th September, leaving on 20th October; whilst 72 returned for a longer stay on 20th October, leaving for Biggin Hill on 22nd March 1942.

It was in March 1941 that three new Canadian squadrons had arrived in the UK under the Commonwealth Air Training Plan. They were renumbered using the prefix of 400 before their own original squadron number. No 1 Squadron RCAF became No 401 (Ram) Squadron of the RCAF and it was this unit that first introduced the Canadians to Gravesend. Equipped with the VB mark of Spitfire, they arrived on 19th March 1942 from Biggin Hill. They carried on the offensive sorties over France, flying from a far smaller airfield than they had been used to. At this time the grass landing areas measured 993 yards in the N-S and E-W direction, with the NE-SW direction 50 yards longer. The main SE-NW landing strip was considerably longer at 1,333 yards. However,

110

during 1942, the N-S and E-W landing areas were lengthened considerably even though the airfield remained grass. To allow a fair degree of all-weather serviceability, Sommerfeld Steel Tracking and Drem Runway Lighting were installed on the main runway.

Joining 401 at Gravesend on 1st May 1942 came another Spitfire unit, No 124 (Baroda) Squadron. Their motto of 'Danger is our opportunity' was very apt as they returned from taking part in Operation Fuller, the German battleship breakout. Whilst at Gravesend they took part in Ramrods, escorting bombers over enemy territory. Though they moved to Eastchurch in June, they came back for a further period on 13th July and converted to the Spitfire VI.

No 350 Squadron flew in from Debden on 30th June. Apart from a few RAF officers, the unit was manned entirely by Belgians who had fled to England as their own country was overrun. Again it was a time of rapid change with 350 staying a few days before Nos 124 and 401 Squadrons returned for a similar period. Another squadron to spend two short periods at the airfield was No 65 (East India) Squadron. Like 92 Squadron which bore the same name 'East India', it was manned by a large proportion of Commonwealth personnel. The unit carried out

Armourers rearm a 66 Squadron Spitfire at Gravesend. (The Times)

72 (Basutoland) Squadron at Gravesend in 1942. The CO, Sqd/Ldr Masterman is right of the centre in the light flying suit. (Kent Messenger)

165 Squadron Spitfire VBs. (IWM)

low level attacks on enemy transport and shipping reconnaissance operations and was based at Gravesend from 29th July until 14th August and again from 20th August to 26th September 1942.

The Eagle Squadrons were RAF units manned mainly by American personnel. The first to form in the UK was No 71 which flew into Gravesend on 30th June 1942. The second to use the airfield was No 133, the third Eagle Squadron to form. Both stayed for brief periods over the summer and autumn of 1942 together with further Spitfire squadrons, mainly No 232 (14th until 20th August) and 165 (Ceylon) (14th August until 1st November 1942).

With all of this activity at the airfield, it was deemed necessary to base an Air Sea Rescue unit at Gravesend. Formed on 22nd December 1941 at Stapleford Tawney in Essex, No 277 Squadron, whose motto was 'We save by seeking', had sent ASR detachments to Martlesham Heath, Hawkinge, Shoreham and Tangmere. Its aircraft covered the busy area between South East England and Northern France over

114

which large numbers of RAF and American fighters and bombers operated. On 7th December, the squadron moved to Gravesend although the detachments were still at the aforementioned bases. It operated a variety of aircraft including Defiants, Lysanders and the faithful Walrus. Commanded by Sqd/Ldr Linney, it stayed for a longer period at Gravesend than any other squadron, finally leaving on 15th April 1944.

With the extensions to the runways completed in 1943, the airfield was now able to accommodate larger and more powerful aircraft. One of the new breed of aircraft, the Hawker Typhoon, came to Gravesend on 24th March 1943 with No 181 Squadron. Despite earlier teething troubles, the Typhoon had proved to be a devastating gun and rocket platform for the RAF both in a defensive and offensive role. The time at Gravesend was spent working up for the period when they would become part of the 2nd Tactical Air Force during the middle of 1943.

More Typhoons arrived on 27th March when No 245 (Northern Rhodesia) Squadron arrived from Peterhead. Staying just over one month, Sqd/Ldr S.S. Herndern took them to Fairlop on 28th May to be replaced by No 174 (Mauritius) Typhoon Squadron. After the Spitfires, the Typhoon was a noisy aircraft with its sometimes unreliable Sabre

245 Squadron and a Hurricane IIc, at Gravesend from March to May 1943. (IWM)

115

engine. Local residents were soon complaining about the noise levels at Gravesend but their misery was to last some time longer as a further Typhoon squadron, No 244 (China-British) arrived for a short stay before secondment to the 2nd TAF. All of these units carried out fighter sweeps over northern France. Rhubarbs and Rodeos became ever more frequent as the fight was carried back to the enemy. Low level attacks against enemy transport and fighter sweeps looking for enemy aircraft lairs became an everyday occurrence. This was the start in building up a tactical air force for the invasion of France that was to come a year later.

Thankfully, on 2nd June 1943, the local populace watched the last of the noisy Typhoon units depart, to be replaced by the Spitfire VBs once again in the form of Nos 19 and 132 (City of Bombay) Squadrons, led by Sqd/Ldr V.H. Elkins and Sqd/Ldr J.R. Ritchie respectively. Within six days both squadrons had moved onto the new ALGs at Bognor and Newchurch although No 19 were to return to Gravesend for a longer stay at the end of the year.

The squadron numbers 300 to 309 had been allocated to Polish squadrons, one of which, No 306 (Torun), was manned entirely by Polish personnel. Sqd/Ldr Karwewski brought his squadron down from Catterick on 11th August 1943 as part of the 2nd TAF, again for a very short period only.

To the dismay of the locals, the Typhoon returned on 17th August when No 193 (Fellowship of the Bellows) Squadron came in from Harrowbeer. The aircraft of this unit were used to catch enemy fighter/bombers attacking seaside towns as well as acting as escorts to our own fighter/bombers attacking enemy shipping. They were joined by another Typhoon squadron, No 257 (Burma), once again making Gravesend a very noisy airfield. A further Spitfire squadron arrived at the same time as No 64 came in on 19th August. Led by Sqd/Ldr V.H. Elkins, who had been at Gravesend with No 19 in June, they carried out offensive operations over the coast of France.

As the autumn of 1943 approached, the tide was turning and time was running out for the Third Reich. At Gravesend, the arrival of No 266 (Rhodesia) Squadron with its Typhoons once again shook the neighbourhood but three days later they had gone and it was back to Spitfires from then until April 1944.

It was Nos 19 and 65 (East India) Squadrons that once again returned after a spell elsewhere. Flying in on 24th October 1943, both converted to the Mustang III in December and as part of the 2nd TAF, prepared for the invasion of Europe. Taking the role of fighter/bombers, they

ME 109s prepare for take-off. They escorted the bombers which attacked British airfields with devastating results before turning their attention to the cities (MAP).

continued the softening up process in advance of the Allied landings, attacking any target that might possibly hold up the invasion. The two squadrons were joined in November by No 122 (Bombay) who also converted to the Mustang III whilst at Gravesend. The three units stayed until April 1944 when, two months before the invasion, they moved down to Ford on the Sussex coast.

It was now the turn of the twin-engined Mosquito FBVI to make its mark on the grass of Gravesend. First to arrive were the aircraft of No 464 (Australian) Squadron who flew in on 17th April 1944 from Hunsdon and were joined by No 21 on the same day. No 487 (New Zealand) Squadron flew in next day, departed to Swanton Morley on the 26th and came back on 30th April. Though 21 sent a detachment to Dunsfold, the three squadrons formed No 140 Wing of the 2nd TAF. They carried out mainly night raids again in preparation for D-Day. The Mosquitos would waken the local residents as they carried out up to three sorties a night. The better weather ensured that there was little interruption in their schedule and for the two months until the landings, Gravesend was the scene of much frantic activity.

An indication perhaps of the future down-grading of Gravesend came in March 1944 when the usual CO of Wing Commander rank was replaced by Sqd/Ldr A.A. Shaw. With D-Day a success, the final run to global victory was accelerated but Gravesend's days were numbered.

Despite this, the Mosquitos continued operations from the airfield until 13th June when they left for Thorney Island.

Their leaving was in fact brought forward by the first of the V1 attacks on the capital. The robot crashed at Swanscombe, just a short distance from the airfield and it became obvious that with Gravesend laying roughly along the flight path of the rockets, further operations would prove hazardous. With the departure of the Mosquitos, it became a command centre for the large number of balloons surrounding the area to hopefully help prevent some of the rockets reaching London. Many V1s were to fall foul of the balloon barrage but when the campaign petered out in the autumn and with the war now being continued on the Continent, no further use was made of Gravesend.

With no squadrons destined to use the base, it was placed under Care and Maintenance. Essex Aero had maintained a factory on the site throughout the war making self-sealing petrol tanks for aircraft. They continued their work until 1956 when Gravesend Borough Council refused permission to consolidate the wartime extensions into the post-war airfield. This caused Essex Aero to go into liquidation and apart from a period of Air Cadet gliding, no other flying took place. The Air Ministry relinquished the field in June 1956 and it was sold for a large housing development called Riverview Park. Today the only visible reminder that there was even an airfield at Gravesend is a plaque on the wall of the new Cascades Leisure Centre in Thong Lane. It commemorates the 14 pilots of 501 and 66(F) Squadrons who lost their lives flying from the airfield during the Battle of Britain. Sadly, the name of Fl/Lt P.A.N. Cox was omitted.

In 1990, the residents of the new housing estate were evacuated from their houses whilst soldiers of No 33 Regiment, Royal Engineers removed explosive pipe mines laid in 1940 to deter any German use of the airfield had Operation Sealion succeeded. The last remnants of Gravesend's war had been removed.

6
HAWKINGE

The rapid progress of the German army through the Low Countries brought a feeling of elation and supreme confidence to the German High Command. As they surveyed the remnants of the BEF that were left behind at Dunkirk, it was felt by some commanders that the invasion of England should go ahead whilst the British people were still in a state of shock and the RAF was in a maze. One commander, Generaloberst Milch, proposed that all available airborne troops should immediately commence an aerial attack on England. One of the airborne targets was a grass airfield perched high above the coastal town of Folkestone. Once landed, the troops were to consolidate their position and make the airfield available to the Luftwaffe. As we know, the plans did not quite work out the way the Germans would have liked

A No 2 Squadron Lysander at Hawkinge. (MAP)

them to have done and the airfield later became the most used forward airfield in Fighter Command. It went by the name of Hawkinge.

It was a Dutchman, W.B. Megone, who first used the field when he built a flying machine in a shed situated in a field running alongside Barnhouse Lane. Dubbed the 'Mayfly', it only managed a few hops into the air and never really flew. Totally disillusioned, Megone returned it to its shed, locked it and was never seen again. Hawkinge was however now placed on the aviation map.

It came into use again during the First World War and in 1918, with the creation of the RAF, it was to continue in a peacetime role. It began a long association with No 25 Squadron who arrived at Hawkinge during 1920 with Sopwith Snipes. At the time they were the sole fighter defence unit in the UK. They converted through a series of aircraft, Gloster Grebes, Armstrong-Whitworth Siskins, Hawker Furies, Hawker Demons and Gloster Gladiators before leaving Hawkinge for Northolt on 22nd August 1939.

No 2 Squadron flew their Hawker Audax biplanes in on 3rd November 1935. The Empire Air Display of 23rd May 1936 attracted a crowd of 3,000 visitors. The squadron had converted to the Westland Lysander by the time of the 1939 Empire Air Day which this time attracted a crowd of 9,000. The centre of attention was held behind a guarded enclosure by the RAF Police. The intense security was necessary at this time as the first of the many was seen for the first time. The Hawker Hurricane was the star of the 1939 show and it saw the beginning of a long relationship with Hawkinge.

The Munich crisis brought the airfield to its first state of readiness. Camouflage was hastily applied to hangars and domestic buildings as the once pretty little grass airfield took on a rather austere and wartime appearance. As 25 Squadron left to go to Northolt and convert to the Bristol Blenheim, there was time for a small celebration for they departed after 19 glorious years at the airfield. They were to return briefly during the Battle for two days but the inter-war years would always be remembered as the best for the squadron.

War reared its ugly head on 3rd September 1939 but with No 2 Squadron preparing to move to France as part of the air component of the BEF, Hawkinge became No 3 Recruit Training Pool, an assignment that betrayed its future use. Almost as soon as war was declared the sirens in nearby Folkestone and the village of Hawkinge began to wail.

'Blimey, Jerry's wasting no time,' one airman was heard to say as everyone prepared to take to the newly dug shelters. Donning their tin hats, the 6th Buffs Regiment who were on airfield defence duties clutched their light machine guns a little tighter and rested their fingers on the triggers. As the sirens stopped their wailing, an aircraft was heard approaching from seaward. A telephone call to Hawkinge from the local Observer Corps established the aircraft was in fact friendly. It turned out to be His Royal Highness, The Duke of Windsor flying into Hawkinge to offer his services as a qualified pilot!

The first Hurricanes to fly from the field arrived on 17th December 1939 with 'D' Flight of No 3 Squadron from Croydon. As Sqd/Ldr P. Gifford, DFC led his detachment in, once again the sirens began to wail as the first enemy aircraft seen overhead flew slowly past at a high altitude before turning back for France. Of far more interest to the men, however, was the arrival of the first Waafs at Hawkinge. They had been trained to operate the Chain Home Radar Station at Dover and were to be billeted at the airfield. Somehow, life would be a little more bearable for the male population.

The Christmas and new year period of 1939/1940 was one of the worst on record. The snow came thick and hard with the overnight frost ensuring the laying snow was covered in ice. The Hurricanes of No 3 Squadron saw little activity over this period except for the constant running up of their engines. As the snow continued well into the new year, Hawkinge became virtually cut off from the rest of the county. No transport could get up or down the hill that led to Folkestone. With every available man and woman put to snow clearing on the airfield, it was left to the more senior members of the station to cut a road through to Folkestone. At least the toil kept everyone warm.

A second snowfall a few weeks later again paralysed the station. With no flying possible, No 3 prepared to move to Kenley whilst the Recruiting Pool closed down. No 16 Squadron had become the first Lysander squadron to form in the UK and it was with these aircraft that they arrived at Hawkinge on 16th February 1940. They operated in the Army Co-operation role and as better weather followed the heavy snowfalls, the station was transferred to Fighter Command and No 11 Group. At the same time a convoy of Queen Mary lorries rolled through the main gates bearing equipment and a number of pilotless aircraft. No 1 Pilotless Aircraft Unit had formed at Henlow and was now ready to put theory into practice. The aircraft were radio controlled models to be used for target practice by the fighter squadrons. The next day several scientists arrived from the Royal Aircraft Establishment at Farnborough, set up a control room and warned everyone to duck as Queen Bees and other pilotless aircraft began buzzing around the local area!

Whilst this period of the 'Phoney War' dragged on with very little happening on either side of the Channel, two RAF officers, Fl/Lt Scott Farnie and Fl/Lt Allway arrived at Hawkinge. Shrouded in secrecy, they locked themselves away in a hut at the end of the runway, seemingly for days on end. When they did occasionally come out for air, their faces gave no indication of life whatsoever until on one occasion, they came out all smiles. Sometime later it was established that the men were operating new radio equipment in an attempt to listen to German pilot radio transmissions. For some time they had no success until, on the day that they came out smiling, they received a transmission. From these humble beginnings came the 'Y' Service, in which linguistic Waafs operated high frequency equipment which enabled them to listen to German transmissions on a 24 hour basis. Eventually the service outgrew the buildings on the station and it moved to Maypole Cottage in the village of Hawkinge.

With the arrival of spring and better weather, the 'phoney' period came to an end. More German activity was taking place over the Channel with attacks on British convoys, the action of which could clearly be seen from the cliffs at Folkestone and Dover. May 1940 was to see Fighter Command well and truly under strain as the main German assault began on the 10th of the month. By this time, many squadrons of Hurricanes had been sent to France to assist the French Air Force in attempting to stall the advance of the German army. Nos 1, 73, 85, 87 (United Provinces), 607 (County Durham) and 615 (County of Surrey) Squadrons had been joined in France by Nos 3, 79 (Madras Presidency) and 504 (County of Nottingham), all equipped with Hurricanes. Working together with the Blenheims and Battles of the Advanced Striking Force, it was hoped that the enemy would be stopped in its tracks. In fact, the air attacks did nothing of the sort and the worries of Air Chief Marshal Dowding had become reality. He allowed no further squadrons to be sent to the aid of the French despite the insistence of Winston Churchill.

By May, it had become evident that these units in France plus the army of the BEF had to be brought back to England. Hawkinge became an important part of Operation Dynamo as the returning aircraft and crews landed there to refuel before being dispersed to other airfields in the country. Many aircraft showed signs of battle and air crews and ground crews were suffering from wounds and fatigue. No 2 Squadron based at Hawkinge over this period had also suffered badly as they flew over the retreating army dropping water and food supplies. Several of the slow flying Lysanders were shot down by intense ground fire whilst the rest, though damaged, made it back to Hawkinge.

Standing fighter patrols were flown over the beaches by squadrons using the station as a forward airfield. Arriving at dawn, they would refuel before crossing the Channel, returning several times during the day to refuel and re-arm before finally returning to their own airfields. For No 41 flying Spitfires and Nos 245 (Northern Rhodesia) and 605 (County of Warwick) flying Hurricanes, this ritual became a way of life throughout the withdrawal from Dunkirk. The same routine applied to No 17 Squadron who had arrived at Hawkinge on 13th April 1940. Sqd/Ldr J.H. Edwards-Jones had led his Hurricanes in from Debden and they were to make the airfield their home for the entire Dunkirk period before leaving on 22nd May to return to Debden.

With the Battle of France over, Goering instructed his Luftwaffe to clear the skies above Britain prior to the German invasion. As it became obvious to all that Hitler did not intend stopping at the Channel coast, the Air Ministry ordered all airfields to strengthen their defences. Further trenches and dug-outs were cut at strategic points around the airfield with four 200 mm Hispano cannons and one Oerlikon gun being sited around the perimeter. Three Pickett-Hamilton Retractable Turrets were placed alongside the landing area in case of an airborne invasion. Wg/Cdr W.L. Payne, the CO of Hawkinge, regretfully ordered that the hangars and anything that was painted white, including the neat kerbstones, were to be painted black or brown.

The installation of a Parachute and Cable Defence System brought many comments from station personnel. A rather wild idea, it consisted of rockets which were fired into the air from tubes, each rocket trailing a length of wire. When the projectile reached about 600 feet and the rocket was expended, a small parachute was released which suspended the wire in the path of oncoming aircraft, hopefully with the desired result! Only one occasion at Hawkinge can lay claim to it ever working successfully and even this is doubtful. All of these precautions, however, ensured Hawkinge was ready for the forthcoming battle.

June and July saw the tension increase as the Battle of Britain got underway. A detachment of No 245 (Northern Rhodesia) Squadron arrived with Hurricanes on 5th June and were joined by No 79 (Madras Presidency) who brought their Hurricanes in from Biggin Hill on 1st July led by Sqd/Ldr D.C. Joslin. They were sent immediately into the fray, losing several Hurricanes to German fighters. They were in action every day until they left for Sealand on 11th July.

Together with other squadrons that used Hawkinge as a forward operating base, the protection of our Channel convoys continued. By

32 Squadron at their forward base in 1940: P/Os (l to r) R. Smythe, J. Procter, K. Gillman, P. Brothers, D. Grice, P. Gardner and A. Eckford.

15th July, it was evident that the pattern was changing as the coastal towns came under attack. Each day enemy reconnaissance planes would fly at least two early patrols gathering information to relay back to German intelligence. On this particular Monday, the entire morning was given over to reconnaissance, giving a hint of new tactics.

The 19th July dawned showery but bright. No 141 Squadron had brought their Defiants in early from West Malling. As we have read in earlier chapters, they were scrambled at 12.32 pm and were attacked by a superior force of Me 109s flying directly out of the sun. In as many minutes, the Germans claimed twelve Defiants shot down with several more damaged. It was only the timely arrival of No 111 Squadron that prevented every Defiant being shot down. At the sight of the Hurricanes approaching, the enemy turned and headed back to France. It was a disastrous day and what was left of 141 Squadron was withdrawn from the front line and posted to Prestwick. The atmosphere during the afternoon was very melancholy as 32 Squadron arrived from Biggin Hill. Soon after their arrival, the radar stations warned of a big gathering of aircraft over Calais and 32 were scrambled.

They fared better than the other squadrons even though Hurricane P3144 flown by F/Sgt G. Turner was attacked and set on fire. Managing to bale out, he was admitted to Dover Hospital whilst his Hurricane crashed at Hougham at 4.25 pm.

It was about this time that Dover, so heavily attacked since the beginning of July, became known as 'Hellfire Corner'. It was very apt as 32 Squadron, back again at Hawkinge for the day, were scrambled in the afternoon to protect a Channel convoy from attack. The two sections took it in turns to cover the ships but at 5.40 pm an attack by Ju 87 Stukas escorted by Me 109s materialised. Weaving and diving amongst the enemy formation, 32 damaged two Stukas though not fatally. Within seconds however, Hurricane P3679 was attacked by Hauptman Tietzel of 11/JG51. Sgt W.B. Higgins, although wounded himself, managed to land his damaged Hurricane back at Hawkinge. The CO of 32, Sqd/Ldr J. Worrall was also attacked and damaged by Oberfw. Illner of the same unit. Not wounded but with an aircraft leaking glycol and liable to burst into flames at any time, he too landed safely just before the Hurricane did indeed become a fireball. Not so lucky was Sub Lieutenant G.G.R. Bulmer, on detachment from the Navy, who was shot down by Oblt. Priller. Sadly, neither the pilot or his aircraft were ever found. Just 20 years old, Sub Lieutenant Bulmer is remembered on the Lee-on-Solent FAA Memorial.

Back on the ground, the airfield was beginning to look like a graveyard for crashed aircraft as the Hurricanes returned from battle. All of this put a tremendous strain on the ground crews at Hawkinge as they attempted to repair the less damaged aircraft to allow them to fly back to their respective airfields.

The rest of July saw the pattern of shipping attacks continue as more squadrons used Hawkinge as a forward airfield. Together with 32 from Biggin Hill came No 64 from Kenley, 610 (County of Chester) also from Biggin Hill and 501 (County of Gloucester) from Gravesend. Hectic scrambles were the order of the day with losses and triumphs for all squadrons. Out of fuel and ammunition, they limped back into Hawkinge to replenish all that was necessary. For the tired pilots and ground crews, rest and sleep was snatched whenever possible until the jangling bell of the telephone set their adrenalin racing once again. As yet, the Luftwaffe had not directed their attacks to the airfields but very soon, this was all to change.

On Monday, 12th August the duty personnel at Hawkinge woke at an early hour to a fine day with early mist. The lull in enemy activity over the past few days had enabled the ground crews to tidy up the airfield ready for another week of squadrons coming early and leaving late. A new pattern was, however, about to emerge as the Observer

Spitfires of 610 Squadron, Hawkinge 1940.

Corps, high up on the ramparts of Dover Castle, trained their binoculars across the clear Channel water. Straining their eyes to the limit, they detected a black swarm in the clear sky above the Pas de Calais and promptly reported this to Bentley Priory. Within minutes of the report reaching them, the black swarm had turned and was now heading towards the Kent coast. Immediately 610 were scrambled from Biggin Hill as were 501 from Gravesend. Soon both squadrons were heavily engaged in dogfights stretching from Deal to Dungeness.

The attacks were divided into five phases moving back and forth along the coastline and inland. At 9 am, the radar stations were attacked and two convoys came under heavy fire in the Channel. In the ensuing dogfights, 501 fared badly. Sqd/Ldr A.J. Holland was forced to land outside Dover at 11.30 am when his Hurricane P3397 was hit by fire from Me 109s. One hour later, F/O K. Lukaszewicz went missing after an attack in the Ramsgate area flying Hurricane P3803 whilst Sgt J.H. Lacey and Fl/Lt J.A. Gibson suffered undercarriage problems with their Hurricanes and were damaged on landing back at Hawkinge. 610 also lost four Spitfires with no loss of life.

At noon 32 came in to relieve the other two squadrons and sat around until 2.30 pm when the scramble came. Climbing to 800 feet, they patrolled between Folkestone and Dover whilst the other units were being refuelled and re-armed. At around 4.45 pm fifteen Ju 88s of the 2nd Gruppe of KG76 operating out of Criel, formed up over the French coast and headed for the Kent coast. 32 spotted them coming in and turned to attack. Suddenly the force split into two with one section heading for Lympne whilst the other approached Hawkinge.

The first bombing run was off the target but the second was definitely accurate. With a loud bang, one of the workshops disappeared and No 3 hangar received a direct hit which pushed the roof in and buckled the immensely strong rolling doors, unfortunately trapping several people inside. The equipment stores was a victim of the third bombing run as smoke and flames engulfed the entire airfield. The landing area was a mass of craters with piles of earth and chalk alongside. As the raid subsided, the station personnel began to pick their way through the rubble that was once their airfield. With the ambulance and fire tender in attendance, they helped look for the dead and injured. For the first time in this war, Hawkinge looked a sorry sight.

No 32, now low on fuel, turned back from their patrol, unaware of the devastation that the enemy had caused. Some of the Hurricanes returned directly to Biggin Hill but five of them, desperate for fuel, made for Hawkinge. Led by Sqd/Ldr Michael Crossley, they looked down on the airfield that earlier that afternoon had looked pristine. Calling on the radio to the watch office that was remarkably still intact, he requested permission to land if possible. The reply from the controller was very precise. 'Hello Jacko Red Leader. [Call sign for 32.] We've had a spot of bother here. Permission to pancake granted. Good luck.'

Although there were some unexploded bombs around the landing area, one by one the Hurricanes landed safely, weaving in between the craters as they did so. Quickly jumping down from their aircraft, the pilots went to help the ground crews to begin refuelling. As they did so, the hum of approaching aircraft became audible. Looking anxiously up, the crews saw a small formation of twin-engined aircraft approaching. Someone suggested they were British but the Balkan Cross and Swastika became clear all too soon. The tannoy roared, 'Take cover' and everyone fell over each other in their rush to the shelters and trenches. Almost immediately the crump, crump of exploding bombs rung in their ears as the enemy aircraft swept low over the field. In five minutes it was all over and although No 5 hangar had taken a full blast, the Hurricanes had escaped unscathed. Finding Hawkinge very unhealthy, the aircraft were refuelled in double quick time and returned to Biggin Hill. That night the BBC announced that the Battle of Britain was on! Wg/Cdr E.E. Arnold AFC, the CO of Hawkinge, felt that he could have broken that particular piece of news very much earlier.

All through the night, station personnel toiled to fill in the craters and move much of the rubble. By next morning extra troops from a neighbouring army camp had arrived to assist in the task. Over the next two days the Luftwaffe concentrated on the other Fighter Command airfields in Kent but on 15th August 1940, with a ridge of high pressure over the British Isles, Hawkinge was once again on the enemy's list.

The early morning of this particular Thursday passed quietly for the airfield. 501 Squadron had arrived from Gravesend and were dispersed around the field. By mid morning the radar stations had picked up large formations forming up over France and warned Bentley Priory that something big was up. Included in this massive formation were the Ju 87 Stukas of LG1 under the command of Hauptmann von Brauchitsch. Leaving Tramecourt, they were to form the spearhead of an attack on Hawkinge. Loaded with 500 kilo and 250 kilo bombs and escorted by the Me 109s of JG26 under the command of Major Adolf Galland, their intention was to finish off what had been started on the previous days, to knock Hawkinge out of the war.

As the telephone rang at the 501 dispersal, the pilots braced themselves for the duty airman's message. '501 scramble. Patrol Dover.'

In five minutes, the Hurricanes were groping for all the height they could get as the Stukas approached the Kent coast. They were too late to stop the enemy from hitting Hawkinge although their presence did prevent a far more serious attack. Down on the ground, the roar of the airfield defence guns plus the crump of exploding bombs and the scream of the Stukas' sirens was enough to cause panic in the best of men. One building used by the sergeant pilots went up in smoke and once again the grass runways were cratered. The Hurricanes of 501 and the Spitfires of 54 Squadron tore into the enemy as they left both Lympne and Hawkinge. In seconds, a Ju 87 flown by Leutnant von Rosen was shot down followed by two more shot down by Sgt Lawrence of 54 Squadron. Minutes later he himself became a victim when he was shot down by one of Galland's 109s. He was admitted to Dover Hospital with shock. Three further Spitfires of 54 were lost by enemy action, all the pilots baling out safely. 501 from Gravesend lost three Hurricanes but once again, the pilots were uninjured.

In the afternoon the onslaught continued as Fighter Command put up eleven fighter squadrons consisting of 130 Hurricanes and Spitfires. It was the biggest attempt so far by the Luftwaffe to conquer the air but by nightfall, it became obvious it had failed dismally. They had employed every available type of aircraft to wipe the RAF from the air and had flown 1,786 sorties in the 24 period. The fighter airfields, though thoroughly battered, had survived this day and had remained operational throughout.

The 18th August saw Hawkinge receive a further attack as the massed formations of enemy aircraft returned. It was the turn of 615 (County of Surrey) Squadron to be at readiness that day. Led by Sqd/Ldr J.R. Kayll DSO, DFC, the Hurricanes had left Kenley at first light and were now dispersed around the field. At 12.40 pm they were scrambled to intercept a force of Me 109s. One of the first Hurricanes to be attacked was that of P/O D.J. Looker. His machine, L1592, was hit by enemy fire and struggling with the controls, the pilot attempted to make Croydon. As he approached the airfield, the ground defences opened up on him and although his aircraft suffered further damage, he made a crash-landing on the airfield and was rushed to hospital with severe shock and concussion. It was not recorded just what he said to the gunners when he became fit for duty! Four further Hurricanes were lost to 615 but this was nothing compared to the losses incurred by the Luftwaffe.

32, 501 and 610 Squadrons were to fly from Hawkinge for most of August, until 32 left for a rest period. Although based at Biggin Hill,

P/O Keith Gillman of 32 Squadron, killed on 25th August 1940. (Plaistow Pictorial)

Hawkinge had become just as familiar to the pilots as their home base. During this period they had earned one DSO and five DFCs but in the process had lost five pilots killed with one taken prisoner of war. Sadly, their last few days in Kent were marred by the loss of P/O K.R. Gillman when he failed to return from combat over the Channel flying Hurricane N2433. A portrait of Keith Gillman taken in July 1940 at Hawkinge became well known as the epitome of a fighter pilot and this very popular officer was to be sadly missed. His memory is forever enshrined on Panel 8 of the Runnymede Memorial.

Their place was taken by No 79 (Madras Presidency) Squadron who flew into Hawkinge for readiness on 28th August. Airfield attacks began from 8 am but Hawkinge on that day was not on the Luftwaffe list.

The end of the month saw 79, 501 and 615 Squadrons using the airfield by day. Friday, 30th August began badly when 79 lost four Hurricanes with no loss of life, with 501 losing another which was repairable. The next day proved even worse with 79 losing nine Hurricanes, with Sgt H.A. Bolton killed and another five pilots injured. 501 fared no better with six Hurricanes shot down with F/O M.D. Doulton missing and three pilots injured. Though no consolation whatsoever for the loss of our pilots, the enemy over the same two days lost over 100 aircraft.

The late afternoon of Sunday, 1st September saw Hawkinge attacked again. With the Dover radar station out of action due to the morning attacks, several Messerschmitts carrying bombs flew low over the field as the ground defences opened up. Eight 125 kg bombs were dropped but did little damage. That same day, No 72 (Basutoland) Squadron had flown into Hawkinge from Croydon for readiness. Apart from having to suffer an enemy attack, they lost seven Spitfires with one pilot killed and two injured. Once again, the situation with pilots was becoming critical as many were lost and those that continued to fight were becoming very tired and badly in need of a rest.

Of that there was very little as September continued in similar vein to August. Friday the 6th saw three main attacks develop which cost Fighter Command 23 fighters with the pilots of twelve unhurt. German losses continued at a vast rate with 35 aircraft lost including Me 109s and eight He 111s from KG2 yet still there was no let-up in the airfield attacks. One of the escorting 109s on this day, hit by anti-aircraft fire, was forced to land at Hawkinge.

Saturday, 7th September 1940. Reichmarschall Hermann Goering, disappointed that his Luftwaffe had not managed to clear the RAF from the skies, now took personal control of the battle upon Britain. His target was London. As his personal train rolled to a stop in the Pas de Calais, both he and his entourage got out and looked upward and across the Channel. If they had looked through stronger binoculars, they may well have seen Hawkinge but on this day, they watched the mighty armada assembling overhead. With his hands over his ears to blot out the overpowering sound of aircraft engines, he joked and laughed that with the attacks upon the capital, Britain would soon capitulate.

Unaware what was going on across the Channel, Hawkinge prepared for another day. At 11.15 pm, four raids developed in addition to the big one on London. One headed for the airfield consisting of Me 109s and Me 110s. A warning had been given by the local Observer Corps that a formation was crossing the Channel but they did not know the precise target. As the sirens sounded, the first wave appeared overhead with the 109s machine gunning the gun emplacements. They were followed by the bomb-carrying 110s who dropped their deadly cargo from 1,000 feet. The station headquarters received a direct hit as did the landing area but tragically, some bombs fell in the village of Hawkinge, one hitting a dug-

Hawkinge at the time of the filming of The Battle of Britain. *It shows the accommodation area and one of the original hangars. (Kent Messenger)*

out killing six people. There were other serious casualties and a visit by the Secretary of State for Air resulted in a dispersal scheme for personnel and certain sections away from the airfield.

Events on the 15th September brought about another change of plan for the enemy. Now celebrated annually as Battle of Britain Day, the 15th was a Sunday. The weather was misty but, with a promise of fine weather later, the Luftwaffe commenced a massive attack on London. By 11 am, the radars showed mass formations building over Calais and Boulogne. No 11 Group put up eleven squadrons, No 10 Group one and No 12 Group five. With 17 squadrons engaging the enemy, accurate bombing by the Luftwaffe was out of the question and bombs were dropped oblivious to the civilian population of London. After a two hour break, the second attack materialised with the last raid of the day coming at 6 pm. That night, families all over the country listened to the radio newscaster declare, '185 enemy aircraft shot down'. Even though the actual figure was whittled down to 60, it was still a tremendous achievement. Whilst Hitler, Goering and the entire Luftwaffe had fully expected the RAF to be obliterated on this day, their returning aircrew told them that it appeared as though the RAF had gathered strength. Once again, the invasion was postponed.

The end of September and beginning of October saw further concentrated attacks on both London and the airfields of Kent. Hawkinge was to receive several when Me 109s carrying bombs came in low under the radar, dropping their bombs before turning instantly and heading back across the Channel. With these hit and run attacks it was necessary to find another source of observation on enemy aircraft in addition to the radar coverage. This resulted in No 421 Flight being formed at Gravesend on 8th October 1940. Consisting of six Spitfire IIAs, their job was to daily patrol the Channel coast at high altitude and identify any German raid forming up, relaying the information back to sector control. They were further briefed to attack and destroy any lone raider when the opportunity presented itself. These patrols became known as 'Jim Crows'.

On 15th November, they moved to Hawkinge, thereby becoming the first resident unit at the airfield since the war began. Before that however, No 303 (Warsaw) Polish Squadron had flown in to be at readiness on Saturday, 5th October. They were scrambled to intercept a force of Me 110s escorted by 109s heading for Maidstone. During a ferocious dogfight, the Poles accounted for four 110s shot down but sadly, when Fl/Lt W. Januszewicz attempted to land his damaged Hurricane at Hawkinge it somersaulted onto its back, killing the pilot.

Four days later the airfield came under attack and on the 11th, the town of Folkestone and the city of Canterbury were hit. It was not, however, only the guns and bombs of the Luftwaffe that were bombarding the coastal towns and airfields for the long-range German guns across the Channel were constantly lobbing shells across the water. On a fine day the flashes coming from the barrels could be seen from the cliffs at Dover but most of the time with cloud cover, the first that the people knew of the shelling was when they exploded. With the right conditions the shells could reach some distance inland and in fact the water tower at Hawkinge was to become a victim of one attack during October.

The month also saw what has been deemed the end of the Battle of Britain. The blitz on London was to continue by night but attacks against the airfields became few and far between. Squadrons were still using Hawkinge as a forward airfield but it was No 421 Flight that was to dominate action from the airfield. As if to forecast a successful time ahead, Sgt McKay on his way to Hawkinge, spotted a lone Do 17 over the coast and in full view of the people of Folkestone, promptly shot it down. October ran into a miserable November but still success came the way of 421 when on 20th November, a Do 17 was badly damaged by Fl/Lt B. Drake and on the 24th, P/O Lawrence shot down a Me 110 that had been spotting for the long range guns along the Pas de Calais.

The success continued for the rest of the month but an incident on the 20th highlighted a problem that was to continue throughout the war, that of aircraft recognition. The day turned out to be very dull with low cloud. Around 11 am, a thin, twin-engined aircraft was seen to enter the circuit. As it prepared to land, all hell was let loose by the airfield defence guns who, acting on their own initiative, had thought it to be a Do 17. The aircraft pulled up for the cloud cover immediately, signs of a hit very obvious. As the gunners were about to slap themselves on the back, the telephone in the gunnery control room rang. 'Don't shoot, you stupid b******'. It's one of ours'. Minutes later a damaged Handley Page Hampden bomber landed at nearby West Malling airfield and a very hot telephone call was made to Hawkinge!

On 5th December, three 109s appeared from beneath the cloud cover and dropped bombs on the airfield, the first for many months. Very little damage was caused but it was a vivid reminder that the airfields were still a target for the Luftwaffe. It had however, been a successful year and had earnt the airfield its first DFC of the war when Fl/Lt Drake was decorated, together with a DFM for Sgt McKay, both of 421 Flight. Following the attempts by the Luftwaffe to put the coastal radar stations out of action, an autogyro, the predecessor of the helicopter, was based at Hawkinge to carry out essential calibration work in ensuring these vital installations returned to work as quickly as possible.

A far quieter Christmas was had by all than the 1939 one and it was with an air of expectancy for better things to come that Hawkinge looked forward to 1941 under the leadership of Wg/Cdr E.E. Arnold, AFC who had taken over from Sqd/Ldr H.B. Hurley during the height of the battle. The excellent work by 421 Flight which began during 1940 continued. Despite a heavy fall of snow, 7th January saw Fl/Lt O'Meara and Fl/Lt Drake damage a Ju 88. Around this time rumours abounded that the strength of the unit was to be increased. Notification finally came on 11th January 1941 when it was announced that 421 were to be renamed No 91 (Nigeria) Squadron and were to be brought up to full squadron strength.

On 16th January, Fl/Lt C.P. Green handed the reins over to Sqd/Ldr F.C. Hopcraft only to take them back two days later with the rank of Squadron Leader. Dedication of the new 91 Squadron Standard took place on 16th February when the Archbishop of Canterbury arrived to conduct a church service and parade.

Three more raids were carried out on Hawkinge, one of them demolishing Sgt McKay's Spitfire. The following month of March saw further damage caused by hit and run raiders. On Friday, 16th May, the field was attacked four times in one day. 91 Squadron, however, continued their success with Fl/Lt Andrews shooting down a Ju 88 which crashed on the beach below the long-range German guns. As he touched down at Hawkinge, he could see the smoke from his adversary rising into the air. He had been chased back across the Channel by a FW 190 intent on revenge. Back at the airfield his flight commander, Fl/Lt Le Roux, was scrambled and shot the 190 down, watching it fall into the sea.

Although the Luftwaffe had lost the Battle of Britain, they still held high hopes of defeating the RAF. The Me 109E was the standard German mark during the battle but by 1941, a new mark known as the 109F began to reach operational units. The F proved to be an excellent fighter and outclassed and outflew the Mk II Spitfires of 91 Squadron. Help, however, was at hand and 6th May saw the squadron re-equip with the Spitfire VB. Having an up-rated Merlin engine and armed with two 20 mm cannons in addition to the four Browning machine guns, the VB gave 91 Squadron a new dimension in the war. As if proof were needed, Sqd/Ldr Green and Fl/Lt Lee-Knight were over Beachy Head getting to know the new aircraft when they tangled with two of the new

Me 109Fs. In seconds, Fl/Lt Lee-Knight had shot one down with the other turning and running for home.

At the same time as the conversion to the VB, the squadron initiated their association with the then British Colony of Nigeria. 91 were so named because the Government of Nigeria paid for and presented 15 aircraft to the squadron. The usual practice with such presentation aircraft was for each one to carry the name of a town or province beneath the cockpit. 91 were no exception and the new aircraft proudly bore names such as Warri Plateau, Ilorin, Kano, and Abeokuta. Even with the strong connection with Nigeria, 91 was a very cosmopolitan squadron with pilots from France, Belgium, Holland and Norway as well as Britain.

With much of the aerial combat taking place over the Channel, it seemed sensible to have an Air Sea Rescue unit based as close as possible to the sea. Hawkinge was allocated a flight of two Lysanders equipped with sea markers and dinghies during June 1941. A month later, two Walrus single-engined amphibians arrived to assist the Lysanders in what was fast becoming a very dangerous duty. Many airmen were shot down within sight of the enemy coast and owed their lives to the ASR units when they flew to the rescue before the Germans could reach them, in the most appalling conditions.

The Jim Crow squadron were still finding success in shooting down the enemy and now had the additional task of acting as escorts to the Lysanders and Walrus. This was to prove dangerous, for the slower rescue aircraft were very tempting to the Luftwaffe as an incident on 27th October proved. A Lysander was scrambled from Hawkinge to assist a pilot who had been shot down in the Dover area. The crew of F/Sgt Hartwell and Sgt Jones reached the area and began a search pattern which, with a watery sun reflecting on the sea, proved difficult. As they peered over the side looking for the pilot, the sharp staccato sound of a machine gun was heard and bullets began hitting the Lysander. Sgt Jones swung his gun round to see a Me 109 flash past. At the same time, F/Sgt Hartwell took evasive action and dived down to the sea. As he levelled out, Sgt Jones managed to fire and was astonished to see pieces fall off one of the 109s. Realising that the Lysander was no match for a 109, both men had prepared for the worst when two escorting Spitfires of 91 arrived on the scene. Taking advantage of the extra firepower, the Lysander continued at wave-top level to head for Hawkinge. Pulling up to clear the high ground, F/Sgt Hartwell dropped his aircraft onto the Hawkinge runway. They had only just made it home.

On 22nd December 1941, No 277 Squadron was formed at Stapleford Tawney in Essex and embraced all the ASR detachments that had been stationed at various bases around the south coast. Thus the year ended with 91 and the newly formed 277 Squadrons in residence at Hawkinge.

February 1942 saw the German battleships break out from Brest and sail through the English Channel late on the 11th. Due to a series of blunders, it was not until Sqd/Ldr Oxspring and Sgt Beaumont took off from Hawkinge to fly a patrol over the Channel at 10.30 am on the 12th that the breakout was finally reported. Landing back at 10.50 am, the pilots reported sighting a convoy of 'about 30 to 40 ships escorted by 5 destroyers or E-boats'. The interrogating officer at Hawkinge showed Sgt Beaumont a book of German warship silhouettes and asked if he could identify any of the larger ships. Carefully turning the pages, he stopped at the outline of a German battleship. 'That's it,' he confirmed. A report was immediately sent through to Fighter Command but still the authorities were not convinced it was the German 'Channel Dash'. The German convoy had it all their own way and sailed through the Straits of Dover. 91 Squadron and Hawkinge only played a very small part in the fiasco and when Operation Fuller was over, it was back to their lone reconnaissance sorties.

The Lysanders of 277 Squadron were supplemented in May 1942 by the addition of six Boulton Paul Defiants. This much maligned aircraft had acted in the day fighter role, the night fighter role and now was to be part of the ASR organisation. Modifications were made to accommodate the all essential dinghy but the type, once again, only lasted a year in this new role before it was replaced by ASR Spitfires.

With the RAF now definitely on the offensive, Hawkinge once again became a host station to many squadrons. The first to arrive were the Spitfire VBs of 65 (East India) Squadron when Sqd/Ldr A.C. Bartley, DFC led them in from Great Sampford on 30th June. They carried out fighter sweeps and Rhubarbs and were joined by No 41, again flying Spitfires, for similar duties. Their stay was short-lived, however, as both units were destined for operations overseas.

Operation Jubilee, the Dieppe raid, saw a strict security cordon thrown around Hawkinge. As with all the other airfields in the South East, personnel movements were cancelled and special security precautions were put in place. On 14th August a Canadian squadron, No 416 (City of Oshawa) arrived with Spitfire VBs. Sqd/Ldr H.L.I. Brown DFC brought No 616 (South Yorkshire) Auxiliary Squadron in from Great Sampford the same day, both units flying operations connected with Dieppe. As the run-up to 19th August continued, No

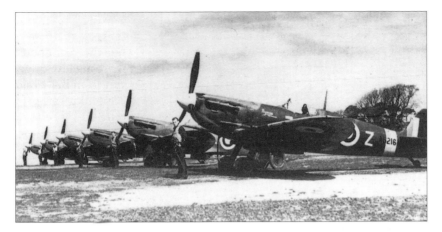

A line up of 91 Squadron Spitfire VBs in May 1942.

91 carried out reconnaissance over the Channel between Le Havre and Ostend whilst the other two squadrons provided top cover. By 06.00 hours on the 19th, three Spitfires of 91 were the first to be scrambled from Hawkinge followed an hour later by 416 and 616. All the squadrons tangled with FW 190s, claiming much success, but the ultimate failure of the landings and the many deaths dampened any enthusiasm for celebration. With Dieppe over, the Spitfire squadrons returned to their home bases leaving Hawkinge to 91 and 277 once again.

For the latter, there was plenty of business and plenty of frights. P/O Hilton, an Australian pilot, was flying his Walrus on 31st October 1942 to pick up Fl/Lt Van Schek of 137 Squadron, then stationed at Manston. Despite a ferocious crosswind blowing, he managed to land his aircraft between two rows of mines just off the French coast. Just as Van Schek was scrambling aboard, one of the mines broke free and began to head for the Walrus. Giving his engine full power, P/O Hilton began his run, bounced the Walrus over the mine and landed safely back at Hawkinge. For this and other daring rescues, he was awarded a DFC.

Later that evening, a hit and run raid on Canterbury was carried out by ten FW 190s but 91 caught the enemy turning for home and destroyed five with four damaged for no loss. Described as 'the best day in the squadron's history', the only sad moment was when F/O F.G.V. Gibbs did not return after he was seen being chased by four FW 190s.

With airfield defence now becoming more sophisticated, 6th

91 (Nigeria) Squadron at Hawkinge in September 1942. (South Eastern Newspapers)

November saw Sqd/Ldr Palmer, VC, MM, a veteran of the First World War, arrive to command the newly formed RAF Regiment. A few days later, Air Marshal Leigh-Mallory presented the 91 Squadron badge to Sqd/Ldr Demozay, with the motto 'We seek alone' seeming very apt. On the 23rd of the month they moved over to nearby Lympne but were back at Hawkinge on 11th January 1943. Before they moved however, 29th November saw 91 and 277 scrambled to look for the crew of a 149 Squadron Stirling that had ditched in the Channel. Finding the crew in the water, dinghies were dropped and both the Walrus and the ASR launch out of Dover Harbour picked them up, with the exception of the pilot, F/Sgt Middleton, an Australian. He had apparently flown the bomber back from a raid on Turin and although virtually blind, had refused to leave his stricken aircraft despite telling his crew to bale out to safety. He was awarded a posthumous VC and when, on 4th February 1943, his body was washed ashore, he was conveyed to his home base at Mildenhall.

On 20th April, 91 moved over to Honiley and converted to the Spitfire XII. Their last operational flight from Hawkinge was on the 15th when Fl/Lt Mathews and F/O H.D. Johnson were acting as spotters to a sweep carried out by the USAAC. Just off North Foreland, they came across a dinghy with two Thunderbolts circling around. The Walrus was scrambled and picked up Lt Col C.G. Peterson, the most decorated officer in the USAAC. At the conclusion of the day's operations, 91 left and 41 Squadron flew in to replace them for the month.

Conversion to the new type went well and they returned to Hawkinge on 21st May. The new mark of Spitfire was powered by the Rolls-Royce Griffon engine and was more than capable of dealing with the low flying FW 190s which were making a nuisance of themselves all along the Channel coastline. It did not take 91 long to prove their new aircraft in action when on 25th May, Sqd/Ldr Harries, P/O Round, F/O Maridor and P/O Davy were scrambled. Fifteen FW 190s were seen approaching Folkestone at sea level, intent on bombing the civilian population. Attacked by 91, they scattered around the local area with just one bomb dropping on Folkestone. Within seconds, Harries shot down two, Maridor and Round shot down one each and Davy probably destroyed another. All of this with no loss to themselves.

One month later rumours abounded that they were to leave Hawkinge. Amidst sadness at the prospect of a move, it was a time to count the score: 77 enemy aircraft destroyed, 27 probables and 78 damaged. The awards had been one DSO, eleven DFCs plus four bars and five DFMs. A very considerable achievement for a squadron that

One of the mobile 'tea and wad' wagons at Hawkinge 1943. (R. Humphreys)

began life as a flight. Now they were to move over to No 85 Group of the 2nd TAF, which they did on 28th June. Farewell Hawkinge, we will never forget you!

Just prior to their going, No 501 (County of Gloucester) Auxiliary Squadron returned to Hawkinge flying the Spitfire VC. Now commanded by Sqd/Ldr B. Barthold, they formed part of the Tangmere Wing and carried out intensive escort work, Rhubarbs and the occasional Jim Crow sortie. They were not the only Spitfires at Hawkinge for around the latter end of 1942, 277 Squadron had received the Spitfire IIA for ASR duties.

As the war was carried back to Germany, more and more heavy bombers, both British and American, used Hawkinge for emergency landings. Because of this increased use, the landing area was extended and further Blister hangars and hardstandings were erected. At the same time, 501 converted to the Spitfire IX and were joined by No 313 (Czechoslovak) Squadron flying the Spitfire VI on 21st August 1943.

Operation Starkey, the feint large scale operation designed to fool the enemy into thinking a landing was being planned along the Pas de Calais, involved the Hawkinge squadrons. As the Royal Navy travelled the length and breadth of the Channel for a week covered by a huge umbrella of American and British fighters, the Germans took the bait and the Luftwaffe came out in force.

Over the autumn period, Hawkinge saw rapid changes in squadrons using its facilities. Nos 64, 165 (Ceylon), 350 (Belgian) and 322 (Dutch) all arrived at different periods through until 1944 for short stays. They carried out Ramrods and Rhubarbs until April 1944 when the fighters departed, leaving Hawkinge with just 277 Squadron. The Walrus aircraft had been supplemented by the addition of a Sea Otter. Though of similar design, it differed in having its single Bristol Mercury engine in the front and pulling instead of pushing as on the Walrus. With virtually twice the range of the latter, 277 used the aircraft to good advantage. Just how they used it to its full potential is illustrated by the fact that on 18th March, a Mitchell of No 320 (Dutch) Squadron had ditched in the Channel under the nose of the enemy along the Pas de Calais. The crew managed to abandon the aircraft and did not wait long before the Sea Otter spotted them and put down on the sea. With the Mitchell carrying a crew of five and the Otter a crew of three or four, the cabin became very crowded and the weight of all the crewmen would not allow the aircraft to take off. Not to be outdone and in a hurry to get out of the area lest the German E-boats came after him, the pilot began taxiing for the English coast to be met by the Dover ASR launch half-way.

Rescue at last as a Walrus reaches a downed airman in the Channel.
(Kent Messenger)

Another saviour of downed pilots, a Sea Otter II Amphibian. (MAP)

The last full year of war saw Hawkinge still in the role of a forward airfield. January froze into February and as the forward planning for 'Overlord', the Allied invasion of Europe was now at an advanced level, the day and night skies over the airfield reverberated with the thunder of large four-engined bombers as the softening up process began. General Montgomery became a frequent visitor to the airfield when he landed on his way to some high level conference or other at Dover.

In preparation for the invasion, Hawkinge suddenly saw a very unusual type of aircraft use its facilities when 24 Grumman Avengers of the Fleet Air Arm arrived. Part of No 157 Wing of RAF Coastal Command, No 854 Squadron flew in from Machrihanish on 23rd May 1944 followed by No 855 from HMS *Ocean* on 31st May. Both units commenced anti-shipping patrols over the Channel, their presence hopefully keeping the enemy ships in harbour prior to the invasion. They left shortly after the D-Day landings.

As 'Overlord' got underway on 6th June 1944, Hawkinge became a very busy airfield indeed. The squadrons that used the field over this period were mainly tasked with creating a false impression of just where the landings were going to be. In addition, the Avengers had been fitted with depth charges and were entrusted with keeping the Channel free from enemy U-boats during the crucial crossing by the Allies. All of the aircraft participating in the invasion had black and white invasion stripes painted on them for identification purposes. One of the busiest units at this time was 277 ASR Squadron whose complement of aircraft now stood at 20 Spitfires and five Walruses plus the Sea Otter. They did sterling work with one day seeing over 22 separate sorties being flown and many pilots rescued in quick time from a very cold, rough Channel. 'Overlord' was a success but seven days after the invasion, a new and deadly weapon was unleashed upon the civilians of Great Britain as a last ditch attempt by Germany to bring the country to its knees.

The V1 'Doodlebug' caused widespread deaths and destruction over a very short period. In order to combat the menace, No 402 (Winnipeg Bear) Canadian Squadron arrived flying Spitfire IXs on 8th August. They converted to the Spitfire XIVE shortly after their arrival when they shot down three V1s on the 16th August. They were joined by No 350 (Belgian) Squadron, also with Spitfire IXs and who also found success in shooting down the rockets before they crossed the coast. Both units carried out anti-diver patrols until September when 350 moved over to Lympne and 402 to the Continent and B70/Deurne.

As the V1 campaign petered out, No 451 (Australian) Squadron arrived together with No 611 (West Lancashire) Auxiliary Squadron. Both of them flew Spitfires with 451 being equipped with the mark XVI which carried eight rockets under the wings. These they used to great effect when attacking enemy military columns. This type of operation continued until the new year when, with the rapid advance of the Allied troops towards Germany, victory came clearly into sight.

By February 1945, the Australians had left for Manston and 611, who had begun to receive Mustangs at Hawkinge, moved up to Hunsdon. 277 ASR Squadron officially disbanded the same month but two Walrus aircraft were transferred to a detachment of 278 Squadron and remained at Hawkinge. As the run-down to victory commenced and as the war moved ever further into the Continent, Hawkinge became used less and less. The surrender of the Germans on 8th May 1945 brought celebrations for service personnel and civilians alike. The last real wartime use of the base was when, like many others, it received returning prisoners of war for documentation purposes.

With the collapse of the Far East war on 14th August, peace had finally arrived but already the words 'Care and Maintenance' had been bantered about for this war-torn grass airfield. It did survive a further period of activity when No 3 Armament Practice School became based there but on 3rd September, Hawkinge did indeed close as an RAF station.

It found a new lease of life in July 1947 when it became a WAAF

Technical Training Unit and in December 1955, the Home Gliding School arrived to instruct Air Cadets in the art of gliding. All of this, however, did not secure the airfield's future and on the cold, windy evening of Friday, 8th December 1961, the RAF Ensign was lowered for the last time as a lone bugler played the Last Post.

Always a grass airfield, Hawkinge had no place in the peacetime jet-powered RAF. Many were the squadrons that used it over the six years of war and many were the men and women of those squadrons that were proud to have served there. Signs still remain of its existence and a memorial erected on the airfield by a local historian, Roy Humphreys, will ensure Hawkinge will never be forgotten. The Hawkinge Aeronautical Trust has its museum of wartime artifacts in one of the old buildings, another reminder of a time when Kent had its back to the wall.

7
LYMPNE

In 1923, the *Daily Mail* newspaper began to take an interest in private aviation and in order to encourage the apparent enthusiasm of the public for flying, organised a series of races at Lympne. They offered a prize of £1,000 to the winner and the Duke of Sutherland, himself an avid aviator, also offered £500 for the longest flight on one gallon of petrol. The first weekend of October 1923 saw an unusual selection of aircraft being transported into Lympne. During the morning they were assembled and test flown by the competitors with the race being held in the afternoon. The eventual winners of this particular race were Mr Walter Longton in the English Electric Wren and Jimmy James in W.S. Shackleton's ANEC. Both aircraft covered 87 miles on one gallon of petrol. Such economy in those days!

This was just one of many such competitions held at the little airfield in those between the wars days, all of them putting Lympne on the aviation map of Great Britain. It came to the notice of the military around 1927 when the RAF showed an interest in the airfield, using it for the tented two week summer camps of Nos 600 (City of London) and 601 (County of London) Auxiliary Air Force Squadrons, although when they left it was to be eight years before the RAF returned. In the meantime however, the airfield became a mecca for light aviation and was the starting point for many record breaking flights.

For Lympne, the changeover from civil to military occurred on 3rd November 1936 when, with the setting up of a Station Headquarters, the Hawker Hind bombers of Nos 21 and 34 Squadrons arrived. It was also a time of change for the local Cinque Ports Flying Club when the 'Youth of Britain Flying Training Association' was established. This became the Civil Air Guard in 1937 when the Air Ministry instructed all flying clubs to take on and teach potential military pilots at the Ministry's expense.

The arrival of the Hinds allowed the airfield to open as a temporary unit in No 1 (Bomber) Group. The aircraft were hangared in the remaining Belfast Truss hangars whilst the personnel of both squadrons had to make do with tented accommodation. On 11th July 1938, when it became obvious that Britain might go to war again with Germany, the two squadrons moved to a permanent bomber station at Upper Heyford and strangely, Lympne was reduced to Care and Maintenance on 1st October 1938. With the increasing tension and the knowledge that Kent would take the brunt of the German air campaign, it was assumed that the airfield would be included in Fighter Command. It was then, rather a shock when it went to No 24 Group Training Command and became the School of Accounting Clerks.

It appears as though someone had realised the error of their ways though when, seven months later, the School left and Lympne was indeed transferred to Fighter Command, although as a unit encompassed within No 22 Group with the option of being handed over to the Admiralty! Two months later it was commissioned as HMS *Buzzard*. The 1st July saw six Blackburn Skuas and three Blackburn Rocs disembarking from HMS *Ark Royal* for a short period followed by the arrival of the naval Air Mechanics School in September 1939 as the airfield was recommissioned as HMS *Daedulus 11*.

With the departure of the naval aircraft back to *Ark Royal*, the airfield fell strangely quiet throughout the opening phases of the war. This persisted until May 1940 when, with the rapid advance of the German army into Belgium and Holland, several units of the Advanced Air Striking Force arrived at Lympne. There was hardly parking space now at the airfield as the Lysanders of No 2 Squadron and the Bristol Blenheims of Nos 18, 53 and 59 Squadrons jostled for space before departing to other airfields. Two remaining Lysander squadrons, Nos 16 and 26, remained at Lympne to fly tactical reconnaissance sorties over the Dunkirk evacuation. In addition the squadrons were engaged on water supply dropping operations to the British army trapped in Calais by the advancing Germans. When it became obvious that this army could not be rescued from the Channel port and would be taken prisoners of war, the supply drops ceased and No 26 went to West Malling on 8th June whilst No 16 went to Redhill.

Before this however, the Air Mechanics School had moved and Lympne was transferred back to Fighter Command to become a forward airfield in the Biggin Hill sector of No 11 Group. Throughout June, a few squadrons used the field on a rotational basis, arriving in the morning and leaving in the evening. However, before what is now termed the first phase of the Battle of Britain began, the Luftwaffe had Lympne on its hit list.

With the main attacks in June 1940 concentrating on shipping in the Channel and the Channel Ports, a force of ten aircraft wandered over the coastline on 3rd July. They saw Lympne basking in a July sun and promptly dropped their bombs around the area, doing no damage to the airfield whatsoever but causing confusion and fear among the civilian population living in the locality. It was a sign of things to come.

Not until Monday, 12th August 1940 did the airfield suffer another attack, this one far heavier than the July raid. The sister forward airfields of Hawkinge and Manston together with six radar stations in Kent, Sussex and the Isle of Wight, the naval dockyard at Portsmouth and a convoy in the Thames Estuary were also included. This was the final interpretation of Hitler's 'Directive No 16', which in addition to destroying the RAF, called for the Luftwaffe also to attack early warning radar stations, naval ports and aircraft manufacturing plants.

By 9 am, the Do 17s of the first Gruppe of KG2 were airborne from Epinoy. Thirty minutes later they approached Lympne at little more than 800 feet and opened their bomb doors. In seconds, three hangars were hit together with the SHQ, several camouflaged buildings and the old clubroom of the Cinque Ports Flying Club. The landing area was badly cratered and several vital cables were severed putting the airfield out of action for several days. A total of 141 bombs were dropped in

A rather unusual Ju 87 Stuka in that it is in camouflage. (MAP)

what seemed to be seconds. As the raiders turned for home, they were attacked by the Hurricanes of 43 Squadron from Tangmere and the Spitfires of 54 Squadron from Hornchurch, both squadrons downing several enemy aircraft although they themselves had several aircraft damaged by return fire.

The damage to Lympne was increased when another raid developed during the afternoon. Just after 3 pm, aircraft from Luftflotte 2 again attacked the airfield dropping a further 242 bombs, although 70 of them fell in the fields surrounding the site. More damage was inflicted on buildings that were still standing and further craters were left on the landing area. Despite this, two Spitfires of 54 Squadron managed to crashland safely without going down into any of them.

With an isolated raid taking place in the late afternoon of 13th August, the next heavy raid came on the 15th, known now as the hardest day. In their greatest effort of the battle so far, all three Luftflotten were airborne at some time during the day. Although the early morning began quietly, from 11 am onwards five main attacks developed. For Lympne, still repairing damage from previous raids and partially out of use as a forward airfield, it was to be hoped that they were not on Goering's list. Not so unfortunately, as just after 11.15 am, a force of 40 Ju 87 Stuka divebombers of Stukageschwader 2 and escorted by Me 109s of JG 51, 53 and 54 delivered a ferocious attack, destroying the station sick quarters and several of the remaining buildings. Again, and only just repaired, the main water supply pipes were cut through together with the main electricity cable. Various sections had to be evacuated to nearby houses with the attack rendering Lympne once again unserviceable.

It is true to say that the airfield played no significant part in the Battle of Britain, although damaged aircraft were grateful for its position and meagre facilities. A few further isolated attacks took place but the full potential of Lympne did not come to fruition until 1941. In October 1940, 421 Flight had been formed from 66 Squadron for the specific task of carrying out high altitude coastal patrols to intercept enemy aircraft coming in over the coast. These types of operations became known as 'Jim Crows'. (See West Malling chapter.) The flight received squadron status on 9th January 1941 and became No 91 (Nigeria) Squadron based at Hawkinge, a short distance from Lympne. It was felt prudent to base a detachment at the latter airfield and in March 1941, Sqd/Ldr C.P. Green DFC sent 'A' flight to Lympne. 91 began 'Rhubarb' operations with their Spitfire VBs shortly after, the low level strike sorties over enemy occupied territory proving a challenge. With the arrival of the

Bomb craters are clearly visible on the grass landing areas at Lympne, 18th August 1940. (RAF Museum)

detachment, it was decided to bring Lympne up to full satellite standard and a period of reconstruction began. Dispersed hardstandings were built together with several fighter pens and the erection of three Blister hangars saw the airfield back to a front line base.

For the rest of the year and into 1942, 'A' flight continued to operate from Lympne. The squadron had also been given the additional task of escorting the Air-Sea Rescue Lysander and Walrus aircraft that went out to pick up aircrew floating in their dinghies. Flying was not, however, left entirely to 91 as during this period, several other Biggin Hill squadrons rotated through the airfield for weekly stays.

August 1942 and the ill-fated Dieppe operation codenamed 'Jubilee' brought a flurry of activity to the airfield which was to continue until the end of the war. In support of Jubilee, Nos 133 (Eagle) Squadron arrived from Biggin Hill on 30th June and 401 (Ram) of the RCAF also from Biggin Hill, on the 14th August. Both flew Spitfires though different marks and were tasked with keeping the skies over Dieppe clear of enemy aircraft.

The Lympne squadrons in common with many others, held their own against the Luftwaffe as the Canadians became pinned down on the beach at Dieppe. For 91 Squadron, the operations proved a little dismal for whilst other units fought over the beaches, they were given the task of carrying out anti-shipping patrols between Ostend and Le Havre. They saw very little action as they spent their time looking for dinghies in the water. During the final stages of withdrawal it fell to 133 Squadron to escort the last remaining boats back from Dieppe. It saddened them and indeed every squadron to learn of the dreadful loss of life.

With 'Jubilee' over, both 133 and 401 left Lympne and it was not until 2nd October 1942 that a full squadron arrived in the shape of No 65 (East India) who flew their Spitfire VBs in from Drem. They commenced a series of sweeps, Rhubarbs and patrols but stayed only until the 11th of the month before returning to Drem in Scotland. The 23rd November however saw the entire squadron of 91 move into Lympne and carry on similar operations in addition to its ongoing Jim Crow activities. Further upgrading of the airfield commenced with the work taking up until the spring of 1943.

No 1 Squadron were very proud of their motto 'In Omnibus Princeps' (Foremost in everything). They had a proud record of achievement from the First World War and continued this pattern throughout the Battle of Britain. Conversion to the Hawker Typhoon in July 1942 whilst at Acklington ensured that they would soon move

Officers and NCOs of No 1 Squadron in front of their Typhoon FI, with CO Sqd/Ldr 'Tony' Zweigbergk centre, Lympne 1943. (L. H. Pilkington)

No 1 Squadron at Lympne. F/O Tony Scrope-Davies poses with his admin team outside the orderly room. (No 1 Squadron Archives)

south into No 11 Group and this they did on 9th February 1943 when they arrived at Biggin Hill. For some reason, the CO of Biggin, G/Cpt 'Sailor' Malan did not want the noisy Typhoon on his base and with a clash of personalities between him and the CO of No 1, Sqd/Ldr R.C. Wilkinson, OBE, DFM, the squadron moved to Lympne on 15th March, 'to be nearer the Germans' as he put it! Once again the beautiful mansion of Port Lympne became the officers' mess, although most ranks were accommodated in mansion type houses. They found a great friend and ally in Mrs Davis, whose husband had been killed just before No 1 had arrived. They had been the owners of Lympne pre-war and she continued to look after the place as if it were still a little flying club. She drove the Naafi wagon around the dispersals, never missing a day through illness or bad weather. For No 1, life at Lympne was very good.

Not so for the residents who were constantly complaining about the noise the Typhoon made. The Sabre engine was very temperamental and in order to ensure the aircraft would start in the early mornings, it was sometimes necessary to run the engines up at intervals throughout the night.

Being near the coast, there was now plenty of action for the squadron.

A typical operation took place on 9th April when P/O Higham and Sgt Sutherland were scrambled from Lympne to investigate some 'bogeys' across the Channel. Taking off in double quick time, they reached Cap Gris Nez and saw four FW 190s escorting a German destroyer. Going straight into the attack they saw to their horror, ten further 190s appear out of the cloud. Breaking off the action, they were relieved to see two further Typhoons arrive from Lympne and turned to re-engage the enemy. Sgt Hornall shot down one for no loss and all the aircraft returned safely to Lympne.

The next three months saw No 1 operating in a similar role. Additional sorties included train strafing and shooting up enemy convoys, at which the squadron became very adept. With Lympne still just a small grass airfield, the Typhoon proved a difficult aircraft to operate and numerous incidents took place.

A detachment of No 245 (Northern Rhodesia) Squadron had arrived at Lympne on 30th March 1943 equipped with the bomber version of the Typhoon, the 1B, universally known as a 'Bombphoon'. Just a little envious, No 1 were detailed to act as escorts to them but by the end of 1943 and in common with many other Typhoon squadrons, the aircraft of No 1 were fitted with bombracks. They commenced Ramrod operations, day bomber raids escorted by fighters. The Typhoons would climb to a height and then dive on their target releasing their two 500 lb bombs just prior to pulling out of the dive. Using this method, 90 per cent accuracy was assured.

By 28th May the 245 detachment had moved to Fairlop and had been replaced by No 609 (West Riding) Squadron of the Royal Auxiliary Air Force who brought their Typhoon 1Bs to Lympne on 18th August. The CO, Sqd/Ldr A. Ingle AFC was due to hand over the reins of the squadron to Sqd/Ldr P.G. Thornton-Brown shortly after their arrival as No 1 became involved in Operation Starkey, the unsuccessful operation intended to tempt the Luftwaffe into large-scale combat. When this was over, it was back to the Ramrod ops with 609 acting as fighter escort to No 1 who were dive-bombing targets of opportunity in Europe.

This pattern continued until 609 left for Manston on 14th December 1943 to be replaced by the rocket-firing Hurricanes of No 137 Squadron who came in from Manston. The squadron had been the second to be equipped with the unusual Westland Whirlwind twin-engine fighter. In 1942 they were modified to fighter/bomber configuration but by June 1943, conversion to the Hurricane IV had taken place. Led by Sqd/Ldr J.R. Dennehey DFC, they carried out anti-shipping strikes before moving to Colerne in January to convert to the Typhoon. They brought these back to Lympne on 4th February 1944 as No 1 Squadron left for Martlesham Heath after a very successful stay.

137 began their escort duties in February and graduated to fighter/bomber work before leaving for Manston in April. In their place came No 186 Squadron from Tain. Although they had flown Typhoons since November 1943, it was the Spitfire VB that they brought to Lympne on 1st March 1944. With these the squadron became operational on the 15th of the month when they flew a close escort sortie to Martin Marauders who were bombing Coxyoe airfield. The next four or five days they flew convoy escort duties before disbanding and being renumbered No 130 (Punjab) Squadron on 5th April 1944. The Spitfires continued their missions over northern France until 30th April when they left for the Sussex ALG of Horne and became part of the 2nd TAF.

With the invasion in mind, Lympne now entered a very busy period of its life when Nos 33, 74 (Trinidad) and 127 Squadrons arrived for pre-invasion sweeps and bomber escort work. Arriving from the 15th to the 17th May 1944, 33 and 74 were flying the Spitfire LF IXE whilst 127 had the Spitfire HF IX. They flew fighter/bomber missions attacking marshalling sites, ammunition dumps and generally becoming a

137 Typhoons and 403 Spitfires at Lympne February 1944. (C. H. Thomas)

155

nuisance to any type of enemy transport that moved on the ground. On D-Day itself, the squadrons escorted the airborne glider formations, coming into daily contact with the Luftwaffe. No 74 were diverted to anti-diver operations in June with the other two squadrons attacking Noball sites. Transfer to the 2nd TAF for all three units in July took them to Tangmere in Sussex, allowing the first Czech wing to fly from Lympne to arrive.

Nos 310, 312 and 313 Squadrons were mainly formed from Czech refugees in July 1940 under a British CO. They found success during the Battle of Britain and in the years to follow. By 1944 bombs had been fitted to their Spitfires and they were engaged in a heavy programme of Ramrods. By the time they arrived at Lympne on 3rd July, they had reverted back to UK defence duties as part of the Air Defence of Great Britain and were carrying out anti-diver patrols against the V1s. They carried out these duties at Lympne for just over a week before leaving and being replaced by Nos 1, back at their old haunt, 41 and 165 (Ceylon) Squadrons flying varied marks of Spitfires.

Anti-diver patrols were the order of the day as the number of launchings increased from across the Channel. Whereas previously the fighters had been allowed to attack the V1s anywhere they found them, a new strategy was now in place. Batteries of heavy guns had been moved down to the Kent and Sussex coastline so that the gunners would get an uninterrupted view of the doodlebugs. The fighters were then given two patrol lines, one in mid Channel and the other behind the gun barrage but ahead of the balloon barrage. This way, if one method did not get the V1s, the other one surely would. The squadrons did not like the new idea and found it hard to adjust initially but there is no doubt that with this method, fewer rockets reached the capital.

As the offensive declined in the middle of August, Nos 1 and 165 left for Detling with No 41 resuming its Channel sweeps. Although the end of the war was fast approaching, there was no slackening of the pace. With the Allies well established on the Continent, the Germans were attempting a last push to come out on top. One of the weapons used in this final flurry was the Me 262, the first jet-driven fighter to attain operational status. Programme 223 had called for a production rate of 60 aircraft from May 1944 but with the constant Allied bombing of German industry, production was severely slowed down. However, the type did enter service with the Luftwaffe during late 1944 and was beginning to prove a problem for the aircraft still carrying out the daylight raids on Germany. In order to combat the new fighter, 41 Squadron converted to the Griffon-engined Spitfire XIV which could

A fine shot of Lympne just post-war showing a variety of aircraft. Plainly visible are the bases of the three original hangars and the wartime Blister hangar. (MAP)

operate at the same altitude as the Me 262. Success against the German jet came swiftly and in August 1944, 41 were joined by two other Spitfire XIV squadrons, Nos 130 (Punjab) and 610 (County of Chester).

The end of 1944 saw No 130 being replaced by No 350 (Belgian) Squadron, who flew their XIVs to Lympne in September and began Ramrod operations in support of the Arnhem landings. With the battle now taking place on the Continent, the time was approaching when many of the Kent airfields would no longer be essential to the war effort. To Lympne, it came in December 1944 when all three squadrons moved to continental airfields and the 2nd TAF. The airfield reverted to an emergency landing ground until April 1945 when two units of the Royal Australian Air Force, Nos 451 and 453 brought their Spitfires in for one month as victory fast approached. When they left, the ATC facilities were withdrawn and Lympne entered a period of Care and Maintenance.

The military found no further use for the airfield and it returned to its civilian role. During the post-war years Lympne regained its status as the perfect civil airport with scheduled services being opened to the Continent with the Dakotas of Silver City Airways, plus flying clubs offering a very good social life. When the Dakota service moved to a purpose built airfield at Lydd called Ferryfield, Skyways Coach and Air

Services took over, also with Dakotas but later with the then modern Hawker Siddeley 748 turbo-prop. For many years the service operated from Lympne, or Ashford Airport as it was then called, but peacetime prosperity brought its own problems with more and more people choosing to holiday further afield. The Coach/Air service struggled on but suddenly ceased trading in January 1970 whereupon it was taken over by Air Freight Ltd, renaming the service Skyways International. A year later Dan Air made a successful bid for the company and started up the coach/air service from Ashford to Beauvais until October 1974 when they too moved to Lydd. This time Lympne had reached the end.

Sadly, industry took over most of the site and today only a few signs of the historic airfield remain. These are mainly wartime buildings and shelters in Otterpool Lane and of course, the lovely mansion of Port Lympne, now part of Howletts Zoo Park. From civil to war and back to civil aviation, Lympne has seen it all.

8
MANSTON

At 11am on Monday, 16th February 1942, five men met in London to open the first and only judicial inquiry into the conduct of a battle during the Second World War. It was a dreary day adding to the already dismal atmosphere in the room. Eleven months had passed since the French dockyard fitter informed the Admiralty that two German battleships had reached the safety of Brest harbour. With the constant bombing by the RAF, the ships were virtually trapped in the harbour. The German Navy needed them back into the Atlantic to carry on their plundering and had two choices. Take the long route round Ireland and Scotland and into the North Sea or the quickest route through the English Channel. They chose the latter and successfully reached Germany virtually unscathed. For the Navy and the RAF it became known as the 'war's biggest blunder' and led to the inquiry. For RAF Manston, it was the airfield's most humiliating period.

Like so many airfields in Kent, Manston's origins were as a Royal Naval Air Station. Opened in 1916, No 3 Wing arrived from RNAS Detling on 29th May of that year and in October, they moved into France. On the formation of the RAF on 1st April 1918, three day-bombing training squadrons arrived. Two months later, Manston was listed as an aerodrome for military and civil use, a combination that remains today – although only just! From 1919, it became a training establishment used by various units and also a popular venue for the RAF summer camps.

On 1st March 1931, a Special Reserve Squadron was formed at the base aptly named No 500 (County of Kent) Squadron, equipped with the Vickers Virginia for daylight bombing. During 1936 the station was transferred to No 24 (Training) Group and with the signs of another war fast approaching, 500 were reclassified from the Special Reserve and given full auxiliary status. Now flying Hawker Harts and Hinds, they were partnered at Manston by No 48 (General Reconnaissance) Squadron who were flying the then new Avro Anson. The RAF expansion scheme required large numbers of air crew and No 48 were enlarged during this period to an establishment of 80 Ansons to cope with the flood of 'would-be pilots'. In September 1938 they moved to Eastchurch, handing over their aircraft to the School of Air Navigation that had formed at the base. On 28th September 1938, 500 moved to their wartime base at Detling.

The airfield began to prepare for war with the issue of gas masks and for certain officers, an issue of small firearms. Trenches and shelters were dug, machine gun posts were in position and manned and training was being carried out in anti-gas procedure with the thought that this would be the first weapon the enemy would use. The Munich crisis brought the airfield onto a war footing as the station build-up continued. The School of Air Navigation expanded and more temporary living accommodation was built. When Neville Chamberlain returned with his little piece of paper, the immediate crisis was relaxed allowing Nos 600 (City of London), 501 (County of Gloucester) and 616 (South Yorkshire) auxiliary squadrons to arrive for a two week summer camp. They found a very different Manston, with its camouflage and preparations for war. Unfortunately, the national crisis again reared its head and the last summer camp was cut short as General Mobilisation was ordered on 1st September 1939. All leave was cancelled, the machine gun posts became active and Manston prepared to go to war.

The School of Air Navigation moved out and on 4th September, the School of Technical Training was dispersed. On the 10th, No 3 Squadron arrived at Manston 'for operational purposes' as the diarist put it, equipped with the Hurricane I. They moved to Croydon seven days later returning to Manston on 12th October 1939, which was deemed a fighter station in No 11 Group, Fighter Command.

Wg/Cdr Hanmer arrived to take command as Nos 235 and 253 (Hyderabad State) Squadrons reformed at the station after having disbanded at the end of the First World War. They were scheduled to receive Blenheim Ifs but in the end they got the Miles Magister trainer and the Fairey Battle light bomber, both types being used in the training role by the two squadrons. Before No 3 Squadron left on 13th November

One of the many mishaps at Manston, due perhaps to the length of the first runway.

1939, they had suffered several mishaps with their Hurricanes. One had landed heavily and broke its undercarriage whilst another went missing after an interception sortie over the Channel. As they departed to Croydon, No 79 (Madras Presidency) Squadron arrived from Biggin Hill to begin a four month stay at Manston. They shot down a Do 17 shortly after their arrival, the first for the squadron and for the airfield.

No 600 (City of London) Auxiliary Air Force Squadron had worked hard to come up to operational status when they received the Blenheim IVs equipped with the earliest form of airborne radar. Northolt, west of London, was not the ideal place to carry out nightly patrols from and the squadron was detached to Manston on 27th December 1939. The reasoning behind this move was that since war had been declared, the enemy had sent over He 115s to lay mines in the Thames Estuary by night. 600 were detailed to patrol the area each night in the hope of detecting them. Sadly, good luck was not on their side and with a very early and often unreliable airborne radar, they found it impossible to even find the aircraft.

The Christmas of 1939/40 was one of the worst. Sitting as it did on the barren Thanet coast, Manston was frozen up for a considerable period. The new year had already started off pretty badly when a Miles Magister of 79 Squadron on a training flight, crashed at Garlinge killing the two crew instantly. The bad weather lasted until February when Nos 235 and 253 Squadrons moved out, with 79 going back to Biggin Hill on 8th March 1940. 32 Squadron moved in from Gravesend for two weeks.

600 Squadron, now the senior unit on the airfield, were still flying at night virtually blind, and they had their fair share of losses. The 11th March 1940 was a good clear night, just right perhaps for finding the enemy minelayers. F/O Tollemache and his gunner LAC Smith, together with a passenger on a familiarisation flight, 2nd L/T Sperling of the Welsh Guards, were detailed for a patrol. Again with no success in finding the enemy, Tollemache returned and whilst attempting to land, the Blenheim suddenly dropped and crashed just outside the airfield boundary. The pilot and gunner managed to scramble clear of the aircraft before the fuel burst into flames but not so 2nd L/T Sperling who was trapped inside. With no thought for his own safety, Tollemache attempted to get back into the burning aircraft to rescue him but was beaten back by the intense heat and flames. For this act of bravery, F/O Tollemache was awarded the Empire Gallantry Medal, later exchanged for the George Cross.

May saw the rapid advance of the German Army through the Low Countries. With the situation on the ground critical, in the air it was even worse. The RAF in France had 400 aircraft in 25 squadrons, most of them equipped with obsolescent and slow aircraft. Air Marshal Dowding doubted that sending further fighters to help the French and Belgians was of any use and told the Under-Secretary of State at the Air Ministry just that in a letter dated 16th May 1940. Shortly after, it became clear that the RAF component of the BEF could no longer fly from French airfields with the enemy knocking at the door and on 19th May, the remaining units were told to leave and fly back to the UK. It was just in time as an incident involving 600 Squadron clearly illustrated. A 74 Squadron Spitfire was damaged in the air but managed to make it back to Calais Marck airfield just before the Germans arrived. A 600 Squadron Blenheim was ordered to fly to Calais carrying some of the Manston ground crews, a radiator and some glycol in order to repair the Spitfire. The job took longer than anticipated and with the Blenheim having returned to Manston for more parts, the poor ground crews found themselves captured by German troops as they entered Calais Marck airfield.

Operation Dynamo began on the evening of 26th May and with

Manston being one of the airfields closest to the action, it became very busy indeed. The Boulton Paul Defiants of No 264 (Madras Presidency) Squadron were detached to Manston for the duration of 'Dynamo' but suffered grievously at the hands of the Luftwaffe as they got the measure of the limited firepower of the Defiant.

With Dunkirk over, Manston returned to normal. The operation had taken a heavy toll on Fighter Command and the month of June saw British fighter defences at their lowest ebb, with the loss of over 100 fighters and 80 pilots. In the period 10th May to 20th June 1940, 944 RAF aircraft were lost of which 386 were Hurricanes and 67 Spitfires. What was left of 'Dowding's Chicks' as they had been named, had arrived back and the real fighting was about to begin.

No 600 were still the only resident squadron at Manston as the prelude to the Battle of Britain began. They had made some contact with the enemy prior to Dunkirk when on 10th May, P/O Anderson on a night patrol over the Channel in his Blenheim, came into contact with two He 111s. Managing to get the airborne radar to stay active during the stalking, he attacked one of the enemy aircraft but the German gunner on the Heinkel managed to retaliate and in the process, shot P/O Anderson's hydraulics away, though he managed to crashland safely. The second contact with the enemy was made when 600 Squadron were ordered to carry out a daylight raid on Waalhaven airfield in Holland. Six Blenheims left Manston, one returned. The next day the squadron returned to night flying duties.

As 'Adlertag' approached, many squadrons within No 11 Group came and went using Manston purely as a forward airfield. It was on the 12th that the Luftwaffe crossed the coastline with the aim of bombing radar stations and coastal airfields. The first armada came at 9 am when five radar stations were attacked but it was just after midday when it became the turn of Manston. 54 Squadron had flown in on that Monday morning from Hornchurch. Having settled in to the dispersal huts, ten minutes later the telephones were ringing as 54, whose call sign was 'Hornet', were scrambled to intercept a large force of Do 17s. With engines at full boost, the Spitfires climbed up through thin cloud.

On the ground, warning had been given that an attack was imminent and many personnel had taken to the newly constructed shelters. As the Dorniers droned overhead and dropped their bombs, the airfield erupted in a mass of noise and flame. Almost immediately the first bombs found their targets with two hangars being hit and badly damaged whilst inside, a Blenheim and two Spitfires were destroyed. Many of the workshops disappeared in a sheet of flame and the

Manston under attack during 1940. The large white areas are exploding bombs. (US National Archives)

runways resembled a domestic colander.

As the bombs fell, No 65 Squadron who had just flown in from Hornchurch, were lining up their Spitfires to take off and join the fight. With the noise of their own engines, the pilots did not fully appreciate what was happening until they saw great clods of earth being hurled high into the sky. Flying through a huge cloud of smoke, they managed to get airborne and join in the melee above. They caught the enemy just as he was turning for home and tore into the attack, downing several of the 109s in minutes.

As the dogfight continued over the Channel, Manston began to lick its wounds. When the dust had settled, leaving just the crackling of flames to hear, it was found that the landing area was pitted with about 100 bomb craters. This together with the hangars and buildings destroyed rendered the airfield unserviceable for 24 hours. Despite the craters, both 65 and 54 Squadrons managed to land safely and refuel before going back to their parent airfields. As evening came, the German propaganda machine swung into action claiming heavy damage on several airfields with No 65 Squadron being entirely wiped out at Manston. It continued by saying that 46 Spitfires, 23 Hurricanes and one French Morane 406 had been destroyed. In actual fact, the Germans lost 31 aircraft and the RAF, in the course of 732 sorties, had suffered 22 casualties.

'Eagle Day' came and went with no attacks on Manston. On 15th August, a crack Luftwaffe unit, Erprobungs Gruppe 210, attacked the airfield at 12.10 pm. Flying from Calais Marke airfield, the Me 110s came in low machine gunning and dropping their bombs. As they approached Manston, the ground defence guns opened up and in seconds, one 110 had fallen to the gunners of a Royal Artillery Bofors gun whilst another was brought down by an RAF Hispano machine gun fitted to an RAF truck. Damage was caused to the remaining hangars and once again, the runways were cratered. Further bad attacks came over the next two days, these forcing 600 Squadron to take their Blenheims, or what was left of them, to Hornchurch.

Manston was a sorry sight and definitely not a healthy place to be. More low level attacks came on 20th and 22nd of August and although squadrons were still using its limited facilities as a forward airfield, no defence as such was available for the airfield itself. A decoy airfield was set up at Ash Level Marshes in the hope that it would take the heat off Manston. But on the 24th, the airfield suffered its worst attack of the war so far. It was a Saturday with the early part of the morning fine and bright. The radar stations and the controllers at No 11 Group headquarters watched and waited anxiously for signs of a build-up. They did not have to wait long for by 9 am, a large force was assembling over Cap Gris Nez. The first attacks were aimed at Dover but several hours later, the target was definitely Manston.

No 264 (Madras Presidency) Squadron had arrived at first light. Led by Sqd/Ldr Philip Hunter, they flew the Defiant in the day fighting role despite the earlier tragedies with the type. Scrambled just before the first bombs fell on the airfield, they struggled to get into some sort of formation and to gain height against the enemy aircraft. The chaotic take-off may have been the reason that within minutes, tragedy came to the squadron. Defiant L7021 flown by P/O D. Whitley with Sgt R.C. Turner as gunner, was hit in the tail by return fire from a Ju 88 and was forced to land back at Manston, though with no injuries. Defiant L6966 was shot down shortly after, P/O J.T. Jones and P/O W.A. Ponting missing in the lost aircraft. Defiant L7027 failed to return with F/O I.G.

Shaw and Sgt A. Berry lost and the CO, Sqd/Ldr Hunter and his gunner, F.H. King, failed to return from chasing a Ju 88 in Defiant N1535. In an earlier incident, Defiant L7013 was attacked by 109s and severely damaged, with F/O E.W. Campbell-Colquohoun and P/O G. Robinson surviving a crash landing. In another attack on Manston later in the afternoon, Defiant L6965 with P/O R.S. Gaskell and Sgt W.H. Machin was shot down by 109s from JG 51. The pilot was badly injured and Sgt Machin sadly died from his wounds later. It had been a catastrophic day for 264 and proved once again that as a day fighter, the Defiant was severely limited.

The airfield had also suffered a great deal from the raid. Seven people had been killed, unexploded bombs lay everywhere, every single communication line had been cut and Manston lay entirely isolated. What remained of 264 Squadron had flown back to Hornchurch and as a serviceable airfield, very little was left standing. Although buildings and hangars were still on fire, the local Fire Brigade and RAF firemen fought bravely to dampen them down. It was not only the airfield that had suffered for many bombs had fallen on the village of Manston and the houses and farms surrounding the airfield. If ever a piece of humour could be extracted from this dreadful raid, it was when one local

The pilot and a Waaf sticking stamps onto a bomb before it is delivered to enemy territory. (F/O Frazer)

resident chose to call the station commander, Sqd/Ldr G.A.L. Manton, complaining about the amount of attention that Manston appeared to be getting from the Luftwaffe and could he, the CO, do anything about it!

With no communications between the airfield and No 11 Group, the controller at the latter telephoned No 1 Observer Corps at Maidstone to see if the Corps could tell him what was going on. The HQ contacted the nearest Observer post to the airfield and asked one of the men to cycle over and take a look at things. This he duly did and, appalled by what he saw, reported back that Manston was in dire straits and almost uninhabitable. As word got back to No 11 Group, it was decided to evacuate the airfield and reduce it to the status of an ELG. A further raid later in the day did nothing to endear the airmen and women to the airfield as they moved their belongings to lodgings at Westgate, a little further around the coast.

At the end of a long day, it had become obvious that the airfields had been the main focus of the attacks. Fighter Command had struggled to cope with the sheer number of enemy aircraft losing many good pilots and aircraft in the process. If the remainder of the fighter airfields were in the state that Manston was, it could only be a question of time before they were all finished.

Hearing of the plight of the airfield, Winston Churchill himself paid a visit on 28th August 1940. He found the place barely serviceable with craters and flags indicating unexploded bombs everywhere. He was visibly shocked and the next day he wrote to the Secretary of State and the Chief of the Air Staff saying that he was perturbed at the time being taken to repair airfield damage and was it not a good idea to organise and form mobile repair units? It is not recorded whether or not his letters had the desired effect but somehow, Manston managed to get itself together and was back on the air in 36 hours.

By September it was back in operation though on a very limited scale. Two Lysanders of No 4 Squadron then based at Clifton, arrived to work in conjunction with the Air-Sea Rescue launches operating out of Ramsgate Harbour. Although only minor air attacks took place during September, October and November, they still hampered the full operating capacity of the airfield. Apart from the Lysanders, no squadrons were based there over this period although fighter squadrons did begin to use the forward facility again. Of far more interest was the arrival of an enemy aircraft in a wheels up landing. The incident took place on Thursday, 17th October when a unit of Me 109s from No 3 Gruppe of JG 53 had left Sempey and Brest on a freelance

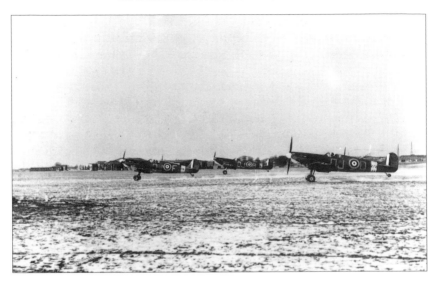

'A' Flight of 92 Squadron's Spitfire IIBs on snow, Manston January 1941. (IWM)

patrol over Kent. Flying at between 22,000 and 24,000 feet, the group was attacked by No 74 Squadron from Biggin Hill. Flying low over Gravesend, Oberleutnant Walter Rupp was damaged in combat by P/O Draper. Hit in the radiator and leaking glycol badly, Rupp turned for home but realised that he could never make it. With his engine rapidly overheating, Rupp crossed over Thanet and saw a badly battered Manston below. Attempting to land, he found that he had no hydraulic power to lower his undercarriage so he prepared himself for a belly landing. This he achieved with very little damage to his aircraft and immediately upon his coming to stop, got out and surrendered himself to the station police. The Me 108E-4, serial no 1106, became the object of intense scrutiny. It had dark green upper surfaces, the fuselage and sides were grey with a light blue under-surface and a spinner and engine cowling and rudder painted in yellow. It bore two white victory markings and had a yellow figure 1 outlined in black. The next morning saw scientists and high ranking officers fly into Manston to inspect the prize before it was later taken to the Royal Aircraft Establishment on a trailer for examination and assessment. It later returned to the county and was put on display at a number of towns. For Oblt Rupp, it meant a prisoner of war camp for the duration of the war.

The next month saw a similar incident with the capture of another intact 109. This aircraft was made airworthy and was delivered to Rolls-

Royce on 14th December 1940. It later passed to the Aircraft and Armament Experimental Establishment at Boscombe Down and then Duxford and today is to be seen, fully refurbished, in the RAF Museum at Hendon. Once again, it had been a very exciting day for Manston.

Christmas 1940 came and went and with the new year came a spate of raids on the airfield once again. Mainly carried out by bomb-carrying Me 109s, they proved more of a nuisance than dangerous although light damage was sustained on the field.

No 92 (East India) Squadron became the first in many months to be based at Manston when Sqd/Ldr J.A. Kent DFC, AFC brought his Spitfires in from Biggin Hill on 9th January 1941. Arriving with the Mk I, they quickly converted to the mark VB and first found success in shooting down the enemy on 3rd February when F/O A.C. Barkley shot down a He 111 over the Channel. One month later the Blenheims of No 59 Squadron arrived from Thorney Island to carry out reconnaissance missions over the Low Countries. They stayed until 1st March before leaving for Bircham Newton. February also saw 92 Squadron replaced by No 74 (Trinidad) Squadron who carried out fighter sweeps whenever the weather allowed.

In the new year the enemy attacks resumed. In January, two bomb-carrying Me 109s intent on flattening what was left of the Manston hangars, failed dismally when they were beaten off by fighters and the station defence. The same month saw the temporary dispersals and living accommodation at Westgate attacked by Ju 88s causing substantial damage but no injuries or loss of life. In February yet further attacks resulted in one airman being killed whilst running to take cover in a trench.

By spring 1941, Manston was involved in the 'Channel Stop' operation. This was an air operation designed to stop German shipping passing through the Straits of Dover. In order to prevent their passage, a detachment of Blenheim IVs from No 101 Squadron arrived. The Channel Stop sorties were indeed dangerous due to the fact that the enemy had recently been employing flak ships to protect their convoys. These proved fatal to 101 Squadron and the loss of the Blenheims prompted the Air Ministry to send No 242 (Canadian) Squadron with their Hurricane IIbs to Manston to protect the Blenheims. Whilst the squadron was Canadian in name, by the time it arrived at the airfield in July 1941, it was a very cosmopolitan unit with Pole, Czech, Australian, French and British pilots within its ranks.

74 Squadron moved to Gravesend in April, their place being taken by various units such as No 3 with Hurricanes, 23 with Havocs and 239,

the latter carrying out ASR and fighter reconnaissance over Belgium flying Tomahawks. The Channel Stop sorties ended in September 1941 after the loss of many aircraft, shot down by the flak ships. Whilst Manston-based squadrons had sunk 44,600 tons of shipping and damaged a further 27,500 tons, the losses were simply not acceptable and the operation stopped. Little did the Air Ministry know at the time that had it continued with Channel Stop, it may well have prevented the 'biggest blunder of the war' from happening.

The months of July and August 1941 were busy ones with No 601 (County of London) Auxiliary Squadron bringing their Hurricanes in from Northolt to be replaced after one month by No 222 (Natal) Squadron whose Spitfires stayed for 19 days. Both units were engaged in bomber escorts and fighter sweeps. 242 Squadron moved to Valley in Wales in September 1941 to be replaced by No 615 (County of Surrey) Auxiliary Squadron. Led by Sqd/Ldr D.E. Gillam, DFSO, DFC and Bar, they endured two months of intense activity flying Rangers and Rhubarbs whenever the weather allowed.

Despite the increased activity at the airfield, it was still a shambles with very little repair work having been done. Wg/Cdr R.P. Gleave was appointed station commander with a mandate to rebuild and get Manston fully operational again. Looking around him, he wondered how on earth he should begin. The skeletons of the hangars and bombed out buildings were still standing like sentinels with rubble and burnt wood laying around everywhere. Although most of the personnel were still living off the base, the ones that had remained through choice were found sleeping and living in the old chalk tunnels that ran beneath the airfield. These were a relic from the First World War and were totally inadequate for such a purpose, rats being the main inhabitants.

Wg/Cdr Gleave issued an order that anyone found living in them would be on a charge. The practice stopped instantly. Complaining to the Air Ministry about the condition of Manston and stating the fact that for a forward airfield, it offered very little in the way of comfort for the visiting squadrons, did have some effect and groups of local builders would suddenly appear on the odd occasions. It was however to be some time before the work was finally finished. Still a grass airfield, the landing runs were extended towards the end of 1941 to cope with the ever increasing number of damaged bombers that used Manston after returning from raids over German cities. The E/W and NE/SW runways were extended to 4,800 feet and 5,700 feet respectively with the promise of a tarmac runway at a later date.

Further squadrons came for short term stays with No 607 (County of

Durham) bringing their Hurricane IIbs in from Martlesham Heath and staying until 20th March 1942. One particular sortie worthy of mention took place on 24th November when two Tomahawks of No 26 (Army Co-operation) Squadron were detailed to undertake an offensive photo-reconnaissance of the beaches at Hardelot and Pointe de Lornel. The squadron had flown into Manston originally on 12th October but had been sent to Gatwick nine days later, returning to Manston on 22nd November. Until now they had not made contact with the enemy but the 24th was to change all of that.

With the briefing over, Sqd/Ldr Hadfield and P/O Baring took off from Manston flying at zero feet until they came to the French coast where they climbed to take their photos. Sqd/Ldr Hadfield then saw an enemy training plane and turned to attack. As he did so, P/O Baring in the other Tomahawk saw that it was a decoy aircraft and noticed several Me 109s just above it. He was yelling over the radio to his comrade to break off and head for home, when one of the enemy aircraft attacked him and shot him down over the Channel. Hadfield saw the aircraft fall into the sea near Ambleteuse and that Baring had swum clear. The Me 109s then came down and dived on the swimming pilot as Sqd/Ldr Hadfield engaged them, trying to at least frighten them off. Already low on fuel, he broke off the engagement and flew back to Manston just as P/O Baring managed to climb into his dinghy.

Upon landing and telling his story, three Hurricanes of 615 Squadron took off to look for the downed pilot. Making a series of sweeps they eventually saw the yellow dinghy and with the aid of smoke floats, the rescue launch managed to find him and pulled him aboard to fight another day.

The rest of 1941 continued in similar vein with Wg/Cdr Gleave somehow managing to restore morale by suggesting that further Waafs should serve at Manston. It took until spring 1942 before a full contingent did arrive but with morale rising and the airfield beginning to look like an airfield again, he was satisfied that Manston was returning to normal. And then came February 1942.

As far back as 29th April 1941, the Air Ministry had warned the RAF and the Navy that it was possible that the Germans might attempt a break-out from Brest with the two capital ships, *Scharnhorst* and *Gneisenau* together with the heavy cruiser, *Prinz Eugen*. Operation Channel Stop was initiated but as we have seen, this was cancelled in the autumn of 1941. Hitler badly wanted the ships back to carry on plundering in the Atlantic and had told his senior naval commanders that if they could not do it, he would have the armaments on board removed and used as shore batteries. This urged the German navy into considering a 'Channel dash'. Although the two British services considered a break-out was possible, the Navy reduced the number of submarines patrolling outside Brest harbour from seven to one. The first error had been made! Meanwhile for some time, Coastal Command had been flying three dawn-to-dusk patrols outside Brest whilst Fighter Command had organised daily sweeps of the Channel by No 91 (Nigeria) Squadron, known as the 'Jim Crow' Squadron.

The Germans planned their escape from Brest for the night of 11th/12th February 1942. Their aim was to leave the harbour overnight and travel through the Straits of Dover in daylight. To cover the fleet, the Luftwaffe would provide 200 fighters in total and the large ships would be supported by destroyers and the very nimble E-boats. The German naval commanders, despite their meticulous planning, felt that the British would never allow them to get away with such an operation.

If the Germans did break out and head for the Channel, the British plan was to activate Operation Fuller. This would involve an attempt to stop the enemy fleet by means of a series of attacks by six Motor Torpedo Boats (MTBs) based at Dover, Beaufort torpedo bombers, six Fairey Swordfish torpedo-carrying aircraft and six 20 year old destroyers which would have to sail from Harwich if needed.

During the evening of 11th February, RAF Wellington bombers carried out a raid on the German ships in Brest. They dropped their bombs but not on the target and took photos which when developed, showed the three ships tied up in the harbour. To the photo interpreters, it seemed obvious that the Germans were not going to move that night and thus, the tense atmosphere was relaxed a little. Unfortunately, the Germans did move that night, just a short time after the Wellingtons had left the area.

The next sorties by the British were three separate patrols by Hudson aircraft. The night was cloudy and dark and the first aircraft had to rely entirely on its radar system to spot any movement in the harbour. This patrol, known as 'Stopper', was plagued by a faulty radar set and the aircraft returned to St Eval in Cornwall. A second Hudson on stand-by refused to start and by the time the third aircraft was ready to go, the German fleet was well on its way. A fourth Hudson failed to spot the fleet as the fog closed in whilst the Commanders of the battleships passed Le Havre, hardly believing their luck. At dawn, two Spitfires of 91 Squadron took off on a Jim Crow sortie but due to heavy cloud, failed to spot the enemy who by now had come within the range of the Chain Home Low radar station situated on the top of Beachy Head. The operator accordingly advised the RAF that something big was happening in the Channel but that it was shipping movements rather than aircraft. The RAF lost interest instantly and advised the radar controller to contact the Navy. This he did but at the mention of aircraft, the Navy told the controller to contact the RAF. And so it went on with no real decision being taken.

As the morning went on, further radar stations were picking up the movements and at last the penny dropped. An officer from Biggin Hill rang Uxbridge, No 11 Group headquarters. 'I think it is Fuller,' he said, to which the officer on the other end replied, 'Sorry, I think you have a wrong number.'

'No, no, it is Fuller,' insisted Biggin Hill but his words were lost for no one at Uxbridge had heard of 'Fuller'. More precious time was lost.

Fl/Lt Gerald Kidd was the radar controller at Swingate radar station, just a short distance in from the coast. He was convinced that the blips on his screens were the fleet and attempted to pass the information on to the Navy at Dover Castle. The telephone line was down and so was the scrambler telephone. Therefore Dover knew nothing of what was going on in the Channel. At the forward airfield of Hawkinge, two aircraft were airborne to check on the radar traces and at Kenley airfield in Surrey, G/Cpt Victor Beamish, the station commander, was tired of sitting behind his desk and thought he might like a quick trip in the Spitfire. Taking Wg/Cdr Finlay Boyd for company, the two aircraft headed for the coast and breaking cloud over the Channel, found themselves above the biggest ships that they had ever seen.

Obeying radio silence, they tore back to Kenley to break the news. Likewise, the two Hawkinge Spitfires also fell upon the fleet as Sqd/Ldr Oxspring instantly broke radio silence and reported their presence to Biggin Hill. No one in the control room believed him and for another hour, the British defences did nothing. Landing at Hawkinge, he attempted to speak to Air Vice Marshal Trafford Leigh-Mallory, the commander of 11 Group. Oxspring was told that he could not be reached by telephone and it was not worth sending a special messenger when all that had been seen may just have been a collection of fishing boats. 'Bloody big fishing boats,' retorted Oxspring. In desperation, he insisted that a message was got to the commander. Meanwhile, when he had landed at Kenley, G/Cpt Beamish also attempted to reach Leigh-Mallory but failed. He did however, contact Biggin Hill and this, together with Sqd/Ldr Oxspring's account, convinced the controller that the German ships were at sea. Twelve hours after they had sailed from Brest, the British were finally convinced.

At Manston, six flimsy Swordfish aircraft from No 825 Squadron of the Fleet Air Arm based at Lee-on-Solent in Hampshire were already armed with a torpedo apiece and were ready fuelled for action. Lt/Cdr Eugene Esmonde had already been briefed on the operation and it was therefore a question of waiting for the signal to go. Around 11.45 pm, as word got around that the ships were in the Channel, the Dover based MTBs had been the first to engage the enemy. The superior firepower of the enemy plus the E-boats made a mockery of the attack. Although all the torpedoes were launched, none hit and the craft suffered badly at the hands of the enemy. The beaten, battered force limped back to Dover.

With snow swirling around them, the crews of the Swordfish had made their way to the dispersal shortly after breakfast to begin a series of practice attacks. They had as yet not been summoned to the attack but shortly before the first flight was due to get airborne, a car raced over to the dispersal. Screeching to a halt, the messenger told Esmonde that the attack was on.

Wg/Cdr Gleave came over to see the crews shortly after. He said there was no confirmation from the Admiralty that the ships were in the Channel because they still did not believe the Germans would dare do it. However, the fighters and the radar plots all pointed to the fact that they were there and if confirmation were needed, 11 Group had just signalled that the Swordfish would be getting fighter escort. For a time, Gleave and Esmonde stood grey and very drawn before confronting the other Swordfish crews. Each one of them knew that their chances of survival were very small. As Esmonde spoke to them, he apologised for not warning them that a day attack was possible. He continued to state that at all costs, the ships must be stopped. Wishing all of his men God speed and good luck, he shook the hand of every one of them.

At 12.15 pm, the engines of the Swordfish were started, yet overhead there was no sign of the promised fighter escort. As they taxied out, the weather began to throw its worst at them. Taking off in a snow flurry, they circled Manston waiting for the escort. Ten minutes after the agreed time, just ten Spitfires arrived instead of the promised sixty. The other four squadrons never made the rendezvouz. Despite this, the Swordfish turned into the wind and headed for the Channel.

It did not take them long to reach the ships. As they approached, they encountered the most ferocious barrage ever. Not only this but the German 109s on top cover to the ships, pounced on the little biplanes immediately, knocking pieces off them. The futile British escort could do nothing to protect the Swordfish as they attempted to drop their torpedos as close and as accurately as possible. Flying into this terrible firepower, in seconds all six aircraft were destroyed with the loss of 15 of the 18 air crew. No torpedo hits were registered and the German fleet sailed on, unscathed. The award of a posthumous Victoria Cross to Lt/Cdr Esmonde and various awards to other members of the crews did nothing to quell the anguish and sadness back at Manston and elsewhere.

Next, it was the turn of Coastal Command to attempt an attack. Seven torpedo-carrying Beauforts from Thorney Island had requested a fighter escort. None were available but before any protest could be forthcoming, it was found that two of the seven aircraft were armed with bombs instead of torpedos whilst a third developed a technical fault. Putting these matters right took over an hour but eventually the Beauforts took off for Manston. No one there had been informed that the Beauforts would arrive late and so the Spitfire escort continued circling the airfield for some time. Eventually it was decided that the Spitfires would rendezvouz with the Beauforts in the vicinity of the fleet. As they headed for the Channel, the Beauforts arrived at Manston. The station attempted to radio the aircraft that the Spitfires had just crossed the coast but someone had forgotten to inform Manston that

A Typhoon IB of 56 Squadron, at Manston May 1942 to August 1943. (MAP)

the Beauforts had recently changed from Morse signals to Radio telephone and therefore they could not hear Manston. They eventually got fed up with waiting and headed out to sea, only to miss the Germans altogether.

Yet more Beauforts came down from Leuchars in Scotland but further hitches became apparent and they too failed to strike a blow. By mid-afternoon, further Beauforts and Hudsons had attacked without success and as darkness began to close in, 'Fuller' began to wind down as the enemy ships moved out of the Channel and into open sea. Later on, *Scharnhorst* was to strike a mine as she continued her voyage but it was not a fatal blow. Meanwhile, on our side of the Channel, accusations and recriminations were coming thick and heavy. Altogether, 675 British aircraft took part in the action made up of 242 bombers, 398 fighters and 35 Coastal Command Beauforts and Hudsons. When notified of the German success, Winston Churchill uttered just one word. 'Why?'

And so it was, four days later that a judicial enquiry began into what went wrong. When the Committee of Inquiry issued their report some time later, its findings made astonishing reading. It found no serious mistakes, even though it was painfully obvious to all who took part in the operation that this was a total whitewash. The Germans had achieved the impossible and unthinkable and it was due to the blundering and mistakes of many that they did so. The echoes of the 'war's biggest blunder' were to be around for a long time.

Slowly Manston came to terms with the loss of so many gallant airmen. The 3rd March 1942 saw the long awaited arrival of the WAAF contingent who were aptly billeted in the Ursuline Convent at Westgate. Most of the men were still in accommodation outside the camp for the threat of an attack and invasion was still very real. In fear of an airborne invasion, Manston was provided with a whole battalion of soldiers to defend the airfield and everyone on the base was trained and armed to defend themselves and the station buildings.

No 174 (Mauritius) Squadron was formed at Manston on 3rd March from a nucleus of No 607 (County of Durham) Squadron. Seventeen Hurricanes and eight pilots were detailed to start operations on the same day. Fighter/bomber missions were flown against enemy shipping and coastal targets. The Havocs of 23 Squadron were still carrying out intruder sorties whilst No 56 (Punjab) Squadron arrived from Snailwell on 29th May bringing the first Typhoons to fly from the base. They fulfilled a promise from Air Vice Marshal Leigh-Mallory to Wg/Cdr Gleave that he would send some Typhoons to Manston following the Baedeker raids on British cities. It was felt that Canterbury was a likely target and the airfield was ideally suited to deal with the intruders. The system was very reminiscent of today's QRA (Quick Reaction Alert) operations with Tornados in that the Typhoons worked in pairs and the pilots sat in their cockpits with engines frequently warmed up, standing by during the dawn and daylight hours.

June started very tragically when an incident occurred that was becoming all too familiar. With a striking resemblance to the FW 190, the Typhoons of 56 Squadron were used to the occasional ground gunner having a pot at them but what happened in early June caused one pilot to lose his life with serious injuries to the other. Airborne from Manston on the first operation from the base, 56 were detailed to carry out a fighter sweep over the French coast. Also airborne on a similar mission were the Spitfires of No 401 (Ram) Squadron of the RCAF operating out of Eastchurch. Seeing the Typhoons in the distance and over France, they mistook them for 190s and promptly shot two down. One pilot managed to bale out seriously injured and was picked up in his dinghy two hours later but of the other, there was no sign. It was a tragic mistake and with a repeat happening a month later, it prompted the RAF to paint a yellow band across the upper wing and black and white bands across the lower wings on all Typhoons to distinguish them from the FW 190.

It was now time for 174 to leave for Warmwell but they returned to Manston on 21st September. The airfield was also fast becoming a haven for returning bombers in distress, bringing further dangers as one incident illustrates. On 12th August 1942, a Stirling bomber was returning after a raid. It had been badly damaged and could not lower its undercarriage. The watch office advised the pilot to belly-land but as the aircraft came in on its final approach, the engines cut. Failing to make the Manston threshold, the aircraft came to rest on an Anderson shelter in the garden of a house in Broadstairs. Luckily only light injuries were sustained by the crew but on emerging from the stricken aircraft, they were horrified to find out that children were in the shelter. They, however, had survived the incident without so much as a scratch and were found busy arguing whether it was a Stirling, Wellington or Halifax that had descended upon them!

The middle of August saw the North Weald Spitfire Wing arrive under the command of Wg/Cdr Scott-Malden. Consisting of Nos 242 (Canadian), 331 (Norwegian), and 332 (Norwegian) Squadrons, they came in for Operation Jubilee, the Dieppe raid. The month also saw the rest of No 23 Squadron arrive, now equipped with Mosquitos. With this aircraft they were able to carry out long-range intruder operations over Northern Europe. Further units connected with 'Jubilee' arrived in early August when No 403 (Wolf) Squadron of the RCAF flew their Spitfires in from Catterick. On the 19th August, as the invasion ships were ploughing through the Channel, all the squadrons participated in giving top cover to the landing troops. All day heavy dog-fighting took place over the beaches with FW 190s and Me 109s. The wing scored some success when they shot down seven 190s for the loss of four Spitfires. 403 also scored when they shot down two 190s and one 109 with a further three enemy aircraft damaged although they too lost three Spitfires. Fighter cover was maintained by Manston throughout the day and by nightfall the airfield tally for the day was 40 enemy aircraft destroyed or damaged against the loss of nine Spitfires. It had been a busy day for the airfield.

With the Dieppe operation over, the Spitfire squadrons departed, leaving behind No 23 with their Mosquitos. Still carrying out intruder missions, they were to go to Bradwell Bay on the 14th August, then return to Manston seven days later before leaving for Malta around December. Unusually, another FAA squadron arrived from Middle Wallop on 23rd August when No 841, commanded by Lt/Cdr R.I. Williamson DSC, RN, flew their Fairey Albacores to the station. They operated at night against enemy shipping and E-boats in the Dover Straits and the English Channel making around 99 attacks in all. They were to stay at Manston until 7th February 1943 when they moved up to Coltishall.

In the meantime, Wg/Cdr Gleave, worried at the number of emergency landings at his airfield, continued to press for a hard runway. The size and number of large bombers that had used the airfield and the number of over-shoots that had occurred due to the length and width of the landing area caused many headaches. The 28th August was the final straw for the CO when just one night brought sheer chaos to Manston.

It began shortly after 8 pm when the Polish Spitfire Wing from Northolt began landing. Nos 302 (Poznan), 306 (Torun), 308 (Krakow) and 317 (Wilco) Squadron had returned from carrying out a Ramrod operation over Dieppe. Forty five aircraft landed in quick succession and were dispersed at various points around the landing area. Shortly after, a Wellington bomber of No 305 (Wielpolska) Polish Squadron crash-landed on the flarepath. Just before 1 am, another three Wellingtons and three Stirlings had crash-landed with another Stirling landing heavily at 4 am. With the other large aircraft still sitting across

Wing Commander R. Beaumont, at Manston. (R. Beaumont)

the landing area, this Stirling had to land further across the field and consequently, swept through a line of the Polish Spitfires. One burst into flames before the Stirling continued to career into the line of FAA Albacores. As the aircraft came to rest amongst a pile of tangled metal, yet another Stirling force-landed and in doing so, demolished one of the Bellman hangars whilst as dawn approached, a further Wellington and Stirling also crash-landed. Photographing the entire scene, Wg/Cdr Gleave pleaded with Air Vice Marshal Leigh-Mallory for a tarmac runway and extensions to the airfield. Permission was granted in principle but again, it was to be a long time before it actually came about. It came too late for Wg/Cdr Gleave to see as he handed the command of Manston over to Wg/Cdr C.R. Hancock, OBE, DFC.

The Westland Whirlwind was the first single-seat twin-engined fighter to be used by the RAF. With the first deliveries being made in June 1940, its early days were plagued by trouble with the Rolls-Royce Peregrine engines but later production models found success in the role of long-range escorts to light day bombers. The second squadron to be equipped with the Whirlwind was No 137 who came to Manston on 17th September 1942. Commanded by Sqd/Ldr H.St J. Coghlan, the

Kapt Haabjoern had force-landed without oil after an encounter with a flak ship, Manston 1943. (609 Squadron Archives)

squadron ceased operations for a while after their arrival to allow the aircraft to be fitted with bomb racks and its pilots to practise bombing techniques. Operations commenced in October, the first being a Rhubarb to a camp near Etaples which resulted in the loss of three aircraft. The squadron was later engaged in bombing attacks on shipping and the Continent with the Whirlwind before converting to rocket-firing Hurricane IVs.

The Manston Operations Record Book for September 1942 remarks: 'The station is now well stocked with bombers, being Albacores, Hurribombers and dare it be said, "Whirlibombers".' Perhaps news of this large number of aircraft sitting on the ground may have reached the ears of German intelligence for October saw a return of enemy activity when a series of low level attacks by FW 190s and Do 217s resulted in further damage to the airfield. The airfield defence,

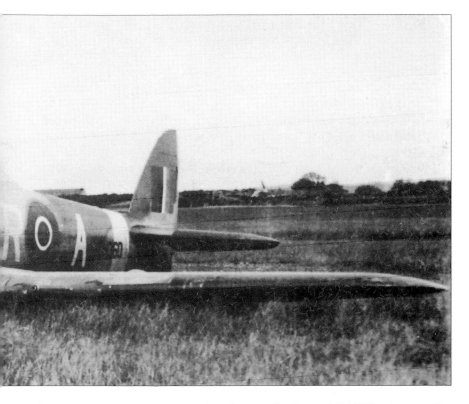

however, was now entrusted to the newly formed RAF Regiment who soon found success when they shot down a FW 190 to loud cheers and applause.

No 331 (Norwegian) Squadron returned to Manston in October for a short period partnered again by No 332. As they left, No 609 (West Riding) Auxiliary Squadron arrived for what was to be a short stay but turned into a very long one. The 'West Riding' Squadron was a very cosmopolitan unit which had within its ranks Belgians, Frenchmen, Americans and again, Norwegians. The CO was Sqd/Ldr Roland Beaumont DFC, later to become famous for his test pilot flying. Equipped with the Hawker Typhoon, it began intruder operations by day and by night, achieving a lot of success.

Further Albacores arrived at Manston to supplement the anti-shipping work of 841 Squadron at the same time as Wg/Cdr Hancock, injured in a car accident, handed over the reins to Wg/Cdr D.F.B. Sheen. Taking his first look at Manston, he was appalled to see some 17 wrecks around the station perimeter, evidence of the emergency use that the airfield offered. Rarely a night went past that the bombers were not asking for help. The emergency frequency, called 'Darky', was now manned by Waafs, their calm, reassuring voices giving strength and comfort to the struggling bomber air crews. Despite all of this, the extensions and hard runway still had not materialised.

No 174 now went to Odiham leaving 137 and 609 to continue the fight from Manston. The Albacores were still attacking enemy shipping whilst 609 began Rhubarb operations. Towards the end of the year there was another mention of an extra long emergency runway with the possibility of it being 3,000 yards in length. An Air Commodore from the Airfield Board came down making it all look very official but again, not much happened.

The year ended with the airfield coming near to disaster. An Albacore of 841 Squadron flown by the new CO, Lt Garthwait, had just touched down when a burst tyre caused the undercarriage to collapse. Scraping along the ground, the aircraft suddenly burst into flames. Leaping from the cockpit, Lt Garthwait and Sub/Lt Waiting ran to safety before the petrol tank exploded. This in turn set off the 100 lb bombs followed quickly by the four 250 pounders. The ensuing explosion shut the airfield for a period despite the threat of further bombers making emergency landings.

1943 was to prove a hectic year for Manston. With the dark nights, the detachment of No 3 Squadron were sent out each night on intruder patrols in their black painted Hurricane IIcs, weather permitting. March saw the arrival of No 198 Squadron from Acklington. Led by Sqd/Ldr J.W. Villa DFC, the Typhoons commenced Rhubarb operations alongside 609. With the RAF now firmly on the offensive, this aircraft was proving the best for attacking any ground target.

Yet further Albacores had arrived in the shape of No 823 Squadron of the FAA on 1st January. These were used on anti-submarine patrols in the Channel and for these operations were attached to Coastal Command. They moved over to Tangmere in March of that year.

February for 609 was not a good month. Ordered to intercept enemy aircraft over Folkestone, they were, as so very often happened, fired on by the ground defences. This despite the fact that they had been painted in the black and white stripes for identification purposes. Later that same day, two pilots were vectored on to four Spitfires wrongly identified by ground control as bandits. Recognising them, the two Typhoon pilots turned away, waggling their wings as they did so. To their amazement, the Spitfires opened fire on them but it was luck that their aim was not too good as the Typhoons went flat out for the ground and home. A few days later, Fl/Lt Atkinson pursued a Dornier across the airfield at 300 feet. As the Dornier pulled up into cloud and out of view, the ground defences stopped firing at the enemy and turned their attention to Atkinson, luckily with no result. When he landed safely, he went straight to the commander of the gunners to give him a piece of his mind and a lesson in aircraft recognition!

In April 1943, Manston suddenly became cloaked in secrecy. A number of civilian scientists arrived for a brief stay including the designer Barnes Wallis of Vickers-Armstrong. A lone Mosquito arrived and was promptly hidden from view in a hangar whilst everyone on the station wondered what on earth was going on. That is, all except the CO, now Wg/Cdr G.L. Raphael DSO, DFC. He knew that the aircraft and the scientists were at Manston to conduct trials of a bouncing bomb which was to be tested over Reculver Sands near Herne Bay. Codenamed 'Highball', it was the trial period of the bomb used in the dams raid which was carried out by No 617 Squadron in May 1943.

The Manston squadrons managed to carry on as normal. An incident reminiscent of 1940 was the capture of another FW 190. In the early hours of 20th May 1943, Unteroffizer Heinz Ehrhardt was flying a Jabo (fighter/bomber) operation to London. Flying as Red 9 of 1/SKG10, he crossed the English coast and after receiving several vectors from his base, became hopelessly lost. When his fuel began to run low, he turned around to head in the direction of what he thought was home. However, he mistook the North Kent coast for the French coast and eventually made a wheels-down landing at what he thought was St Omer. It was actually Manston!

In June, the long awaited improvements to the landing area came to fruition as the contract was awarded to John Laing and Son Ltd. Officially starting on 15th June 1943, the hard runway was to be 9,000 feet long, 750 feet wide together with a 6,000 feet dispersal loop and twelve crash bays. It was worth waiting for. Whilst work was going on, flying was continued from a temporary strip alongside. The first Americans to fly from the base arrived at the same time when they used the airfield as a forward operating base for a unit of P47 Thunderbolts. They designated the field as Station 351.

June also saw the rest of No 3 Squadron arrive whilst No 56 (Punjab) Squadron replaced 609 earlier in the year. The latter were to return on 14th December 1943 to stay for a further two months.

No 137 Squadron had been replaced by No 184 who brought their Hurricanes over from Eastchurch. They commenced attacks on enemy shipping but left for the ALG at Kingsnorth on 14th August. Back came

609 Squadron Typhoons taxi off the tarmac at Manston 1944.
(609 Squadron Archives)

137 but not with the Whirlwind. They had converted to the Hurricane IV which was rocket equipped. They went back on operations flying Rhubarbs and then anti-shipping sorties for which both cannon and rockets were used to devastating effect. August was definitely a shipping and Rhubarb month. The most successful night of the month was the 15th when aircraft operating out of Manston notched up five locomotives, five rail trucks, two barges, a railway bridge and an airfield building.

The final months of 1943 were full of action for the airfield. On 30th November 198 Squadron set off for a long range sweep over Dutch bases used by the German Air Force. As they arrived over Deelen, several FW 190s were observed to be landing. The Typhoons fell from the sky like eagles and in as many minutes, four 190s and one Ju 88 were destroyed with another 190 damaged. Leaving the area rather promptly, they spotted some barges and tugs below and immediately sunk two of each for good measure.

1944 was the beginning of the end for the enemy. Carrying the war back to Germany, the 18th March saw the heaviest bomber raid to date when the RAF dropped over 3,000 tons of bombs on Hamburg. Earlier in the year, General Eisenhower had assumed his role as the Supreme Commander, Allied Expeditionary Force. This was in preparation for Operation Overlord, the Allied invasion of Europe.

Manston was now entirely manned by the RAF, the Navy having

taken their leave and moved to Exeter. No 3 Squadron had spent two months at Swanton Morley and were back with bomb-carrying Typhoons. 609 returned, glad to be back in their old haunts, and together with their old sparring partners, 198, were again roaming over enemy territory. As if to give notice of their return, 2nd January 1944 saw the two squadrons destroy two FW 190s, a 109 and a Bucker 131, damaging at least five more on the ground.

February saw Manston classified as No 123 Airfield, No 84 Group of the 2nd TAF. It was a period of massive changes on the base and with the frequent movements of squadrons, the locals got very little sleep by night and day. Added to this was the work of building the new runway which had been continuing since 1943. It officially came into use on 5th April with full Mk 11 runway lighting and the pipe and burners in place for the use of Fido, the Fog Investigation and Dispersal Operation. In the first three weeks of operation, 56 emergency landings were made, all of the aircraft landing safely and not running out of runway. The diarist was happy to record: 'More crashes and forced landings today. Manston is rapidly becoming a pranger's paradise.'

No 137 were back in April, this time flying Typhoon fighter/ bombers. They too were eventually fitted with rockets for this was the heyday of the aircraft when, with rockets and guns, it packed a devastating punch.

As the year progressed, changes were apparent at the airfield. At the beginning of March, No 3 Squadron had left and was followed later in the month by Nos 609 and 198 after a very successful stay at Manston. Following their departure, the base was used briefly by No 123 Airfield comprising Nos 183 (Gold Coast) and 197 Squadrons. When they left it was a gradual change for Manston from an offensive role to a refuelling and emergency landing role. No 605 (County of Warwick) Auxiliary Squadron brought their Mosquitos in as part of the 2nd TAF. They carried out night intruder operations. The FAA returned on 18th April when No 819 Squadron arrived from Lee-on-Solent as part of No 155 (General Reconnaissance) Wing, No 16 Group, Coastal Command under the command of Lt/Cdr D.A.G. Oxley RN. The Swordfish were painted black and were fitted with ASV Mk X. They were joined on the 20th of the month by No 848 Squadron FAA who flew the first American Grumman Avengers to be flown from Manston. This aircraft was one of the most successful torpedo bombers of the war and although some difficulty was experienced with fitting British torpedos to the aircraft, the FAA used the Avengers as straight bombers, minelayers or as rocket firing strike aircraft. In all configurations they performed well.

Meteors of 616 Squadron at Manston. (IWM)

The Beaufighters of No 143 Squadron came in from North Coates to assist in the coming invasion. Their part was to attack E-boat patrols on the eastern flank of the invading forces. Although it was intended that they should return to North Coates after D-Day, they stayed until 9th September 1944.

On 6th June 1944, the Allies invaded and almost immediately gained a foothold on French soil. The following day, Wg/Cdr Raphael, the CO, announced over the tannoy that the second front had begun and that everyone should brace themselves for an increase in activity. His words rang true as more and more used the Manston facilities. The base was bombed on 13th June but not by the Luftwaffe, those days were far gone. The incident happened when a Liberator made an emergency landing with its bombs still on board. As it pancaked on the ground, one of the bombs fell from the bomb door and exploded just behind the aircraft. It left a sizeable hole in the ground which was quickly filled in as more aircraft waited to land.

The invasion, however, did not stop the enemy from trying a last ditch attempt at bringing Britain to its knees. On 15th June, Fl/Lt J.G. Musgrave and his navigator, F/Sgt F.W. Sanwell flying a 605 Squadron

186

Mosquito, were returning from a sortie over the Channel when they encountered a strange phenomenon. A small flying object with fire coming from its tail was just ahead of them. Realising that this was one of the secret weapons that Hitler had spoken about, they gave chase and opened fire. Suddenly the object exploded and fell into the sea as the Mosquito flew through a storm of debris. Coming safely out the other side, the crew realised that they had just shot down a V1 flying bomb, the first RAF crew to do so. That same night the squadron destroyed two more as 605 took on the anti-diver patrols. Together with the Typhoons of 137, also transferred to diver patrols, the Manston score of V1s shot down steadily increased. By the end of June the total had reached 36.

The detachment of Albacores of 415 Squadron which had arrived during 1943 was re-numbered No 119 on 19th July but they still kept the Albacores. They left for Swingfield on 9th August 1944 but it was the anti-diver patrols that kept the Manston squadrons busy and with the arrival of No 616 (South Yorkshire) Auxiliary Squadron, it brought the station up to full strength.

No 616 had just converted from piston-engined Spitfires to the first operational jet aircraft to see action in the war, the Gloster Meteor 1. Though the squadron still had the Spitfire VIIs, they also had the detached flight of Meteors. Their first operation against the V1s was made on 27th July with no success due to the difficulties with the Meteors' guns. Whilst the problem was being sorted out, F/O 'Dixie' Dean of 616 was on patrol in Meteor EE 216 when he spotted a V1 coming across the Channel. Coming up behind it he pressed the gun 'tit' but the cannons refused to fire. Undaunted, he formated on the rocket at 365 mph and slowly brought his wing tip beneath that of the robot. Gradually the disturbed airflow took over and the nose of the V1 tipped and it plummeted to earth. It crashed five miles from the nearest town and F/O Dean became the first pilot to down an enemy aircraft in the Meteor. The same day, another Meteor claimed a V1 using the conventional method of shooting it down.

The Luftwaffe were still making mistakes with their navigation. Not one but two Me 109s landed in error at Manston in the early hours of 21st July, the first being Feldwebel Manfred Gromill of the 3rd Gruppe of JG 301 in his Me 109G-6 (serial no 163240) when he incorrectly identified the airfield. Shortly after, another Me 109G-6 (serial no 412951) also landed in error.

August continued the trend of anti-diver operations together with an increasing number of emergency landings. More squadrons came in to combat the V1s with No 501 (County of Gloucester) Auxiliary Squadron flying Tempests, 137 back again with Typhoons and 605 (County of Warwick) Auxiliary unit flying Mosquitos. 137 were replaced by 504 (County of Nottingham) Auxiliary Squadron whilst No 274 came in from West Malling also flying the Tempest. The diver campaign kept Manston busy until September when the launchings began to dwindle.

September 1944 saw several squadrons arrive in support of the Arnhem operation whilst a No 11 Group Spitfire Wing comprising Nos 118, 124 (Baroda) and 229 Squadrons arrived to carry out bomber escorts. The Fido system was activated many times as autumn and winter approached to clear fog from the airfield for emergency landings. Rapid squadron changes were taking place with No 229 being replaced by 91 (Nigeria) and 118 by No 1. No 406 (Lynx) Squadron of the RCAF brought their Mosquito XXXs in from Colerne for escort and Ranger sorties, remaining over the Christmas period and carrying out business as usual.

And so the last year of war began. Wg/Cdr Raphael handed the reins over to Wg/Cdr A.D. Murray and the new year began with Nos 1, 91 and 124 Squadrons carrying out 'Ramrod 1424', a bombing raid on the Dortmund-Ems canal by Lancasters. In a last minute flurry of activity, a Czech wing comprising Nos 310, 312 and 313 Squadrons moved in from Bradwell Bay with Spitfire IXs for Ramrods and bomber escort. Determined to be there at the end, No 822 Squadron of the FAA arrived on 14th April 1945 flying Barracuda IIIs for anti-submarine work. By this time very little contact was being made with the enemy yet the bombing of Germany went on until Victory was declared. On 8th May 1945 the Station Commander paraded all the personnel and told them that the war was over. He went on to say that Manston squadrons had made a significant contribution to victory with 123 enemy ships sunk, 234 aircraft destroyed and 161 V1s shot down.

So Manston ended its war. It was to remain a peacetime base used by the American Air Force as well as the RAF. It took on the role of a Master Diversion airfield but with successive government cut-backs during the 1980s and 1990s its use today is minimal, although it has the best facilities any airfield could offer. It is the last remaining military airfield in Kent but sadly it was recently announced that the RAF are to leave by the year 2000. The civil use of the airfield will no doubt continue and Kent International Airport, as it is now known, will expand as the main civil airports reach saturation point. The Hurricane and Spitfire Museum which is situated on the military side of Manston will remain and is set to become a major tourist attraction in Thanet.

9
ROCHESTER

Although the Short Stirling was the first four-engined Allied bomber to enter service during the Second World War, it soon became the victim of a lack of foresight on the part of the planning authorities to predict future requirements. Because of this, it failed to reach the status of its later stablemates, the Lancaster and the Halifax. It was, however, conceived and born in the fighter county of Kent and is thus unique in being the only Second World War bomber to be manufactured in the county.

Short Brothers had been manufacturing aircraft at their airfields at Eastchurch and Leysdown on the Isle of Sheppey since before the First World War. They concentrated on seaplanes as well as land planes but it is the latter that this chapter is concerned with. The Armistice brought a gradual rundown in demand for military aircraft. In order to remain solvent, Shorts turned to manufacturing cars and buses, a venture that continued until the 1930s when plans were drawn up for the construction of the now famous 'C' Type Empire Flying Boats. The flying field on the Isle of Sheppey was found to be unsuitable for testing land aircraft and Messrs Shorts began to look for new premises.

By good fortune, in September 1933, Rochester Council had purchased a large area of land on the top of the North Downs alongside the Chatham-Maidstone road with the idea of establishing a municipal airport. A month later the Short Brothers approached the council to allow them to lease the land for test flying purposes, which would at the same time allow the council to continue its municipal airport idea. The levelling of the ground over the next year allowed Alan Cobham to bring his National Aviation Display Tour to Rochester on 25th August 1934. Received with great enthusiasm by the council and public alike, he returned to the field on 16th June 1935 and firmly established the presence of Rochester Airport. With legal requirements satisfied, Short Brothers moved their facility from the Isle of Sheppey to Rochester.

Another aero engineering company by the strange name of Pobjoy Air Motors Ltd also moved in and with the official consent of the Air Ministry, who had looked at the airfield for military purposes, Rochester was deemed open for business. It fell to Short Brothers to make the inaugural landing when John Lankester Parker flew the Short Scion, G-ACJI, over from Gravesend. With the erection of several hangars on the site, the company began building two landplane versions of their highly successful Kent class flying boats for Imperial Airways. Named 'Scylla' and 'Syrinx', they were in service by 1934 but sadly by this time, Horace and Eustace Short had died leaving Oswald to carry on the company through a crucial period.

One of the reasons that Pobjoys had relocated to Rochester from Cheshire was the fact that the Scion was powered by Pobjoy Niagara engines. Moving down in 1933, the company found itself in financial difficulties by 1936 and approached Oswald Short for capital investment. Arrangements were finally made in which Shorts would invest in Pobjoy for a substantial holding in the company and use of the aero engine production line. From this decision came the production of the Scion II and the Pobjoy Pirate though the latter proved to be underpowered and did not even go into production. With the threat of another war looming on the horizon, Shorts eventually took over Pobjoys completely.

Although the Air Ministry had given its approval to Rochester Corporation on the layout and facilities at the airport, the RAF had little interest in it until 1937 when they approached Shorts to form and manage a flying school to train Royal Air Force Volunteer Reserve pilots. By April 1938, No 23 Elementary and Reserve Flying Training School had formed at Rochester with Fl/Lt R.C. Chambers as the chief flying instructor, ably assisted by four other pilots. The school formed part of No 26 Group RAF and was accommodated in a purpose built administration block. In addition, No 1 hangar was built to house the fleet of Avro Tutors, Miles Magisters and Hawker Harts. The school was further expanded in 1938 to train pilots for the FAA but the rumbling of war was already creating waves in military circles.

For Short Brothers, an air staff requirement of 1936 calling for a four-engined heavy bomber resulted in their gaining a licence to design and build such an aircraft. With no past designs to help, for a four-engined high-winged monoplane bomber had not been built before, Shorts decided to build a half scale model powered by four Pobjoy Niagara engines to provide valuable data on the aerodynamic and handling features of the design. This resulted in the S31 M-4 which flew for the

S31 – the Pobjoy half-scale model of the Stirling bomber. (MAP)

first time on 19th September 1938. A near exact scale model of the S9, as the Stirling was called, it had a retractable undercarriage and flew on many occasions, all of them successfully. It was even demonstrated to King George VI and Queen Elizabeth when they visited the factory on 14th March 1939. Given the Royal approval, work went ahead on building a full size Stirling. This entailed big extensions to the factory and main works for with the aircraft having a span of 99' 1", a length of 87' 3" and a height of 22' 9", none of the existing floor areas would have been enough.

Late 1938 and early 1939 saw work carrying on to produce the prototype. The first aircraft, A29 (L7600) was rolled out of the factory on 14th May 1939, this time powered by four 1,375 hp Bristol Hercules II engines. The initial flight was perfect but unfortunately on landing back at Rochester, one of the brakes seized causing the undercarriage to collapse and the aircraft to crash. Luckily no one on board was injured but the prototype proved to be beyond repair and was written off. By this time however, the second prototype was ready to fly (L7605) and with a successful first flight and landing, development work proceeded. So impressed were the Ministry for Aircraft Production by the success of the initial flights that they ordered 100 aircraft directly from the drawing board. With a crew of seven and capable of carrying seven 2,000 lb bombs over 2,000 miles at a maximum speed of 300 mph, the Stirling appeared the answer to the prayers of a very ill-equipped Bomber Command.

The first production Stirling Mk I, now powered by the up-rated Hercules XI engines, was airborne twelve months later and by August of 1940, the type had entered service with No 7 Squadron at Leeming in Yorkshire.

Before the outbreak of war in September 1939, as the manufacturing facility of Shorts grew at Rochester, it became obvious to the German civilian aircraft of Lufthansa flying overhead that the airfield was a centre for aircraft production. It can therefore be safely assumed that they were taking photographs of the large extensions, the prints of which would prove invaluable to the Luftwaffe when war began. For Rochester, plans were going ahead as it became obvious that indeed, war was about to break out. Large air raid shelters were dug around the main manufacturing plant and the defence of the airfield was later entrusted to the 33rd Battalion Kent Home Guard. From pillboxes and trenches around the site, it was their job to defend this crucial airfield.

With the Battle of Britain overhead in 1940, it became increasingly likely that at some period Rochester would be the target for a Luftwaffe attack. Since July, enemy formations had passed close to the airfield on their way to attack and bomb Fighter Command bases. The closest they

Britain's first heavy four-engined bomber, the Short Stirling, pictured here on its roll-out at Rochester.

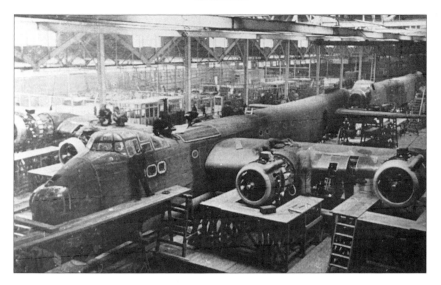

Stirling bomber production at Rochester 1939/40. (Short Bros)

came initially to an attack was on Sunday, 11th August when a high flying aircraft was spotted by the local Observer Corps approaching Rochester. All around the area the sirens began to wail and people ran for cover, either to a shelter or to their own homes. No bombs were forthcoming and as the 'all clear' sounded, it was assumed that the aircraft was on a reconnaissance sortie doing much the same as the past Lufthansa aircraft had done. The decisive day was Thursday, 15th August 1940 which brought a ridge of high pressure over Britain with a little cloud over the Channel. This was the day that the Luftwaffe produced a series of raids on as wide a front as possible. This front also included Rochester.

In Britain, the early hours were quiet but from 11 am, a series of attacks developed. The radar stations had picked up the large formations forming over the coast of France and throughout the morning, raids of varying degrees were taking place all over the county. At 3.30 pm, 100 enemy aircraft were tracked approaching Deal to be followed by another 150 over Folkestone. Included in this formidable armada were the Do 17s of KG3 under the command of Oberst Wolfgang von Charniers Glisczinsk.

As the bombers flew westward over Kent with a strong fighter escort from JG26, it was the second wing of KG3 operating from Antwerp/Duerne that changed course and headed for Rochester.

193

Eighteen aircraft approached the airfield flying low in an arrowhead formation, opening their bomb doors as they did so. With no British fighters to deter them, the enemy had it all their own way. One by one they dropped their 100 lb bombs over the landing area and the factory buildings before pulling up and heading back for the coast. On the ground the sudden appearance of the Luftwaffe overhead set the sirens wailing, albeit a little late. At the same time the warning hooters sounded in the factory indicating that a raid was imminent and all work was to stop. It was also a warning for the employees to take cover in the shelters.

The devastation that followed set the production of the Stirling back a year. A direct hit on the inflammable Finished Parts Store did the most damage as the entire wooden area went up in flames. Most of the essential parts for the Stirling that were ready were lost as were many of the drawings and jigs. A black pall of smoke hung around the entire area together with the stench of burning paint as the stores began to blaze. The main roof of the factory where seven Stirling fuselages were in the course of completion had caved in destroying several of the aircraft instantly. Pieces of the aircraft lay everywhere together with metal splinters, wood, glass and the other debris associated with a bombing attack.

As the Dorniers headed for the coast, they were attacked by No 54 Squadron Spitfires from Hornchurch who achieved some success in shooting down several of the raiders. It was, however, the scale of destruction at Rochester that shocked the factory workers as they crawled out from the shelters. The first thing that confronted them was the smoke. Thick and black, it covered the entire sky above the factory. As they groped their way around, coughing and retching, the 'all clear' sounded as if indicating that all was well. All was not well, as some workers discovered the body of a man inside the Bell Shelter, a round metal structure built to house two or three men who were on guard duty at the factory entrance. At the time of the attack there were just two employees inside, with the other one being badly wounded. Apparently it had been ripped by pieces of red hot bomb casing that had pierced the entire shelter. This was, however, the only death, which was fairly remarkable considering the ferocity of the raid.

The clearing up process was to take many months and in fact, Stirling production at Rochester did not fully recover until a year or so later. When production did resume, certain parts of the aircraft were built at other locations in the Medway Towns. Some aircraft were even assembled at the Great Western Railway factory at Swindon with sub-

The destruction at Shorts after the 15th August 1940 raid. (Short Bros)

contract work being carried out by Austin Motors. Despite the recovery, the prospect of further raids on the factory meant that manufacture of the Stirling was soon to be dispersed to other parts of the country as well as Rochester.

In order to eliminate as far as possible the prospect of further raids, a decoy airfield was set up at Lidsing. Complete with dummy hangars and dummy aircraft and even dummy cars in the car park, it looked every bit the same as Rochester. The ruse certainly proved effective as later in 1940 and in early 1941, the site was attacked. Apparently the Luftwaffe had interpreted the photos they had taken of the site as showing extensions to the main Stirling factory. This interpretation did save Rochester from further large raids.

As a result of the raid on 15th August, the airfield defence force was strengthened when the 33rd Battalion of the Home Guard, already carrying out defence duties on the site, were asked to form a light anti-aircraft unit. This they did equipped with nine 20 mm Hispano cannons deployed at various locations around the buildings.

Production of the Stirling continued at Rochester until the end of the war, the final number, No 537, coming off the production line in early 1945, though this was the later Mark IV. The performance of the aircraft had been limited by a service ceiling of only 20,000 feet, this brought about by its having been designed with a very low aspect ratio wing.

The enemy bombs Rochester. Clearly to be seen are the craters and the smoke from the exploding bombs. (Bundesarchiv)

Another limitation to its use as a heavy bomber was the fact that the bomb bay was divided into sections, restricting the weight of the heaviest bomb to be carried to 4,000 lb. Though the type operated in all the 1,000 bomber raids of 1942, the Stirling was outmoded as a heavy bomber and was allocated to less important targets. It found further use as a mine-laying aircraft and for special duties connected with radar jamming and the dropping of supplies to the French Resistance. The last raid carried out by Stirlings of Bomber Command was on 8th September 1944. From this time on it was mainly used as a Glider Tug and Transport.

Rochester contributed handsomely to the war effort by the production of the Short Stirling. In 1943, Short Brothers were taken over by the Government allowing production of the aircraft to be accelerated, but it was not only Stirlings that used the facilities at the airport. Pobjoys had continued in business at the site making components for Hurricanes and Spitfires. Later in the war, the Air Cadets used it for gliding tuition and of course there was always the odd aircraft in trouble that used Rochester as an emergency landing ground. The worst incident came in 1944 when a P47 Thunderbolt of the USAAF ran into the factory canteen when attempting a landing with failed brakes.

With the end of the war, Stirling production ceased at Rochester. In 1946, the Government decided that Shorts should concentrate their work at Belfast and sadly, although a service facility remained at Rochester, the company left the Medway Towns. Before this however, the prototype Short Sturgeon, a naval reconnaissance bomber, had been manufactured at the airfield. The design was later converted into a high performance carrier based target tug with the first prototype flying from Rochester on 7th June 1946. Five days later came the news that Shorts were to relocate to Belfast. Despite objections from the workforce, the unions and local prominent citizens, the remaining two prototype Sturgeons were crated and sent to Ireland. Some of the former employees formed the Short's Gliding Club and actually constructed a small two-seat aircraft named 'Nimbus', flown for the first time on 18th January 1947, in an effort to keep the company alive in Medway. It was hoped to build improved versions of the glider but sadly it never happened and aircraft production ceased at Rochester.

In 1947 the RAF returned when No 24 Elementary Flying Training School arrived with Tiger Moths and an Admiralty Flight was established to provide instrument and refresher flying for pilots with ground jobs. A mixed bag of aircraft arrived including Oxfords,

Harvards, Fairey Fireflies and Hawker Sea Furys. In the next few years there was a resurgence as the Shorts facility expanded and a Royal Naval Ferry Flight was formed with Percival Sea Princes to carry senior naval personnel around from nearby Chatham Dockyard. Although No 24 EFTS were disbanded in 1953, the period saw a return to civilian use of the airport with flights to the Channel Islands, Paris and Ostend being carried out by the Dakotas of Channel Airways. However, with the stringent requirements set out by the newly created Civil Aviation Authority in 1967, the airfield fell below the standards of most civilian airports and the Channel service was forced to go elsewhere.

The lease reverted back to the Council who appointed Marconi-Elliott to manage the airfield. A merger between Elliott's and Associated Automation Ltd saw the introduction of specialised aviation work in the buildings vacated by Short Brothers. Later mergers were with English Electric and then the General Electric Company, the results of which we see today in GEC Avionics, a world leader in aviation avionics.

It is very apt that they, together with the Rochester Aviation flying tuition company, have ensured that the airfield continues to flourish. Private flying is increasing at the airfield and the site is also the home of the Medway Aircraft Preservation Society, a company in the forefront of aircraft refurbishment. The name of Short Brothers will always be synonymous with the Medway Towns and the local area has many memories of those times when Rochester was the home of the mighty Stirling bomber.

10
WEST MALLING

The station record for RAF West Malling on 16th April 1943 stated that the weather was fine and warm for the time of year. Around midnight, some enemy activity was reported by sector control at Biggin Hill, this prompting the Biggin controller to send up a single aircraft to carry out a patrol in the area of mid Kent. Several searchlight units were active within the vicinity but none of these had illuminated an enemy aircraft. As a navigation aid for the pilots, a single searchlight was switched on over Sittingbourne upon which it immediately began to be orbited by

The FW 190 of Otto Bechtold in front of the West Malling tower, April 1943. (IWM)

several aircraft. Deflecting the beam to the direction of West Malling airfield, one aircraft followed the light and at three minutes past midnight, entered the West Malling circuit. Thinking it to be a Defiant in trouble, the controller ordered the aerodrome beacon and runway lights switched on. With the airfield now visible to the pilots of the orbiting aircraft, the lead aircraft switched on his own navigation lights, fired a recognition flare and turned onto finals to commence his landing. Completing this manoeuvre, the aircraft then turned onto the perimeter track and proceeded to make its way to the watch office beside the control tower.

At this stage, one of the crew of the fire tender which was parked alongside the tower, jumped down and ran towards the aircraft to inform the pilot that he had landed at West Malling. As Gunner Lionel Barry of the 4th (Ulster) Light AA Regiment approached the aircraft he detected a foreign tongue and realised at that moment that the aircraft was German. Running back to the watch office to get his rifle, he shouted to his comrades that it was an enemy plane. By the time he got back to the aircraft, the pilot, Feldwebel Otto Bechtold, had raised his arms in surrender and was being taken into custody by the station police. His aircraft, a Focke Wulf FW 190A-4, was manhandled and pushed back to a position in the front of the control tower.

Several minutes later, a searchlight beam was again deflected towards West Malling and a second aircraft was heard to enter the circuit. With the runway lights still on, it too commenced to land and had its wheels on the grass as the watch office duty crew took a Beaverette gun platform vehicle to head the aircraft off. Twenty yards from the aircraft, they identified it as another Focke Wulf and at the same time, the pilot realised his mistake and attempted to swing the 190 back onto the runway. Seeing what was about to happen, Leading Aircraftsman Sharlock gave the aircraft a burst of fire from the Vickers gun mounted on the truck. Several hits were scored causing a small fire to start in the back of the cockpit.

As the 190 continued across the grass, Sharlock gave it another burst of fire. This time the bullets hit one of the fuel tanks and the aircraft immediately caught fire. As it stopped rolling, the pilot fell out of the cockpit with some of his clothing on fire. One of the men from the Beaverette ran to him and there was a brief struggle as the German managed to dodge behind the fire tender which was now in attendance. As he did so, he ran straight into the arms of the Station Commander, Group Captain Peter Townsend. At this point, with the airmen smothering his burning clothes, Leutnant Fritz Setzer surrendered and was found to be wounded in the leg and shoulder as well as suffering from burns. He was bundled into the ambulance and taken to the station sick-quarters.

By this time his aircraft was well alight and the oxygen bottles in the cockpit exploded throwing pieces of red hot metal as far away as 300 yards. Two members of the fire crew, AC1 Lamb and AC1 Halford, received severe injuries in their efforts to put out the fire with extinguishers and were hit by flying metal from the explosion.

The night, however, was far from over as a third aircraft was heard to orbit the beam. With the airfield defence guns firing into the dark, this Focke Wulf undershot the runway and crashed at Springetts Hill Farm, East Malling. Oberfeldwebel Otto Schulz escaped with only concussion and lacerations, and the ambulance truck arrived to find him taking tea with one of the locals who had rushed to the crash site. Under armed guard, he was taken to the guard room. Not so fortunate, however, was the pilot of the fourth aircraft which crashed at Staplehurst at about the same time. Oberleutnant Kurt Klahn, realising that he was lost, had abandoned his aircraft but too low for his parachute to fully deploy. He was found the next morning by a rescue party from West Malling some distance from where his aircraft had come down.

For West Malling it had seemed like a long night. No further aircraft appeared and at 2.30 am, the runway lights and beacon were switched off. The intact 190 was left in front of the control tower as the station diarist recorded laconically: 'An intensely interesting night.'

After becoming a prisoner of war, Leutnant Fritz Setzer little thought that he would ever see West Malling again. Fate however was to play a hand, for in 1997 he returned to the former RAF station, now a housing and industrial estate, as a guest of honour. Accompanied by his wife, he told guests and civic dignitaries of his previous visit to the airfield. 'If anyone had told me 53 years ago that I would be invited back here by the British, I would have told them they were mad,' he said. He continued, 'I first arrived here as a very much uninvited and unwelcome guest. I landed with a burning aircraft and if it was not for Peter Townsend I would not be here today. With my flying suit burning, he showed great bravery by beating out the flames with his hat. He couldn't understand me but I was screaming for him to stand back because I knew the aircraft would explode any moment. I will never forget him and how he risked his life, together with many other airmen, to save an enemy pilot. It is a privilege to be here today.'

So spoke one Luftwaffe pilot of RAF West Malling but long before this incident, the station had played a very significant part in the opening phases of the war.

In 1930, a company calling itself Kent Aeronautical Services became established at the site then known as Kingshill and classed as an emergency landing ground for nearby Detling. Mr P.H. Meadway, the owner of Kent Aeronautical, founded a flying club on the field, naming it the West Kent Aero Club and changing the name of the landing ground to West Malling. The early test flying of gliders was also carried out from the site by Mr 'Jimmy' Lowe-Wylde, who sadly crashed to his death at West Malling whilst testing a powered sailplane called a 'Plannette' shortly after his arrival. In common with most of the Kentish airfields, Sir Alan Cobham brought his National Aviation Day Display to the airfield on 21st/22nd May 1932. Sadly, even this sort of attraction could not prevent Mr Meadway from becoming an early victim of inflation as he put the airfield up for sale, eventually selling it to a company calling itself Land, Air And Water Services for the sum of £4,250. The new owner, who went by the rather flamboyant title of Count Johnston Noad, turned out to be a little 'phoney' and he too came to the end of the road in January 1934 when he sold the airfield for £6,000. His one redeeming feature, however, was that he changed the name of the airfield to Maidstone Airport, thus placing it firmly on the aviation map.

It was sold to Malling Aviation, a company owned by Mr Walter Laidlaw, who changed the name once again to Malling Aero Club. He managed to bring a new air of respectability to the airfield and under his guidance, Malling Aero Club flourished for the next four years.

These were the halcyon days of flying but by 1938, with another war with Germany looming, Walter Laidlaw was asked to set up a Civil Air Guard Scheme at West Malling. This was a mainly civilian organisation but paid for by the Ministry, run as a military organisation, with a view to training future RAF pilots. It lasted little beyond a year for by early 1939, the Directorate of Public Works had paid a visit with a view to requisition. When the final notice of possession was handed to Mr Laidlaw, it was a sad moment for him as he disbanded Malling Aviation and closed the little clubhouse up for the last time.

The expansion of the airfield began rapidly when building teams arrived and commenced putting up various buildings. Two grass runways were laid and strengthened with Sommerfeld Tracking to ensure maximum all-weather usage. A detachment of the South Staffordshire Regiment came to take up station defence duties, air raid shelters were dug and a 'J' type hangar was constructed opposite the

The unique flak tower situated on the perimeter of the airfield, manned first by the Army and later by the RAF Regiment. It housed a Bofors anti-aircraft gun and a range predictor. (T. Reynolds)

watch office. Two Pickett-Hamilton Retractable gun platforms were placed on the airfield should enemy paratroops ever drop in and with the construction of a hutted hospital, No 4 Casualty Clearing Station was up and running. This, in fact, was the only part of the airfield that was, as the expansion began to take longer than anticipated.

When war finally broke out in September 1939, West Malling was in no way ready to begin its war. Although it was designated as a satellite to Kenley and a forward landing ground for Biggin Hill and Kenley, the opening phases of the battle up until June 1940 saw no use of the airfield at all. During this time the boundary was extended from the old Maidstone Airport to encompass Abbey Wood Farm and Kate Reed Wood. By May 1940 the grass airfield measured 1,100 yards NE to SW, 1,300 yards SE to NW, 1,200 yards N to S and 1,400 yards E to W. The north to south landing area was later extended to 1,666 yards and the main east to west runway was extended by 750 yards. In addition to the 'J' hangar, several Blister hangars were built among the trees that surrounded the airfield.

It was not until 20th June that a resident unit, No 26 (Army Co-operation) Squadron, became established at West Malling. Even then it was only tasked with pin-pointing leaks in the night black-out within the area and to assist the local ack-ack units in reconnaissance and photographic sorties.

'By the end of September 1939, No 26 Squadron had moved to France as part of the air component of the BEF and were based at Abbeville, sharing the airfield with No 2 (AC) Squadron who like 26 Squadron were flying Lysander aircraft. Following our rapid retreat from France as the Germans advanced, we boarded a Royal Navy destroyer from Boulogne on 24th May 1940. We were billeted in Folkestone for about three days, operating from Lympne airfield and flying over the Dunkirk beaches, dropping water to the troops below. These supply dropping flights continued until mid June when we left Lympne and moved to West Malling. At this time we were the only squadron operating from the field and in fact, when we arrived, the nursing staff of No 4 Casualty Clearing Station were in attendance in their new hutted hospital. We ground staff were billeted in what were the hospital huts whilst the officers were using some of the large houses within the area.

'I was with 26 Squadron at the time when all non-NCOs of aircrew status were made up to Sergeant. That was, indeed, a night to remember and I can state that the two holes which were made in the ceiling of the Rose and Crown towards closing time, were genuine 45 slugs from a Colt 455 revolver, these being issued to all aircrew on 26 Squadron at the time. The same can be said of the "Wild West" type running battle which continued along the main street and all the way back to the camp that night! Another humorous item was when our armament section was charged with the production of "Molotov Cocktails", as an aid to aerodrome defence on the understanding that, when the enemy tanks arrived, the best way to destroy them would be for us to clamber onto the tanks, raise the lid and drop this lethal beer bottle into the innards of the tank. We were told not to even say excuse me.'

So recorded Fred Brinton of Herne Bay who was on groundcrew duties with the squadron.

Around this same period, the first CO of West Malling, Wg/Cdr R.W.K. Stevens arrived to find a partially completed station. With the Battle of Britain raging overhead, no use was made of the airfield as No 51 Wing were posted in for engineering duties. Still no other aircraft arrived and the Lysanders of 26 Squadron had the field to themselves. It was not until 12th July that they were joined by another unit as Sqd/Ldr Richardson brought No 141 Squadron in from Turnhouse flying the Boulton Paul Defiant.

As we have seen from the Biggin Hill chapter, the glory of success for this new fighter only lasted a very short time. Though very successful at Dunkirk, their first scramble from the forward airfield of Hawkinge on 19th July ended in tragedy when the Me 109s of the 2nd Gruppe of JG2 operating from Beaumont-le-Roger, shot down Defiants L7001, L7009, L6974, L6995, L7015 and L7016, and damaged L6983. Nine of the air crew were lost and several others were badly injured. But for the timely intervention of No 111 Squadron's Spitfires, the entire squadron would have been shot down. What was left of 141 was posted back to Prestwick. That evening the atmosphere at West Malling was very melancholy indeed.

Once again, 26 Squadron became the sole residents. On 28th July 1940, Wg/Cdr T.B. Prickman had assumed command of the base, to be replaced by F/O F.A. Lewis on 18th August. With a station commander of such a low rank, it was apparent that West Malling was still very much unfinished. This did not, however, deter the Luftwaffe from attacking it during that very hot August. The first of these raids came on the 10th when German activity during the day was seemingly limited to shipping reconnaissance over the south and east coasts. During the morning a lone Do 17 was tracked inland heading towards West Malling airfield. It suddenly appeared out of cloud over the southern end of the airfield and commenced a bombing run. With everyone on the ground taken by surprise, it made two runs dropping 14 bombs in all. Accuracy was not one hundred per cent and some fell beyond the boundary. Those that did land on the airfield blew out most of the windows in the recently constructed buildings together with causing severe injuries to 17 building workers, one of whom later died. Three Royal Engineer Sappers received minor injuries when one bomb landed beside the building they were occupying and two Lysanders of 26 Squadron were damaged by machine gun bullets and flying debris. The ground defences had no time to react and the lone raider escaped into the cloud unscathed. For one enemy bomber, the damage was considerable.

The attack put back even further the completion of West Malling with the next five days being used to rebuild much of the damage. Eagle Day came and went without further attacks on the base despite the rest of the Kent airfields suffering at the hands of the Luftwaffe.

It was not until 15th August that the next attack came although in this instance, the airfield was bombed in error. The day dawned fine and warm with just a little cloud over the Channel. From mid-morning the raids developed but at 6.15 pm a force of over 70 aircraft were plotted coming in from the Calais area. With most of the fighter squadrons in 11 Group on the ground being refuelled and rearmed, Keith Park, the commander of the group, switched four squadrons from the eastern sectors to patrol Kent. Meeting the enemy as they crossed the English coastline, the fighters managed to split up the German force causing them to miss the primary targets of Biggin Hill and Kenley. Instead they saw West Malling from a high altitude and dropped their bombs on the base. Considerable damage was done and two airmen were killed by flying splinters. An ambulance received a direct hit as it waited empty outside the new sick quarters, with the same bomb blowing in all the hospital windows. Again all non-duty personnel were put to the task of clearing up but as the next day dawned hot and sunny, the Luftwaffe returned.

On this particular Friday the plotting tables were clear until 11 am when a series of raids once again developed. Shortly after 11.30 am, 18 bombers came in low and dropped high explosive and incendiary bombs destroying one Lysander and severing many of the main service cables underground. Consequently the airfield was out of service until the 20th but even this did not stop the Luftwaffe from returning on Sunday, 18th August. This time it was obvious that the enemy were out to devastate the airfield before it really came into service.

Once again the day dawned sunny with many people getting ready to go to church early lest the raids prevent them from doing so later. As it was, the first enemy force did not cross the Kent coast until midday but it was this particular force that headed for Croydon, Kenley, Biggin Hill and West Malling. Twelve Ju 88s of the 2nd Gruppe of JG 76 flying from Creil, approached Kenley but seeing a vast bank of smoke from an earlier raid blotting out the airfield, opted to cross to West Malling instead. At 1.20 pm they crossed the airfield and dropped their bombs with great accuracy. Further damage was caused to the buildings, one Blister hangar was demolished and three more Lysanders of 26 Squadron's 'A' flight were destroyed. Fires were started all over the airfield but luckily, no loss of life was recorded. Yet again, West Malling was in a sorry state as Fl/Lt V. Mercer Smith arrived to take over the duties of Station Commander from F/O Lewis.

All non-essential personnel plus the builders who were still constructing various buildings, were put onto clearing up the damage. The rest of August saw no further raids, allowing this work to carry on at a rapid pace. With the threat of further raids however, 26 were posted to Gatwick on 3rd September 1940. They had certainly not enjoyed their stay at Malling and Gatwick was to prove a far quieter place. As if to prove the point, shortly after they had left, the field was subjected to a further raid. Although the 'all clear' had been given by Kenley Operations room, several enemy aircraft came in from the south-east and dropped around 30 bombs. They all landed squarely on the airfield and again, demolished buildings, cratered the grass runways and, sadly, killed one workman.

Several delayed action bombs had also landed and this was about all the civilian workers could take. An airfield was definitely not a healthy place to be and with the punishment that West Malling had received, many had threatened not to turn up for work. It was only the threat of no pay and possibly no job that made them reluctantly think again. There were, however, doubts about their decision on 10th September when a lone Do 17 came in low and dropped six anti-personnel bombs. One landed directly on a gun post, killing six soldiers and wounding three more of the Queen's Regiment who were now on airfield defence duties.

With the constant bombing and the threat of a paratroop invasion, a system of alerts was introduced by the Air Ministry for all 11 Group airfields. Alert 3 meant that invasion was likely but improbable within the next three days. Alert 2 was invasion probable within the next three days and Alert 1 was invasion imminent and likely to occur within the next three hours. When this information reached Fl/Lt Mercer Smith at West Malling and he looked out at his devastated station, it brought a grimace of contempt to his face as he wondered just how much more his station could take.

The next five days were quiet for the airfield allowing reconstruction to continue. Sunday, 15th September broke fair but with cloud patches which persisted all day long. It was also the day which brought to a climax the aerial assault on England. By 10.50 am, Luftflotte 2 were massing over Calais and Boulogne for attacks on London. These persisted throughout the morning and afternoon culminating in a final assault at about six in the evening.

At West Malling, the 'take cover' had sounded around 3 pm as the drone of engines was heard approaching. Thinking it to be another raid, many were already running for cover as a He 111 was seen coming towards the field very low. What was not quite right was that it seemed to have smoke coming from both engines and that it was being pursued by British fighters. Stopping to watch the saga unfold, all thoughts of a further attack fast disappearing, the men and women saw the enemy aircraft drop its undercarriage, turn steeply and land on the grass. At the same time, the two Hurricanes that had been chasing it also landed.

Both pilots were uninjured and ran over to the enemy aircraft to look at their joint prize. As the three surviving German airmen were marched off to captivity, their aircraft became the subject of much attention and was eventually transported to Farnborough for evaluation. For West Malling, it had been an exciting day!

Further light raids came on 17th and 18th September when single aircraft dropped bombs in the vicinity of the airfield but little damage was done. The 28th September saw the penultimate raid on the base, with the last raid of any significance coming on 18th October. By now the Battle of Britain was over, petering out as winter set in. West Malling had suffered badly from enemy bombing, but with the battle over, its slice of the action was about to begin.

It was not until the end of October 1940 that the airfield was considered ready to accept a squadron. 11 Group informed newly promoted Sqd/Ldr Mercer Smith that a Spitfire squadron would soon be moved to his airfield and the 30th of the month saw Sqd/Ldr A.S. Forbes DFC bring the Spitfire Is of No 66 Squadron over from Gravesend. It was a very ignominious arrival when three Spitfires promptly crashed on landing due to the bad mixture used to fill the large craters in the runway caused by the enemy bombing. Apparently clay had been used, causing the aircraft wheels to sink directly into it. Those that did land safely were soon dispersed amongst the trees lest an attack should develop.

The arrival of an entire squadron caused accommodation problems for the station staff. Several cottages next to the old flying club site known as the Sportsman Cottages were hastily requisitioned together with some wooden huts at Kingshill. The officers took over a large rambling house called the Hermitage as their mess whilst the old flying club buildings were brought back into use as a combined watch office and operations room. With 66 Squadron came 421 Flight, formed from a nucleus of the parent squadron. They were to fly Hurricanes on coastal patrols but the October weather proved so abysmal that no operations were carried out by either unit. With no flying possible, the squadron members spent many hours in the pubs of Maidstone and the surrounding area. Fast cars were used to speed them between venues and many hostelries were left with visible reminders of their visit in the form of .38 revolver bullets in the furniture! One week later 66 were posted to Biggin Hill and 421 Flight to Hawkinge. Once again, West Malling was deserted.

Christmas 1940 saw thick snow carpeting the airfield and the rest of the county. With the accidents to the Spitfires of 66 Squadron still fresh in many memories, it was decided that the airfield should have a tarmac runway and the new year saw work begin. A sign that the future use of the airfield was assured came with the building of a public house within the security bounds of the station. It was built in seven months by Whitbread Fremlins and by December 1940 it had been officially opened. Given the name of the Startled Saint, it was a witty speculation on the reaction of St Leonard, who had once found rest at West Malling, and his feelings should he have returned and found the airfield with its wartime aircraft! The landlady was Mrs Alice Baker and she was to remain as 'mine host' for 38 years. Over the coming traumatic years, she was to consider all the airmen as 'her boys' and they in turn were to refer to her as 'their mum'.

A change of command came on 14th March 1941 when Sqd/Ldr Mercer Smith handed over the reins to Wg/Cdr A.M. Wilkinson DSO. With work still continuing to bring the airfield up to the standard of a front line fighter station, 14th April saw the first squadron arrive since the departure of No 66. No 264 (Madras Presidency) flew the short hop over from Biggin Hill in their Boulton Paul Defiants. The aircraft was now flying in a night fighter role since the disastrous operations of 1940 but a single operation from West Malling was to prove that, even in this role, it was a limited aircraft. They stayed at the base for three weeks before receiving orders to leave for Colerne, away from the main battle area. Before they departed however, an advance party of No 29 Squadron arrived to review the situation regarding the completion of the building at West Malling. They found a station ready for war and by the evening of 27th April 1941, had flown their Beaufighter IFs down from Wellingore.

Commanded by Wg/Cdr S.C. Widdows, the squadron had seen action during the Battle of Britain flying from Debden in Essex. Now equipped with the powerful Beaufighter, 29 had come south to attack the enemy by night. By the 30th, the squadron had settled into West Malling. With the help of Wg/Cdr Wilkinson, the crew quarters were established in the old Maidstone Flying Club clubhouse. The officers' mess was again the mansion called the Hermitage and the ground crews were billeted out at Hamptons, another mansion some distance from the airfield. No one really minded this for driving or cycling back and forth to the airfield through the country lanes and orchards of Kent was a sheer delight, especially at this time of year and with the promise of a long, hot summer.

Flying with 29 at this period was Fl/Lt Guy Gibson, who was later to achieve fame as the leader of the dams raid. Though a bomber pilot,

Pilots and navigators of 29 Squadron at West Malling. (Kent Messenger)

the Air Ministry had allowed him and various other bomber pilots to experience operational flying from the night fighting angle in order to give them a greater insight into evading the German night fighters when they returned to flying bombers. By nightfall the entire squadron had settled in and although operations were planned for that night, the weather closed in and no flying was possible. At the suggestion of Gibson, it was down to the Startled Saint which at closing time, was still resounding to the various 'ditties' of the day. It was a different story the next night when aircraft of the squadron were airborne under the control of Sandwich and Wartling ground radar stations. Several Beaufighters were vectored to a height of 15,000 feet above Brighton and, as they continued to orbit the town below, the ground controller called the flight leader.

'Hello Bad Hat 25 [call sign for 29 Squadron]. We have some customers for you. Vector 180 degrees to meet them across the Channel. Angels 12 [12,000 feet] and Buster [full speed].'

One by one the aircraft pulled out of orbit and turned onto the instructed heading. For Guy Gibson and his observer, Sgt James, the mention of 'Bad Hat 17' meant that the ground controller had a target for them. Instructed to call Kenley control, Gibson pressed a button on the side of his radio and heard the voice of the Kenley controller.

'Bad Hat 17. Vector 180 degrees, they're still around you crossing the coast at Hove. Orbit and flash your weapon [switch on your airborne radar].'

Circling to the left, Sgt James switched on his radar and looked for the tell-tale blip of an aircraft on the screen.

'Any joy Bad Hat?' from Kenley.

'Nothing yet, listening out,' from Gibson who a second later saw the exhaust of an aircraft ahead. At the same time, Sgt James got a contact on the set and the stalking began. Taking instructions now from James and not Kenley, Gibson got himself into an advantageous firing position. A minute later the Beaufighter shook with the reverberations of four cannon and six machine guns being fired simultaneously. The effect was devastating and the enemy aircraft lit up as the explosives split his tail. Diving steeply, he fell away towards the sea as Gibson brought his aircraft back over the coast. Another blood to 29 Squadron.

Every fine night the Malling night fighters roamed far and wide bringing further victories to Gibson as well as Fl/Lt Bob Braham and Fl/Lt Alan Grout, to name but a few. The tally of victories began to notch up as the large scale enemy raids reached a climax around 12th May 1941. On that night, 500 bombers were sent over in several raids,

29 were brought down by night fighter squadrons and four by flak.

On 14th June 1941, Wg/Cdr Widdows took command of West Malling, his place as CO of 29 being taken by Wg/Cdr Colbeck-Welsh. Both Guy Gibson and Bob Braham were promoted to Squadron Leaders and given a flight within the squadron. At the same time, a new type of operation was being carried out by the squadron, that of anti minelayers. For some time the enemy had been sending over aircraft to lay mines in the Channel approaches. 29 began practising low level interception at every opportunity. The first hit came to Bob Braham when he shot down a He 111 found laying mines off the Dover coastline. From that time the squadron found great success in the new operations and this showed in the round of parties that usually followed such sorties.

July 1941 saw 29 joined by an experimental unit known as a 'Turbinlite' Squadron. It was formed as No 1452 Flight commanded by Sqd/Ldr J.E. Marshall DFC and began flying training from West Malling on 3rd July. The aircraft used was the American Douglas Havoc which was fitted with airborne radar and an enormous searchlight or 'Turbinlite' in the nose, the purpose of which was to illuminate enemy aircraft at night. The Havoc would fly in company with a fighter aircraft, usually a Defiant or Hurricane, in the hope that the illuminating process would allow the fighter to shoot the enemy down. It was a rather wild idea and in the final analysis, had very limited success during the 15 months they remained at Malling.

29 were still the resident night fighter unit but during the day, many day fighter squadrons used the airfield as a forward operating base. The former were not without problems as bad weather caused many Beaufighters to crash around the Kent countryside. They did however achieve a lot of success in shooting down the enemy and before Guy Gibson left to return to Bomber Command at the end of 1941, he and his navigator had shot down another He 111. This could not beat the score of his ally and comrade, Bob Braham who eventually destroyed 29 enemy aircraft and became the most decorated RAF officer, winning a DSO and two bars, a DFC with two bars and an AFC together with many other foreign awards.

At the end of the year a detachment of No 255 Squadron arrived from Coltishall. They flew the Beaufighter Mk IIF, a version fitted with 1,280 hp Rolls-Royce XX engines instead of the normal Bristol Hercules. Flying in on 21st September 1941, they were not to equal the success of 29 Squadron.

Late 1941 also saw two of the largest parties seen at the airfield. The departure of Guy Gibson did not go unnoticed and in the early evening many of the squadron members departed for the Royal Star Hotel in Maidstone, a favourite haunt for the West Malling squadrons. From the Star it was a short walk across the road to the Queen's Head and when this closed, it was back to the Startled Saint until closing time and beyond. The second party was to celebrate the award of the DSO to Bob Braham and the DFC to his navigator. A lunchtime session began at the Star and of course the inevitable happened. Too much alcohol was consumed and at the end of the afternoon, way after normal closing time, Bob insisted on driving his own car back to the airfield. Being the worse for wear, he collided with a traffic island and was subsequently prosecuted for dangerous driving. Whilst the law punished him by a fine of £5, the damage to the island was permanent and remains to this day. It was, however, a splendid party.

In the new year the Turbinlite squadron was still endeavouring to carry out its duties in appalling conditions. Tragedy first struck on 21st January when a Havoc piloted by WO Hopewell with Sgt Craig as navigator, crashed near the airfield, sadly killing the pilot. A second fatal accident came in February when an aircraft overshot the runway and crashed into orchards killing both crew members. All of this when the squadron had not yet become operational. For 29 Squadron, 1942 meant business as usual as improved radar equipment and new techniques gave the air crews further success. It was rumoured they were soon to receive the new Mosquito night fighter but for the present, the Beaufighter continued to give them good results.

During 1941, two other units had arrived at Malling in the form of No 1426 (Enemy aircraft) Flight and No 1528 (Beam approach) training flight. The former had been established to fly captured enemy aircraft in combat with our own squadrons, thus enabling pilots to learn valuable lessons when confronted by the real enemy. 1528, equipped with Airspeed Oxfords, was another experimental unit concerned with improving ground controlled landings in bad weather. Whilst the enemy aircraft flight remained for some time, 1528 only used the airfield until Christmas 1941.

It was from January 1942 that the dominance of the night fighters was broken as West Malling began to accept many more day fighters. They came mainly to refuel and rearm before carrying out the arduous duties of escorting the bombers which were acting on behalf of Winston Churchill's 'Set Europe Alight' speech. Meanwhile, the Beaufighters of 29 had been equipped with the newer Mk 7 AI radar which resulted in more contacts being made. Bob Braham had been given a new navigator

West Malling airfield in 1942 from 2,500 feet. (RAF Museum)

by the name of 'Sticks' Gregory (the nickname relating to the fact that he once had played drums in a well known dance band). Airborne with the new AI in early June, they shot down a Do 217 off Sandwich but because of fog at West Malling, had to divert to Manston on their return from patrol. Not being familiar with the airfield, the crew overshot the runway and came to an abrupt halt in a ploughed field. Neither were injured but both had very red faces!

A change of command came on 25th June 1942 when Wg/Cdr Widdows was posted to be replaced by Wg/Cdr 'Pop' Wheeler, a First World War veteran. One month later, Wg/Cdr Colbeck-Welsh left 29 and was replaced by Wg/Cdr Cleland. The 6th April had also seen the duty of airfield defence duties change from the army to the newly formed RAF Regiment. No 2767 Defence Squadron arrived at Malling to remain for the duration of the war.

Although fighter squadrons had been using the base as a forward operating airfield, 5th May saw No 32 bring their Hurricanes up from Manston. Part of their task was to fly in conjunction with the Havocs and Bostons of 532 Squadron as well as intruder flights over Europe. With the Turbinlites now operational, it was hoped that success would come their way. This however was not to be and losses continued at an alarming rate with June proving particularly disastrous.

The first tragedy came on the 2nd involving a Boston, the bomber version of the Havoc that 532 also operated. As dusk was falling on that day, the Boston took off with instructions to formate with a Hurricane of 32 Squadron which was already airborne. As the two aircraft approached each other they somehow collided, with disastrous consequences. Falling from around 2,000 feet, both aircraft crashed at East Farleigh just outside West Malling, killing both crews. Part of the aircraft lay scattered around the area, much of it still on fire. A gipsy family working on the nearby farm of Mr Edmunds were woken by the explosion and rushed out to see if they could save any of the pilots. When they realised that this was impossible, they began gathering up large pieces of the aircraft including live bullets which they kept until the ARP and the police arrived. On 21st June, a Havoc (B3470) spun into the ground at Offham, several miles from the airfield, again killing all the crew. The very same night, another Boston (W8296) crashed during a forced landing at West Malling. On this occasion, happily, both crew members survived. With the amount of fatalities in the Turbinlite squadrons, not only at Malling but also elsewhere, serious thought was being given as to the continuation of the operations. During this period, 32 Squadron alternated between the airfield at Friston near Eastbourne and West Malling.

By early August it was apparent to all at the station that an operation of some magnitude was about to break, as day fighters in the shape of Spitfires arrived. All of this extra activity was connected with Operation Jubilee, the proposed Allied landings at Dieppe, which if successful, seemed likely to shorten the war. On 18th August, No 610 (County of Chester) Squadron arrived from Ludham. Led by the legendary 'Johnnie' Johnson, they were to be part of a No 12 Group Wing, the other squadrons being No 485 (New Zealand) and No 411 (Canadian). The wing was commanded by Wg/Cdr P.G. Jameson DFC, all units flying the Spitfire Vb.

Hardly having time to settle into West Malling, they prepared to fly the first sorties in 'Jubilee' on 17th August but bad weather caused the landings to be postponed for 24 hours. At 03.33 hrs on the morning of the 19th, the Malling Wing came to readiness at first light and prepared to cover the invasion. 610 were the first above the beaches and the first to see that a disaster was developing below. The entire wing immediately came into contact with a superior Luftwaffe force of fighters intent on stopping the landings but in the air battle, 'Johnnie'

Johnson shot down one Focke Wulf 190, a Me 109 and shared a part damage to another FW 190. The next morning the Duxford Wing flew in to refuel before carrying on the fight. Returning at noon, they were soon back in the air after refuelling and rearming, achieving some success against the enemy. By 13.00 hrs it had become apparent to all that Dieppe was a total failure resulting in the loss of thousands of lives. As the last of the landing craft returned to the coastal ports, the operation was deemed over.

It was time to assess the contribution the Malling Wing had made. 411 Squadron claimed a half FW 190 destroyed with one probable and a Do 217 damaged, 485 had shot down a FW 190 with another damaged and 610 claimed one and a half FW 190s destroyed, two Me 109s probably destroyed and a Do 217 and three FW 190s damaged. The wing and Malling were well satisfied but the tragedy of 'Jubilee' made depressing news for all.

With the operation over, the Spitfires left the airfield once again to the night fighters. For a few nights after, the enemy sent over a number of Ju 88s, which suited 29 Squadron admirably and in conjunction with the Chain Home Extra Low radar stations that were situated high on the cliffs of Kent and Sussex, trade became very brisk. To mark the success of 29, the Mayor of Maidstone presented a silver cup to the squadron. Suitably inscribed, it was given in recognition of the sterling work done by 29 at night. With the formal part of the ceremony over, it was back to the 'Star' and the 'Saint' before finishing the celebrations at their new mess at Addington Court, a country mansion requisitioned by the squadron.

With the war now being carried back to Germany by Bomber Command, it was not unusual to see a variety of aircraft using West Malling as an emergency landing ground. Many of the Stirlings, Wellingtons, Hampdens and Halifaxes were badly shot up and unable to reach their home airfields. Work to repair these before they could leave entailed long hours for the Malling ground crews. Some that could not be repaired were dismantled at Malling and transported back to their respective airfields. It was proving a very busy time for all.

During the last quarter of 1942, the enemy began to send over bombers and fighter/bombers singly or in small numbers during the day, taking advantage of low cloud and poor visibility to escape attack. It was impossible for day fighters not having airborne radar to find the enemy and as a result night fighters were used for a short period. It meant long duties for the Beaufighter crews of 29 but any chance of attacking the Luftwaffe was welcomed.

29 Squadron at West Malling with their CO, Wg/Cdr Wight-Boycott in 1943. (Kent Messenger)

In September, 32 Squadron left the airfield for the last time. They were replaced in October by No 486 (Royal New Zealand Air Force) Squadron who brought the unfamiliar sound of the Hawker Typhoon to the district. This 400 mph fighter had a very disappointing start in life but went on to achieve great success in the rocket attack role. 486 carried out offensive sweeps over France, Belgium and Holland with considerable expertise.

It was around this time that the 'Baedeker' raids began on some of the major British cities. These were reprisal raids for attacks on German cities and were named after the Baedeker guide books, as they seemed to concentrate on the ancient cathedral cities. The early evening of 31st October began quietly with not much activity in the Biggin Hill sector. Around midnight a force of German bombers was tracked by radar approaching the Kent coast. Once over, the force split and part of it headed for Canterbury. 29 Squadron had been airborne since early evening under the control of the Foreness radar station. Though plagued by a fault in his airborne radar, Bob Braham had shot down a Do 217 and another crew, F/O Pepper and F/P Toone (nicknamed Pepper and Salt for obvious reasons), had got another. On their second

218

sortie that night they shot down two further Do 217s much to the elation of the squadron. For this superlative performance, Pepper was awarded the DFC and Salt the DFM. Two weeks later the entire squadron mourned the loss of these two when the Beaufighter that they were testing after maintenance flew into the ground. At the hearing afterwards it was suggested that F/O Pepper had tried a manoeuvre that even the forgiving Beaufighter could not take. Whatever, it was a tragic loss to everyone concerned.

The arrival of Guy Gibson back at Malling on a visit to his old squadron did help lift spirits a little. Arriving in a Lancaster of 106 Squadron, of which he was now the commanding officer, he renewed old acquaintances and old haunts. Accompanied by his dog Nigger, who flew in the Lancaster with Guy, he stayed two days before leaving for his base in Lincolnshire.

With the year coming to a close, the station and its squadrons felt justly proud of their achievements. A temporary change of command for West Malling came in December when Wg/Cdr C.M. Wight-Boycott DSO was appointed as acting station commander pending the arrival of G/Cpt Peter Townsend. A few weeks before Christmas, Bob Braham was posted away to command 141 Squadron and if this was not enough to generate a party, Wg/Cdr 'Pop' Wheeler was granted his wish to fly again, making him the oldest pilot flying at the time. It is rumoured that the party went on for two days!

On 31st January 1943, the Turbinlite squadrons were disbanded after a very disappointing period. Difficulties were found in two main areas, these being that the squadron was dependent on fighter aircraft being available when they were really needed for day fighting and also that when they were available, it was difficult to clinch the operation if the enemy aircraft took evasive action. In the end the success rate only stood at one enemy aircraft destroyed, one probable and two damaged. Compared with the loss of air crews in the Turbinlite squadrons the operation had proved a dismal failure. The last factor was that by 1943, new and improved types of airborne radar were being installed in the latest Beaufighters and Mosquitos. The new year, however, still saw 29 achieving great success in the night fighting role.

The early evening of 17th January was very busy within the sector with several enemy aircraft operating in the area. About 11.30 pm 50 Luftwaffe aircraft were approaching London as 29 Squadron were scrambled for the eighth time that night. Approaching from behind the enemy and with good visibility helping, the first contact was made by F/Sgt Wood of the Royal Australian Air Force and his observer, P/O

Slaughter. Coming up beneath the belly of the Ju 88, F/Sgt Wood used up all his ammunition without the satisfaction of seeing his adversary crash, though he was seen diving away with fire coming from the underside. The next contact was by F/O Musgrove and Sgt J. Petrie who attacked a Ju 88 sending it crashing in flames.

At the same time the CO of 29, Wg/Cdr Wight-Boycott with F/O Sanders as observer, was diverted from a night exercise over the Sussex coast to intercept a Do 217 which had left the main pack and was heading back home across the Channel. The CO gave the 217 a quick burst, the pilot promptly losing control and diving vertically into the ground. Exhilarated by this quick success, they landed back at West Malling for refuelling and rearming. Immediately taking off again, they pursued another Do 217 that the radar controller had told them was in the vicinity of Sevenoaks. With throttles at full power, Wight-Boycott climbed above the 217 and came down firing at the enemy. They had the satisfaction of seeing it crash near Westerham before another contact came on the airborne radar and the Beaufighter swung left to bring it onto an attack course. The Ju 88 saw them coming and took evasive action. Over the Kent countryside a chase developed as the German pilot tried every manoeuvre in the book to escape the Beaufighter. At an opportune moment, Wight-Boycott gave the 88 two short bursts, after which the enemy aircraft caught fire and swung away. At this point, Wight-Boycott and his observer felt distinctly ill and realised that their oxygen had accidentally been turned off during the heat of the chase.

Wg/Cdr Wight-Boycott recovered in time to see his Ju 88 flying home over Caterham and gave chase. Attacking it from behind, he saw it dive for the ground with the crew baling out. Now low on fuel once again, the Beaufighter returned to Malling. News of his and F/O Sanders' success had preceded them and when they stepped down from their aircraft, tired and hungry, they were met and applauded by the entire station personnel.

The next day the national newspapers were full of the night's exploits and the crew became national heroes. The action earned a DSO for Wg/Cdr Wight-Boycott and a DFC for F/O Sanders. It took a long time for the squadron to let this particular crew forget their success but at the end of the month, Wight-Boycott was promoted and posted to a staff appointment. A huge party was held to celebrate his posting and to welcome his successor, Wg/Cdr Millar, DFC and Bar.

February was to prove a depressing month with bad weather affecting operations both here and across the Channel. West Malling in

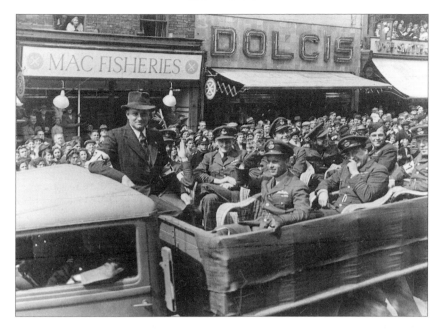

Wg/Cdr Guy Gibson and members of 29 Squadron in a 'Wings For Victory' parade at Maidstone during 1943. (Tovil Scouts)

1943 had one J-type hangar and 16 Blister hangars dispersed among the trees surrounding the perimeter. The airfield had one tarmac runway and one of grass with Sommerfeld Tracking laid to give it all-weather serviceability. Its measurements were 3,300 feet NE/SW, 3,900 SE/NW, 3,600 feet N/S and 4,200 feet E/W. It was a typical layout resembling many of the German-held airfields in France and it may well have been this fact that confused the four Luftwaffe FW 190s into attempting to land at Malling on the night of 16th/17th April.

As we have seen at the beginning of the chapter, it was quite a night for West Malling. The next morning as the news spread throughout 11 Group, the station became the focus of much attention. From early morning on the 17th, a string of visitors began to arrive, among the first being G/Cpt 'Sailor' Malan, then the CO of Biggin Hill. Many high ranking officers from the Air Ministry and civilian experts from Farnborough came to see the enemy planes and, later that evening, the 190 was flown by an RAF pilot for assessment, his verdict being that it was a very potent fighter indeed.

No 515 Squadron had formed at Northolt on 1st October 1942 from

Wg/Cdr John Cunningham at the Manor House, 85 Squadron's mess, in May 1943.

a unit known as the Defiant Flight. It was an experimental unit flying Defiants packed with special equipment to jam enemy radars. The idea was that the Defiants would fly ahead of the Bomber Command raids and jam the radars thus causing confusion for the Germans and thereby giving the bombers a head start. Known as 'Moonshine' operations, the Defiants would position themselves at various advance airfields such as Coltishall, Tangmere and West Malling. Several Defiants came to the latter and stayed at various times from October 1942 until the summer of 1943.

With the station back to normal after the excitement of the German landings, clearance was given to 29 Squadron to carry out intruder missions into France. This came as a welcome change from purely defensive duties and on the very first mission, P/O Cronie and his navigator P/O Colebrook shot up German barges on the Seine near the Pas de Calais. Similar operations were carried out throughout the month together with a continuance of night operations. Peter Townsend as CO of Malling was very keen to encourage the maximum aircraft usage and serviceability and was the first to congratulate the ground crews on their sterling efforts.

One sad piece of news that he had to impart to Wg/Cdr Millar was that a signal had been received notifying 29 Squadron that they were to be posted to Bradwell Bay in Essex. Many did not want to believe it for with 49 kills credited to them whilst at Malling, it seemed that they and the airfield were inseparable. However, their departure did not go unrecognised, with a party at the Startled Saint that continued until the early hours. There were tears in the eyes of Alice Baker as she said farewell to her beloved 'lads' for they had all shared in the triumphs and the tragedies of the squadron. The one good thing about the move was that they were to convert to the de Havilland Mosquito but even this could not dispel the sorrow of their parting on 13th May. One day later, West Malling entered a new phase with the arrival of No 85 Squadron commanded by Wg/Cdr John 'Catseyes' Cunningham DSO, DFC.

The squadron had previously operated from Hunsdon and had been engaged on testing a Turbinlite Mosquito. With the apparent failure of the entire idea, they went over to intruder patrols with Mosquito NF XVs which were capable of flying to heights of 43,000 feet. They had gained a reputation comparable to that of 29 Squadron and the prospect of even better 'Hun' hunting from Malling delighted the entire squadron.

By 10.30 am on 14th May, the aircraft had landed safely at Malling and were busy taking over the dispersals vacated by 29. Peter Townsend, himself a past CO of 85, greeted them all on landing and then went to meet the other personnel that were arriving by special train at West Malling station. By late evening, the unloading and billeting of accommodation had been completed, 'A' flight being housed at the Retreat and the Guest House in West Malling and 'B' flight at Hamptons, a large mansion some distance from the airfield. The officers acquired a lovely house called the Manor House for their own mess. It had previously been used as a convalescent home for elderly ladies. A list of rules which had been applicable to the home had been found by some previous RAF occupants and were on view for all to see, one of them stating that ladies could not be accepted as guests unless they were capable of walking upstairs without assistance. Some hope with the present occupants!

A day after 85 had arrived, Sqd/Ldr F. de Soomer brought the new Hawker Typhoon Ib to Malling in the form of No 3 Squadron who were to be resident for day operations. The aircraft were a little unconventional due to the fact they were filled with a bomb rack, and were universally known as 'Bombphoons'. They operated in the fighter/bomber role with the brief to hit anything that moved behind enemy lines. Remaining for one month, they achieved a fair reputation as the 'train busters'.

With 85 settled into their new home, night operations began immediately with the Mosquitos coming under the control of Sandwich, Wartling and Beachy Head GCI stations. As dusk settled in on 16th May, it was 'B' flight who answered the jangling telephone in the 85 crew room. It was the controller informing them that he had contacts coming over the Channel but that he was sending No 3 Squadron with their Typhoons to patrol the area. Despite the protests from 85 who knew that the Typhoon was virtually blind when flying at night, the patrol went ahead. After flying around for some length of time and not seeing a single enemy aircraft, they were recalled and 'B' flight took over. Getting airborne in record time, they made contact with the Sandwich GCI controller who told them the raiders were heading for home.

With engines at full boost, 85 caught up with them over the coast, promptly downing one FW 190 over Dover. Minutes later another contact was picked up by Geoff Howitt and George Irving over Hastings and as he fled across the Channel to safety they shot him down just off the French coast, in full view of the German coastal batteries. Two shot down and the night was still young! Another 190 was destroyed at close range by Bernard Thwaites and Will Clemo, their Mosquito being hit by pieces of wreckage. Just to make it a foursome, F/O Shaw and P/O Lowton caught a raider near Gravesend and sent it down in flames, themselves receiving a coating of soot-like substance from the disintegrating aircraft. It had been quite an opening night for 85. Four definites and one probable brought the congratulations pouring in, among them one from the sector controller, 'Sailor' Malan in his new appointment.

Around this time of year the weather became idyllic for operations with long warm days and clear nights. The officers' mess at the Manor

P/O Gillingham of 85 Squadron at the Manor House. He was killed in action on 9th July 1943 attacking a Do217.

House became a picture as the flowers bloomed and the cherry and plum trees began to bear fruit. Part of the cellar of the Manor House was converted into a bar-cum-nightclub and was named the 'Twitch Inn'. It acquired an atmosphere of its own with soft lights, secluded corners with candles and ample supplies of wines, beers and spirits. Night after night the 'Twitch' was to echo to the sounds of revelry as the thought of death in the air was forgotten by those not on night flying. When operations were on at night, a dice was placed upon the bar signifying that the air crew were dicing with death and conversely when bad weather prevented operations, a scrubbing brush was on show to signify that operations had been scrubbed. When the latter happened, the bar was full until the early hours of the morning when it was a struggle to get up the stairs to bed.

A regular visitor to the mess was David Langdon, the famous cartoonist. He was a past intelligence officer with 85 Squadron and liked to visit the old unit whenever he could. On the occasions that he came, he drew character cartoons of some of the officers on the hardboard panels that had been put around the walls to protect the ornate plasterwork. Several occasions saw members of the squadron write their names on the ceiling in candle grease, a feature that remains in the cellar today.

And the success continued, with pilots like John Cunningham gradually increasing his score to 17, with 16 of them shot down at night. Peter Townsend was suffering from a wound that he had sustained in 1940 and was sadly advised to relinquish his command of the station. He was replaced by Wg/Cdr Norman Hayes DFC.

With the arrival of July there came a lull in the enemy activity by night. It was later found that the Germans were experiencing severe misfortune with their FW 190 night operations, this becoming even more apparent when they projected two searchlight beams from a point near Dunkirk. This was in order to aid the German pilots when they were returning to France after carrying out fighter/bomber attacks over England. No doubt this idea had been accelerated by the misfortune of the four FW 190 pilots who landed at West Malling earlier in the year. The Luftwaffe was still keeping up its attacks using a mixture of FW 190s, Me 410s and Ju 88s. The Mosquito, with its superior airborne radar was a match for any of these aircraft and the issue of Ross night binoculars helped identification at night. July and August were good months for 85 and, having been the sole residents for some time at Malling, they did not take too kindly when they heard that two Spitfire squadrons were to join the base.

Sure enough, 5th August saw Sqd/Ldr W.H. Wright bring No 130 (Punjab) Squadron over from Honiley, now flying the Spitfire VB, and the next day they were joined by No 234 (Madras Presidency) Squadron, also from Honiley. They were briefed to carry out Ramrods, escorting day bomber formations, English and American, who were delivering the knockout blows to German industry. By night, it was still 85 who went into battle as darkness fell.

As late summer turned to autumn, the squadron were informed that their Mosquitos were to be fitted with the new mark of airborne radar, the Mark X. In order for the navigators to become fully conversant with the new radar, a Wellington bomber was fitted out as a flying classroom and training for 85 began in October 1943. With operations continuing at night and instructional flights during the day, life became very busy for the navigators of the squadron. As the month waned and the darker nights set in, the new radar began to bring in the desired results as many of the crews began to acquire good personal scores. Among these were the partnerships of Fl/Lt Maguire and Lt Lovestad and the Norwegians Per Buege and Claus Bjorn. It was however the mounting personal score of John Cunningham and his navigator that attracted the attention of the press. They had made him a hero and dubbed him 'Catseyes Cunningham', something that he personally hated. His sharpness of sight was attributed to the fact that he ate large quantities of carrots, all of which was pure fallacy but the nickname was to remain with him for the rest of his life.

On 16th September, No 234 took their Spitfires to Rochford followed by No 130 departing to Catterick two days later. Their place was taken by No 64 Squadron who flew their Spitfire VCs in from Gravesend on 6th September 1943. By the 25th they had left for Coltishall after a brief period of flying 'Ramrods' from Malling. Meanwhile, October had been a good one for 85 Squadron with the score for the month being five Ju 188s, three and a half Me 410s and one Ju 88 with a further two Me 410s damaged. On the 20th of the month, they were joined by the third Canadian nightfighter squadron in the UK, No 410 (Cougar). Led by Wg/Cdr G.H. Elms, the Mosquito VIs came in from Coleby Grange to accompany 85 on regular night patrols but on 8th November, they moved up to Hunsdon.

With the motto of 'Nocturni Obambulamus' (We stalk by night), 96 Squadron arrived at West Malling shortly after 410 had left. Led by Wg/Cdr E.D. Crew DFC, they flew the XIII mark of Mosquito, the latest version of the type having a higher loaded weight and a longer range. Having had a pretty miserable time flying from Drem airfield, they greeted the news that they were to move south with great jubilation and together with 85 Squadron, proved a very effective night fighting unit.

During November the squadrons at Malling had some uncomfortable operations when it was discovered that the Germans had fitted a rear-facing radar to some of their Ju 88s. No longer was it possible to come up behind a raider without fear of being spotted, but with more and more of the Mosquitos being fitted with the X mark of airborne radar, it was hoped that this would counteract the new German aid.

With snow covering much of the county, 1944 dawned bright and crisp. This did not really hamper 124 Squadron whose high altitude Spitfire HF VIs were operating up to a height of 42,000 feet in order to catch the high flying Ju 86Bs the Luftwaffe were now sending over. One success worthy of mention was when 124 were providing withdrawal cover for a force of B17s at 28,000 feet they tangled with a force of FW 190s, managing to destroy four and damage another for no loss to themselves.

For 85 and 96 Squadrons, operations continued immediately after the Christmas festivities as the Luftwaffe lull came to an end, and on 21st January 1944, the Luftwaffe put on the heaviest raid since the winter of 1940/1 with nearly 200 aircraft. FW 190s and Me 410s came in first and dropped 'window', strips of tinfoil designed to confuse our radar stations, followed by Ju 88s and Do 217s to inflict damage. It was 'B' flight of 85 who were on standby patrol and in the battle they shot down three and damaged a fourth out of the total of 16 shot down over the British Isles that night. At the end of the night, 85 had reached the magic number of 200 kills by day and night. For John Cunningham and Jimmie Rawnsley, it was their 20th victim and with rumours of Cunningham's departure to group headquarters, it was a fitting last success. For West Malling it was a time to take stock as the airfield's own tally at this time reached 26 victories by day and 93 by night with 12 and 13 probables and 22 and 27 damaged.

Wg/Cdr J.A. O'Neill DFC took over command of the station from Wg/Cdr Hayes on 1st February. The airfield was attacked for the first time since the Battle of Britain towards the end of February when several Luftwaffe fighter/bombers came in low and dropped their single bombs, doing very little damage. None actually landed on the airfield but several chicken houses around the boundary suffered casualties, much to the anguish of the local farmer who demanded compensation from the station commander!

The same month also, the 100th night success was achieved by Fl/Lt N.S. Head of 85. To mark the occasion, a performance of Noel Coward's

Private Lives was performed in the station theatre by Kay Hammond, John Clements and a first class support company. Immediately after the show ended, John Cunningham left his beloved 85 and was succeeded by Wg/Cdr C.M. Miller, but not before he had been sent on his way in the customary manner, that of being hawked around the various departments on a barrow.

It was around this time that the word 'Overlord' was being spoken behind closed doors. For many, the idea of an Allied offensive into Europe had been viable since 1942. By March 1944 the idea had become reality and it brought about a new phase of operations for West Malling. With 124 Squadron taking their Spitfires to Church Fenton on 18th March, No 616 (South Yorkshire) Squadron returned to their former base now equipped with Spitfire VIIs and XIVs and commanded by Sqd/Ldr L.W. Watts DFC. In April they were joined by 91 (Nigeria) Squadron flying Spitfire XIIs and XIVs, both units now part of the recently formed 2nd Tactical Air Force. The end of the month saw the rumours become fact when No 85 received a signal that they were to become part of 100 Group of bomber support aircraft. Though they departed to Swannington on 1st May, fate was to see them back at Malling at a later stage.

The night fighting was now left to No 96 with 91 and 616 flying by day. As the date for the re-entry into Europe came closer, General Sir Bernard Montgomery flew into West Malling to discuss the use of the airfield in support of his troops who would invade the French coast, meetings which were held behind locked doors in strict security.

The dispersals left by 85 did not remain empty long as No 29 returned to its former home the day that they left. They quickly settled in and a day later were joined by No 409 (Nighthawk) Squadron of the RCAF flying the Mosquito XIII. Rapid changes were the order of the day as 616 left for Fairwood Common, leaving West Malling with 29, 96 and 409 flying Mosquitos and 91 flying Spitfires.

As the date of the invasion drew nearer, 91 Squadron with its high flying Spitfires took many valuable photographs of the Allied landing areas as well as enemy movements. This increase in activity brought even more bombers in distress to the airfield. One particular raid in late May saw around 200 B17s take off from East Anglian bases to attack a German ball-bearing factory at Schweinfurt. Crossing the French coast they were confronted by a little light flak but it was not until they reached the target area that the German fighters were waiting for them. Many of the bombers were shot down even before releasing their bombs. One particular B17, having hit the target, turned for home but was badly shot up as he crossed over enemy country. Around 3.30 pm on 29th May the aircraft had crossed the coast and was making for West Malling, losing height all the time. On his approach the pilot flew low over the field indicating that his radio was out of action and that he was in trouble. In the aircraft the order was given to jettison anything of weight to lessen the load before attempting a crash landing. With the B17 managing to gain a little height, the captain ordered his crew to bale out. This they did, many of them landing in the surrounding villages. At approximately 4.10 pm, the B17 pilot managed to bring his stricken aircraft down safely.

Meanwhile the crew, having parachuted to safety, were waiting to be picked up. In wartime, it was the job of the local police to collect all parachutists seen to drop and on this particular afternoon, the job was allocated to two special constables who managed to round up all the crew except one. He had landed in the grounds of a large house belonging to a brewery executive and naturally, the local hospitality had taken over. By the time the police arrived, he was in no fit state to go anywhere. Free whisky and the attention of several lovely ladies had taken their toll!

On 3rd June, Hitler authorised Kesselring to withdraw from Rome and the next day, the 5th Army marched into the city. With foul weather in the Channel, General Eisenhower postponed the invasion for 24 hours and the crews of the West Malling squadrons were stood down. With the promise of a slight improvement for 6th June, the General decided that the risk must be taken and that D-Day had to be on the 6th. At 02.00 on the morning of the 6th, with the Channel somewhat calmer, the first of twelve convoys moved into position and the assault was on. History has documented the results very well and at its conclusion, it was deemed a success though with a substantial loss of life. By 08.00 of 6th June, Allied aircraft had flown 7,500 sorties, both bombers and fighters maintaining close support for the troops below and endeavouring to keep the skies free from enemy aircraft.

At West Malling, all four squadrons took part in the offensive. By the next day the Allies had established a good foothold in France and it was back to normal operations for the squadrons. Normal that is for six days, for at the end of this period, a new and terrifying weapon was unleashed upon the British public.

The night of Monday, 12th June 1944 passed quietly for the county. Not much enemy activity was noted by the sector controllers but at 00.40 in the morning of the 13th, Folkestone reported that it was being heavily shelled by the long-range German guns along the Pas de Calais in France. One hour later Maidstone, just a short distance from the airfield, was also being shelled. At 04.09 the duty crew around the plotting table at Bentley Priory were thinking of bed and a well-earned sleep as they awaited a plot to appear. Suddenly one of the Waaf operators heard the words 'Diver – Diver' in her headset. Repeating the words aloud, the entire control room staff stared in amazement at an extraordinary progress across the plotting table at great speed, heading for London.

The coastal radar stations had reported nothing out of the ordinary, for the words 'Diver – Diver' had been spoken by a Royal Observer Corps member perched high on a Martello Tower at Dymchurch on Romney Marsh. The post was called Mike 2 and was one of the early warning posts in addition to the radar stations. The two Observers on the tower plotted the low flying craft heading towards Pluckley whose post in turn plotted it to the Lenham zone. Leaving their area, it was handed over to No 19 Group headquarters at Bromley when suddenly in between Dartford and Gravesend, the object stopped emitting flame from the back and tipped downwards. It dived to earth and crashed with a terrific explosion on waste ground at Swanscombe. The time was 04.20 and the first Flying Bomb or V1 had crashed on British soil. With the aiming point the Tower of London, the Vergeltungs 1 or Retaliation Weapon had begun its reign of terror.

West Malling became one of the main airfields for coping with the menace and this in turn ensured that the airfield was turned over to the day fighters. The night fighter squadrons moved out, with 29 and 409 leaving on 19th June and 96 following on the 20th. Since 1942, West Malling had been known as the premier night fighter station in Fighter Command but now it was the turn of the day fighters to combat the V1s. With 91 already at the airfield, they were joined on 20th June by No 322 (Dutch) Squadron flying the Spitfire XIV. Together the squadrons devised methods of bringing the robots down, the obvious way being to shoot them down. This could only be accomplished if the attacking fighter stood some way back for fear of parts of the exploding V1 hitting his aircraft. One other method used was to fly alongside the V1, as close as possible, until the flow of air over both of the wings caused the rocket to tip downwards.

Slowly the toll of rockets brought down gathered momentum. In June alone as launchings from France increased, 91 Squadron had a credit of 184 brought down whilst by July, 322 Squadron had claimed 108 destroyed. Fitted with the powerful Griffon engine, the Spitfire XIV was the ideal fighter for the work and the best individual achievement

Mustang IIIs of 316 Squadron. (J. Rawlings)

was by F/O Brugwal of 322 Squadron, who on 8th July managed to claim five rockets.

During June many of the V1s fell close to the airfield and towards the end of the month it appeared as though Kent was littered with pieces of metal. With the daily launchings increasing during July, two more squadrons joined 91 and 322 at the airfield. No 80 and No 274, both flying the Spitfire IX, flew in from Gatwick. Although the V1 campaign seemed to be gathering momentum, the war for the Germans appeared to be falling apart. Hitler on the 20th was, himself, the target of a bomb plot which failed and all over the world, the Allies were proving victorious.

The 21st July saw 91 leave Malling after a very successful period. Their stay was sadly marred, however, during their last days at the airfield when one of the squadron's favourite pilots, Fl/Lt Maridor, a Frenchman, shot down a V1 and when realising it was to crash on Bethersden Hospital, fired again. In the following explosion, Maridor lost his life when his aircraft flew directly through the debris. At his funeral at Brookwood Military Cemetery, the Legion of Honour was pinned on his coffin.

Guy Gibson returned to his favourite station on the 24th, this time with the ribbon of the Victoria Cross pinned on his battledress. Sadly this was his last visit for both he and his observer were to die tragically on 19th September 1944 when their Mosquito crashed in Holland.

On the same day that 91 left, No 322 departed to Deanland and both squadrons were replaced by No 157 and, back again at their former home, No 85. Both these squadrons had been pulled from No 100 Group to help combat the V1s and with their arrival, West Malling became the

No 316 (City of Warsaw) Polish Squadron at West Malling, with Sqd/Ldr Arct in the cockpit.

foremost anti-diver airfield in Fighter Command rivalled only by the Newchurch Wing down on Romney Marsh. (See the chapter on the ALGs.)

By 31st July, West Malling could claim 278 V1s destroyed. The rapid turnround in squadrons indicated the strain that this type of operation had upon the majority of crews, the average length of stay for diver operations varying from one week to four. August saw 274 convert to the Hawker Tempest and on the 4th of the month, No 316 (City of Warsaw) Squadron arrived from Coltishall. For the first time in its history, West Malling was parent to an American fighter for 316 were equipped with the North American Mustang III. They had been taken off the strength of the 2nd Tactical Air Force in order to help Fighter Command in its battle against the V1.

In August, the launchings increased to between 250 and 300 rockets a day. All the squadrons were in daily contact with the robots, resulting in less than half of them reaching London. Not that all of this can be attributed to the fighters for the ack-ack gun barrage and the balloons were also having a successful time in bringing them down. The 17th saw 316 leave and on the 28th 157 departed having done their tour on

West Malling control tower, forlorn in 1991 whilst the rest of the airport is taken apart for industry and housing. (R. J. Brooks)

anti-diver operations. One day later, 85 left again for Swannington and 100 Group and No 80 moved to Manston in partnership with 274. The reason for the sudden departure of all the squadrons was that the end of the month saw V1 launchings dramatically reduced. This was partly due to the fact that the launch sites were being hit heavily by Bomber Command and also that the advancing Allies were overrunning many of the sites. Although the campaign was to continue on a limited scale with V1s being air launched by German aircraft over the North Sea, the main attacks were over. In all, over 8,500 rockets were launched against the United Kingdom, but barely 2,500 got through to their target. For the RAF at Malling, the anti-diver operation had been a great success and the total tally for the airfield was 280 V1s destroyed.

By 31st August the airfield lay abandoned, but it was already earmarked as a major base in peacetime. Tremendous extensions and a new concrete runway would be needed for the post-war RAF and the new breed of jet aircraft and although the closure of West Malling seemed premature, for war was to rage for another year, the station claimed to have been responsible for the destruction of 165 enemy aircraft, together with 34 probably destroyed, 59 damaged and 280 V1s shot down. It was quite an achievement and peacetime was to see the airfield again become the premier night fighter base of the RAF.

The reconstruction took until June 1945 when Sqd/Ldr G.T. Block handed over command of the airfield to Sqd/Ldr H. Baxter MM. At the end of the month, West Malling was once again operational, its first task being that of a rehabilitation centre for returning POWs. No 287 Squadron flew in from Bradwell to open the flying once again and the airfield took part in the final victory flypast over Kent when it hosted Mustangs, Spitfires, Tempests, Mosquitos and the new jet fighter, the Gloster Meteor.

Its role in peacetime is as worthy of mention as its wartime role, when it once more became a major fighting base. Sadly peacetime also brought financial constraints upon the military and in 1960, West Malling was offered to the United States Navy who operated a naval facility flight from the airfield until 1962. When they left, the MOD sold the airfield to the Kent County Council who allowed No 618 Volunteer Gliding School to continue their excellent work with the Air Training Corps. It soon became obvious that such a large area of land as an airfield could not be allowed to fall into disrepair and plans were put forward to turn it into a commercial concern. This attracted such an outcry from the locals that the plan was turned down, the Air Cadet gliding school had to disband and an American concern were contracted to turn the entire site into an industrial and housing estate. This is how we find the airfield today.

For the historian, there is not a lot left to see for the hangars, including the unique 'J' type, have been pulled down. The concrete runway has been removed and the internal grass area of the airfield is now a golf course. The wartime control tower is at present still standing.

11
THE ADVANCED LANDING GROUNDS

With the preparations for the invasion of the Continent in 1944, came the need for selected short term airfields to be built. Known as Advanced Landing Grounds, they were intended to be used as fighter or light bomber bases in support of the main invasion force.

As far back as 1940, the Air Staff had seen the need for 50 or more small strips to be built around southern Britain, though then for a different purpose. Although this part of the country was well catered for in larger airfields, the chance that any of these could become unserviceable due to enemy bombing made the building of smaller, mobile strips essential. They had to be built among trees wherever possible, there were to be no permanent buildings and personnel would be required to sleep and live in tented accommodation. In the event, they were not needed. However, 1941 saw Fighter Command take the offensive and it was then that the idea of using smaller airfields to support the main invasion when it began, came to fruition.

Operation Hadrian was an ambitious plan to land troops in the Pas de Calais during 1941 and again, there was a need for temporary airfields. Though Hadrian did not go ahead, the work of building the ALGs continued. Fifteen such airfields had been planned within the Biggin Hill, Hornchurch, Kenley and Tangmere sectors during 1942. Six sites were selected in Kent but none of these ever actually became an

ALG. Hadlow, Rother Levels, Marden Beeches, Withersdale, Wickhambreux and Stelling Minnis all appeared very favourable but due to water logging and logistical problems, work never started on them.

Early planning for a future invasion of the Continent meant that work started in earnest during the autumn of 1942 and since civilian labour was at a premium due to most of the able-bodied men being at war, the ALGs were built by RAF Airfield Construction Groups and Airfield Construction Groups of the Royal Engineers. Some help was afforded by construction groups of the US Army due to the fact that some of the ALGs were to be used by the USAAF. It was still hoped that the sites would be completed by March 1943 but the grading and levelling of the proposed sites took far longer than anticipated. The weather over this period was also to blame for the delay but of far greater hindrance were the objections of landowners to giving up their precious land. Although inferior ground was usually chosen, there were occasions when good fertile areas had to be used. This resulted in a battle royal between the Ministry of Agriculture and the Air Ministry. Some sites had to be compulsorily requisitioned under the Defence of the Realm Act and when this happened, as a compromise, the Air Ministry allowed some grazing on the sites until the ALG was required.

Out of the overall 72 sites selected, 36 were granted preliminary approval. This number was further reduced to 25 of which 23 were eventually built. They were not all in the south-east corner of the country for some were along the south coast in Hampshire and beyond. In Kent, eleven were finally built, all of them being in use for a very short, but essential, period. With the tented accommodation came the acquisition of farm cottages and barns adjacent to the site for use as accommodation, crew rooms and messing facilities. Bomb depots were situated some way away from the airstrip itself for obvious reasons, and hidden in thick woodland. In Kent, such depots were established at Ham Street and Smarden and supplied the ALGs within their own area.

The problem of ensuring all-weather serviceability was solved by the fitting of Sommerfeld Track across the landing area. Developed by an Austrian, Kurt Sommerfeld, it was a heavy steel netting held in place by angled, metal pins which were secured deep into the ground. Whilst this method was successful initially, the problem of wear and tear arose during operations, especially with the USAAF's Thunderbolts. The ALGs were later fitted with Square Mesh Track. Produced by the British Reinforced Engineering Co Ltd, it consisted of 3" square mesh and came in rolls, 7'3" wide and 7'5" long. SMT was easily and quickly produced

The field kitchen for 421 Squadron RCAF at Headcorn/Egerton. (A. Palmer)

but even this had its problems. Other mesh carpets used were the American Pierced Steel Plank and even later, a prefabricated Bitumen surfacing, which was totally waterproof and covered the grass entirely, rather like a large carpet.

Despite all the problems, the ALGs were ready by April 1944, two months before the invasion took place. They served their purpose admirably and when the units moved onto the Continent after D-Day, the majority were left to return to the landowners and agriculture. A few have continued as private airfields to this day. What follows is a list of the Kent ALGs and the units that used them, together with an in-depth study of one particular ALG, Staplehurst.

ASHFORD – Known more locally as Great Chart, it opened for use on 13th August 1943 when Nos 414 (Sarnia Imperials) and 430 (City of Sudbury) Squadrons of the RCAF arrived with Mustang Is. They were replaced in October by Nos 65 and 122 (Bombay) Squadrons of the RAF flying Spitfires. Allocated to the 9th Air Force during early 1944, the

Drop fuel tanks for the P47 Thunderbolts of 406th BG, Ashford. (Kent Messenger)

406th Bomb Group arrived with the 512th, 513th and 515th Fighter Squadrons equipped with P47D Thunderbolts. This group covered D-Day and claimed the first V1 shot down by the USAAF. They left in August 1944 and the ALG returned to its owner. Reunions were held at Ashford during 1988 and 1989 and again in 1997 when the American veterans visited their former base.

BRENZETT – Opened in September 1943 when No 122 (Bombay) Squadron flew in with Spitfire IXs staying for two days. Unused up to D-Day when Nos 129 (Mysore), 306 (Torun) and 315 (Deblin) Polish Squadrons flew in with Mustangs for anti-diver operations, later carrying out Rodeos. The site closed in December 1944 and is now the home of the Brenzett Aeronautical Museum.

HEADCORN – Sometimes known as Egerton and not to be confused with the present day Headcorn, it was one of the first ALGs to be chosen by Fighter Command. Modified in August 1942, it was in use by June

239

Col A. V. Grosselta checks the bomb fuse on his P47D Maggie's Masher, *Ashford. (Kent Messenger)*

At Brenzett, Sqd/Ldr E. Horbaczewski, CO 315 Squadron, poses with his Mustang III and fellow pilots shortly before his death on 18th August 1944. (IWM)

1943 when it was taken over by the Biggin Hill sector of 11 Group and became the headquarters of No 17 Fighter Wing RCAF. On 20th August 1943, Nos 403 (Wolf) and 421 (Red Indian) Squadrons flew their Spitfire XIBs in and were joined by a detachment of No 405 Repair and Salvage Unit. The Canadians were engaged on Ramrods and returned to Kenley for winter operations on 14th October 1943 whilst Headcorn was upgraded. It was allocated to the 9th Air Force, USAAF and the runway was resurfaced with US Steel Planking before the Thunderbolts arrived with three squadrons of the 362nd Fighter Group of the 100th Fighter Wing. These were Nos 377, 378 and 379 who commenced offensive sorties over northern France and Belgium prior to the invasion. The 362nd finally crossed to France on 2nd July 1944 when the ALG was deserted and returned to agriculture. During the 1980s, the Canadians planted three maple trees and erected a monument to the memory of their fallen comrades. A memorial service is held every autumn attended by No 421 (Red Indian) Squadron RCAF together with a flypast by a Spitfire of the Battle of Britain Memorial Flight and the current equipment of the RCAF, an F18 Hornet.

HIGH HALDEN – Designated a stand-by ALG, it was not used until 13th April 1944 when the 358th Bomber Group consisting of the 365th, 366th and 367th Fighter Squadrons moved in with P47D Thunderbolts. They left in July 1944 when No 616 (South Yorkshire) auxiliary squadron of the RAF used it as a forward operating base for a detachment of Meteor 1s from Manston carrying out anti-diver operations. It closed and returned to agriculture in September 1944.

KINGSNORTH – One of the first sites to be selected, it opened in June 1943 when 122 Airfield and the Spitfire VBs of Nos 65 (East India) and 122 (Bombay) flew in from Selsey and Bognor respectively. They carried out Rodeos with No 602 (City of Glasgow) Auxiliary Squadron who also arrived from Bognor but were replaced by No 19 Squadron in August. They were rather unusually joined by the Hurricane IVs of 184 who stayed for just a few days. The ALG was upgraded in September 1943 and 122 Airfield left in October 1943. Allocated to the American 9th Air Force, the 36th Fighter Group, 303rd Fighter Wing arrived with the 22nd, 23rd and 53rd Fighter Squadrons with P47D Thunderbolts. The 36th Fighter Group moved across the Channel in July 1944 and the land returned to its owner in 1945.

Lashenden 4th July 1944 – Col Bickell, Brig Gen Quesada and Gen D. Eisenhower arrive after a flight over enemy lines. (C. Freeman)

LASHENDEN – Now known as Headcorn which is very confusing when another ALG situated nearby was known as Headcorn during 1943. Opened in August 1943 when No 127 (RCAF) Airfield moved in comprising Nos 403 (Wolf) and 421 (Red Indian) Squadrons with Spitfires. They left twelve days later when the ALG was upgraded. In April 1944, the 100th Fighter Wing Tactical Air Command arrived with the 354th, 353rd, 355th and 356th Fighter Group flying the P51 Mustang. By July 1944 the land had already reverted to agriculture but in 1973, the airfield reopened operated by Shenley Farms (Aviation) Ltd who renamed it Headcorn. Today it is a private civil airfield and parachute centre and is also the home of the Lashenden Air Warfare Museum.

LYDD – This town gave rise to several flying sites, one of them being connected with the Royal Engineers' balloon experiments, but it is the ALG that is remembered. With Sommerfeld Track runways laid by spring 1943, 131 Airfield comprising Nos 174 (Mauritius), 175 and 245 (Northern Rhodesia) Squadrons arrived with Typhoons. They carried out Ramrods and Rhubarbs and tasted bombing themselves when a force of FW 190 fighter/bombers attacked the ALG. Lydd was unique in that five Blister hangars were built for the squadrons but they were little used as the ALG was deserted by September 1944 and was returned to agriculture.

NEWCHURCH – This was one of the most successful of all the Romney Marsh ALGs and was selected and approved during the early summer of 1942. 125 Airfield arrived on 2nd July 1943 consisting of Nos 19, and 132 (City of Bombay) Squadrons with Spitfire VCs. They immediately began escort operations mainly covering light and medium bombers. Newchurch was of such importance that a decoy airfield was built at Burmarsh, something no other ALG had. No 602 (City of Glasgow) Auxiliary Squadron replaced No 19 in August and the Hurricanes of 184 arrived from Snailwell. No 125 Airfield moved to Detling on 12th October 1943 as the ALG was upgraded, receiving several Blister hangars in the process. Newchurch was reopened in April 1944 when 150 Airfield, No 85 Group of the 2nd Tactical Air Force arrived. No 3 Squadron flew the Tempest, 486 (RNZAF) receiving them on 15th May, whilst No 56 (Punjab) Squadron flew a mixture of Spitfires and Typhoons. The wing was led by Wg/Cdr 'Roly' Beamont, DSO, DFC and Bar and they began operations on shipping reconnaissance. With the last squadron converting to the Tempest, they began offensive operations over France. The wing saw little action on D-Day but achieved a lot of success on anti-diver operations. They left Newchurch on 23rd September 1944 and the site was returned to its owner shortly after.

NEW ROMNEY – Like Lydd, New Romney also had two sites of aviation, the first in use during 1914/18 as a School of Gunnery. The ALG was approved in December 1942 with No 124 Airfield arriving

132 Squadron at Newchurch on 14th October 1943 with Spitfire LF VBs.

with Typhoons on 2nd July 1943. Nos 181 and 182 Squadrons were employed in the fighter/bomber role and the aircraft were commonly called 'bombphoons'. They were joined later by No 247 (China-British) Squadron and began anti-shipping strikes which they carried out with great success until moving to Merston, a Sussex ALG, in October 1943. The strip was then put on the list of reserve ALGs but was only used by a ground signals unit waiting to go to France. It was returned to agriculture shortly after.

WOODCHURCH – This ALG was unique due to the fact that it was one of two selected as a light bomber base but due to difficulties with the land, it reverted to a fighter base. The 28th July 1943 saw No 128 Airfield, No 39 (RCAF) Sector, No 83 Group Tactical Air Force established with Nos 231 and 400 (City of Toronto) Squadrons flying Mustang Is. They flew Channel patrols, low level photo-reconnaissance and Rhubarb operations before leaving in October 1943. Like the majority of ALGs, Woodchurch underwent modification and 1st April 1944 saw the 373rd Fighter Group, 9th Tactical Air Force arrive with the 410th, 411th and 412th Fighter Squadrons flying P47D Thunderbolts.

Col W. H. Schwartz briefs his pilots of 373rd Fighter Group at Woodchurch 1944. (Kent Messenger)

They carried out fighter sweeps over Normandy and on D-Day provided top cover over the landing beaches. The Americans left Woodchurch a few days later and the site returned to agriculture.

These were ten out of the eleven most important and active ALGs within the county. There was one other at Swingfield but it was never used for its intended purpose. The rest were used over several hectic months and contributed a great deal to the Allied invasion of Europe. An in-depth study of Staplehurst ALG is indicative of life on all of them.

STAPLEHURST – This was the most westerly of all the ALGs surveyed during the spring of 1942. Lying close to several other ALGs in the Weald of Kent, it was situated on low lying ground near the River Beult. The site was finally selected as suitable for use in July 1942 and in September, a more detailed report recommended that a 4,200 foot runway running east-west and a 3,300 foot runway running north-south was possible. Accommodation for operational purposes was seen to be no problem with two local farms, Chickenden Farm and Spills Hill Farm and their adjoining cottages available.

With acceptance of the plans, work began on 19th January 1943 by No 5005 Airfield Construction Squadron, previously known as the RAF Works Services, operating from a large tented camp on Hothfield Common near Ashford. The work went ahead on levelling and clearance and with no problems, the ALG was finished by March. With no plans to utilise the strip immediately, the Ministry of Agriculture pressed for its use for cattle grazing, a request that was granted on a monthly basis. This privilege had to be relinquished in August 1943 when on the 6th, a large convoy of No 126 Airfield of No 83 Group TAF moved in from Redhill. The next day Nos 401 (Ram) and 411 (Grizzly Bear) Squadrons of the RCAF flew their Spitfire VBs in to be followed one day later by the Spitfires of No 412 (Falcon) Squadron. After the relative comforts of Redhill, the basic amenities of Staplehurst did not endear the ALG to the hearts of the Canadians. Even worse came the realisation that all cooking was to be done in a field kitchen. The workshops and much of the equipment were either contained in specially modified trucks or in one of the local farmers' open barns, and accommodation was in tents except for the chosen few. Like most of the similar sites, the runways at Staplehurst had been strengthened by the laying of Sommerfeld Tracking. Whilst this was fine to land on when the surface was dry, if wet it could cause no end of problems for the unwary pilot.

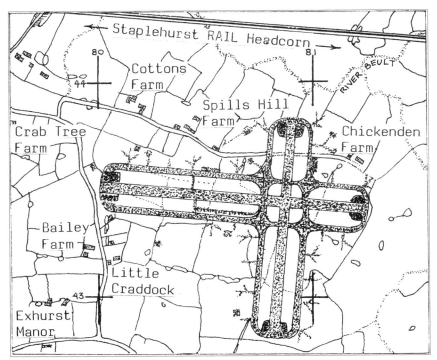

Staplehurst ALG. (R. J. Brooks)

126 Airfield settled into Staplehurst and soon made friends with the owners of Chickenden Farm, the Munns family. Always there to offer a helping hand whenever it was needed, the family also introduced the ways of the Kentish farming community to the Canadians. It was very much a give and take situation as one early episode relates. With cooking being done on a field kitchen and therefore providing a very limited diet, the temptation of so many chickens running around proved too much for one of the young pilots, who, one dark night, committed a number of chickens to the pot. For the next few days, the crews dined on Kentish Fried Chicken. Though the Munns family knew what had happened to them, they did very little about it and some time later, as a gesture of appreciation, the drop tanks of a Spitfire were filled with brandy to be given to the family as a gift. Unfortunately, on its way back to Staplehurst, the aircraft was lost over the Channel!

The first Ramrod was planned for 8th August but bad weather prevented the operation from going ahead. Two days later, the first of many such ops was flown with the wing being led initially by Wg/Cdr

J.E. Walker, DFC and 2 Bars. Shortly after its arrival at Staplehurst, Wg/Cdr K.L.B. Hopson DFC and Bar was appointed CO and it was he who led the wing throughout their time at the ALG.

Once settled in, the Canadians lost no time in carrying out the first operations and Ramrods were to become an everyday occurrence. As August turned to September, the wing became involved in Operation Starkey, the feint attacks intended to deceive the enemy into believing an assault on the French Coast was imminent. On the 8th of the month, the wing were airborne by 9 am and although the squadrons flew provocatively along the French and Belgian coastline, the enemy failed to respond. Not so during the second sortie of the day when the wing tangled with a force of FW 190s, with very little success on either side.

It is worth recording a typical Ramrod operation carried out by the wing. This was Ramrod 258 which was flown on 3rd October 1943. The attack was delivered between 14.50 and 15.00 hours over Bethancourt-Ault. The weather at the time was clear with 4/10th light cloud at 5,000 feet. Led on this occasion by Sqd/Ldr E.L. Neal DFC, the wing was to rendezvous with twelve Bostons ten miles north of Beauvais. It consisted of twelve aircraft from each squadron and left Staplehurst at 13.45 hours to meet the Bostons on the way home and provide an escort.

The air traffic control lorry at Staplehurst – simple and very mobile. (V. Baker)

They were at the appointed point on time only to find no sign of the Bostons. Stooging around for 14 minutes, there was still no sign of the bombers so the wing leader ordered all aircraft to return to base.

With 401 and 411 Squadrons flying at 3,500 feet, 412 were providing top cover at 4,500 feet. When passing over what apparently was a goods train near Aurnal, Red 3 of 410 (Fl/Lt Studholme) was hit by light flak in the starboard wing which was badly damaged. He was however, able to continue with the operation. About ten miles south-east of Ault in the vicinity of Bethancourt, a feinting bounce was carried out by 15 FW 190s on 401 Squadron who were flying line abreast on the starboard side of the wing. The enemy aircraft, however, did not open fire but pulled up and overshot the squadron. 412, who at this time were flying at 3,500 feet line abreast, were bounced by these aircraft who attacked flying line astern after having made a sharp 90 degree turn to starboard. Combats took place during which Fl/Lt Boyd and Fl/Sgt Bowker engaged the enemy.

About four miles off Ault to the north-west, Yellow 1 of 412 Squadron (Fl/Lt Boyd) shot at a range of 300 yards at a FW 190 from almost directly line astern, giving the enemy aircraft a two to three second burst. Strikes were seen on the fuselage by Fl/Lt Boyd and his number two, P/O Dewan. The enemy aircraft broke formation and pouring thick oily black smoke from the wing roots and the belly, was last seen diving towards the sea. This enemy aircraft was claimed as damaged pending the examination of the cine gun.

Blue 3 of 412 Squadron (P/O Heacock) was attacked by two FW 190s while flying at 1,500 feet approximately four miles north and west of Cayeux. Blue 4 (F/Sgt Bowker) who was flying on his port side observed this attack and climbed up into the sun as Blue 3 broke to port in a tight diving turn, followed in a wider turn by the enemy aircraft. By this time the 190s were flying 50 feet in line astern heading towards Ault. F/Sgt Bowker dived down below them and attacked from behind and below, giving a two to three second burst from 350 to 400 yards. This enemy aircraft was seen by F/Sgt Bowker to turn on its back and dive into the sea. P/O Heacock completed his orbit and although he did not see the enemy go into the sea, he did see a large splash just before F/Sgt Bowker passed over the spot. Blue 4 pressed home his attack on one enemy aircraft and closed from 600 to 200 yards, firing the rest of his ammunition. The enemy peeled off slightly to port and crashed into a house on the shore slightly north of Ault and burst into flames. At the end of the action, the wing turned for home and landed safely at Staplehurst. For two of the Spitfires slightly damaged, the enemy had lost two FW190s destroyed and another damaged. Ramrod 258 was deemed a successful sortie. There were to be many similar.

Despite the intense operations, there was still a need for exercises. On 10th October, personnel were dropped at different points in the county and told to use their initiative to find their way back to Staplehurst. Use it they did, when F/O J.T. Murchison and P/O R.M. Davenport crept into 129 Airfield based at the Ashford ALG, managed to open the hoods on two Spitfires and flew them back to Staplehurst. Again from the same ALG, F/O O.P. Kelly flew a Tiger Moth out. Not to be outdone, Fl/Lt W.R. McRae and F/O T. Koch managed to drive an army bus off a camp near Ashford despite the threatening abuse of the army police. The exercise was a success, but news that the wing was to move to the comforts of Biggin Hill came as an added bonus. However, despite the earlier objections to basic life at Staplehurst, the Canadians were sad to leave the many friends they had made over their brief stay, especially the Munns of Chickenden Farm.

Over the winter months, the ALG underwent improvement for its forthcoming use during the invasion of the Continent. Seventy hardstandings were built together with a further strengthening of the runways. The Sommerfeld Tracking had really not stood up too well to the intense operations and so it was replaced by the tougher Square Mesh Track. With work completed on time and the better spring weather approaching, Staplehurst began a new role, that of an airstrip of the USAAF which they chose to call Station 413.

The 363rd Fighter Group had moved to England during March 1943 to join the 9th Air Force. Consisting of the 380th, 381st and 382nd Fighter Squadrons, they received their Mustang P51Ds at Rivenhall during January 1944 and flew their first sortie on 23rd February. In April they moved down to Staplehurst for operations up to and including D-Day, 6th June. Like the Canadians before them, the basic amenities at the ALG came as a shock after the comforts of Rivenhall, even to the extent of landing the P51s on grass! To crown it all, there were as yet no beds for them to sleep on, it was a case of making do with straw bales. After threatening to leave Staplehurst, things did suddenly and rapidly improve and by the end of the first week, life became a little sweeter.

'Saturday April 15th. Our first day at Staplehurst dawned wet and foggy. In spite of the impossible weather we were sent out on a jackpot mission after some enemy building in central Germany. The entire outfit aborted, only one plane getting as far as the German border. That in itself would have been bad but in the process we lost three of our best-liked pilots and nearly lost a fourth. While going over the aborted

The 363rd FG pose at Staplehurst with one of their P51 Mustangs. (Kent Messenger)

area, Lt Canill and T/Sgt Hare spun out of the overcast and into the sea. Lt McRoberts of the 381st crashed while trying to land at a field nearby and was killed instantly. Lt Ringgenberg, 381st, spun out of the overcast over the North Sea and had to bail out. When his chute opened, he lost his dinghy. When he hit the water, he lost his Mae West and he couldn't swim. However, he managed to paddle to his Mae West, inflated it and in ten minutes he was rescued by a small fishing boat. He returned to camp with only a sprained elbow to show for his really miraculous escape.'

So recorded the 363rd diarist. Many similar missions ended in failure as the weather throughout April proved abysmal. In addition to the many escort missions, the group also carried out bombing attacks with the bombs slung beneath the Mustangs' wings. With regard to the former sorties, some of the bombers themselves barely made it back to England and it became a common sight at Staplehurst to see B17s and B24s dispersed next to the orchards awaiting repair to enable them to return to their own bases in East Anglia.

A dive-bombing mission on Saturday, 22nd April saw the group leave the ALG during the late morning and head for Melines in Belgium. Eight and a half tons of bombs were dropped on the locomotive repair sheds and oil tanks at the marshalling yards. Led by Major Ben Irvin and his trusty Mustang, *Lolita*, the pilots showed remarkable accuracy. Extremely well-patterned bombing runs tore the target to pieces and all aircraft returned safely. Again in the afternoon, aircraft of the group went on the first fighter sweep into south-west Germany with airfields around Frankfurt the principal targets. These fields were strafed and two Ju 88s were probably destroyed. In addition, a trainer biplane, a glider and bulldozer were shot up. Sadly, it proved to be an expensive mission for the 363rd as four aircraft failed to return, two of them the victims of heavy flak over the target area.

May was a month of similar operations with both success and loss. As the plans for D-Day came together, the wing prepared itself for the big push. In the run-up to Overlord, 1st June was wet with a little improvement promised for the next day. Even then the cloud did not clear until late afternoon and at 17.00 hours, a bombing mission to Rouen went ahead. The attack was on a bridge which was successfully destroyed even though Lt Webster of the 382nd lost his canopy in a dive and had a blustery ride home! The next day no operations were flown but on Sunday, 4th June, three missions were flown escorting the large bombers. In the afternoon the wing were honoured to receive a visit from the heavyweight boxing champ, Joe Louis, who was in England on a goodwill mission. Attendance in the big hangar was 100% that evening.

Overnight the ground crews had been busy putting the invasion stripes on the Mustangs ready for the big day. Monday the 5th saw no mission flown but intensive briefing went on all day behind closed doors with everyone confined to camp. A tight security cordon was in place around Staplehurst stopping anyone going near or into the ALG. Once again, the diarist recalls the momentous day.

'Tuesday June 6th. THIS IS IT. D-DAY. The field itself was calm and showed little evidence of participating in the greatest military movement in history. All were on alert, each squadron taking its hour in the cockpit. Nothing happened and our only news was via the radio. By the evening, led by Colonel Tipton, we escorted C-47s and gliders to Cherbourg Peninsula. The weather turned bad and many planes had to land in and around Middle Wallop.

'Wednesday June 7th. The war goes well. Very early in the morning, we went out to escort more C-47s and their gliders over to the beach-head. Weather was bad and anyhow we were 50 minutes late so we never found the tugs. We did however escort them back to safety. In the evening it was a dive-bombing mission at the back of the German

A scene typical of many of the ALGs as a P51D Mustang is bombed up at Staplehurst. (Kent Messenger)

lines. It was a great success and all aircraft returned safely to Staplehurst. At last the end is near.'

Friday, 18th June 1944 saw the first V1 that the Americans had ever encountered fly over the base. It was around midnight and the local ack-ack gunners had opened up with all they had. A red alert was given at Staplehurst as it approached and the comforting words over the tannoy system were, 'Look out for rockets and do what you think best!' The majority of the Americans just stood and watched it fly overhead.

On one of the last missions, on Thursday, 22nd June, Major McCall lead his squadron in a dive-bombing attack near Cherbourg. The rest of the group went on a similar mission inland whilst at Staplehurst, the advance echelon was preparing to pull out and head for France. A signal had been received that morning that the 363rd were to leave Station 413 and proceed to Southampton Marshalling Area prior to going to Site B1 – Maupertus.

Like the Canadians before them, the Americans were sad to leave the ALG. Whilst the locals had originally resented them, over the weeks they had begun to welcome them into their homes. Now they were to leave taking their Kentish memories with them.

The Battle of Britain memorial at Capel-le-Ferne between Folkestone and Dover. (R. J. Brooks)

With their departure, Staplehurst had served its short but very important purpose. With the War Agricultural Committee pressing for its de-requisition by October, the Steel Surface was lifted for further use on the Continent. The site was finally de-requisitioned on 18th January 1945. All of the ALGs made short but very important contributions towards the war effort. A few signs of those hectic months still remain today although most of them have returned to their roots, namely agriculture.

When No 412 Squadron arrived in 1943, it already had a Kentish connection dating back to 1940. Within its ranks at that time was P/O John Gillespie Magee. Born of Anglo-American parents, his mother hailed from Deal in Kent and his education had begun at a preparatory school in the town before moving onto Rugby School and thence to the Royal Canadian Air Force and No 412 Squadron. He was killed on 11th December 1941 when his Spitfire collided with a Cranwell-based Oxford training plane. Before his untimely death he composed a sonnet which has since become a classic and portrays every fighter pilot of the last war. It therefore does not come amiss to include it here.

HIGH FLIGHT

Oh! I have slipped the surly bonds of earth
And danced the skies on laughter-silvered wings;
Sunward I've climbed, and joined the tumbling mirth
Of sun-split clouds – and done a hundred things
You have not dreamed of – wheeled and soared and swung
High in the sunlit silence. Hov'ring there
I've chased the shouting wind along, and flung
My eager craft through footless halls of air.

Up, up the long, delirious, burning blue
I've topped the wind-swept heights with easy grace
Where never lark, nor even eagle flew –
And, while with silent lifting mind I've trod,
The high, untrespassed sanctity of space,
Put out my hand and touched the face of God.

Wherever 412 Squadron go, this special sonnet goes with them.

12
CIVILIANS AT WAR

At 9 am on Sunday, 3rd September 1939, Sir Neville Henderson, the British Attache in Berlin, delivered an ultimatum to Dr Paul Otto Schmidt. He declined an invitation to sit down but with deep emotion, read the ultimatum, shook the hand of Schmidt and left. By 11 am, the ultimatum had expired and with no reply from Berlin, Britain was at war with Germany.

After the storms of the night before, the day dawned bright and sunny across the deserted streets of the County of Kent. On that fateful Sunday, every civilian household in England listened to the Prime Minister, Neville Chamberlain. With his broadcast to the nation beginning at 11.15 am and the playing of the National Anthem six minutes later, the sirens began to wail over London and the home counties at 11.28 am. Although it was a false alarm, the civilian population of Kent, together with the rest of the country, had heard the first sounds of war.

As early as June 1936, every local authority in Kent had issued a circular on air-raid precautions. Later on came leaflets on what to do in the case of a gas attack, which was widely predicted, and the formation of the Civil Defence Corps with its headquarters at Mt Ephraim, Tunbridge Wells under the overall control of Sir Auckland Geddes, the south eastern regional commissioner. The taste of what an air raid was really like had come in May 1938 when the biggest exercise so far was carried out in the Medway Towns. Aircraft from Manston simulated bombing attacks with about 2,000 people from the area taking part in the test. It was as realistic as could be made possible.

In Maidstone, the County Town, the council had been recruiting and training air raid wardens, auxiliary firemen, ambulance drivers and other civil defence personnel since 1936. Strangely, the town had been on the Government list of places supposedly not exposed to attack. Therefore no Anderson shelters were supplied to the population. The town council did not agree with the Government and repeatedly

Sandbags are placed around County Hall, seat of Kent County Council in Maidstone. (Kent Messenger)

warned of Maidstone's vulnerability. They pointed out the presence of a large army barracks close to the town centre and in addition, a further encampment of Canadians and Scotsmen in Mote Park. Yet again, the Government insisted that the town would be so safe from attack as to consider it as a main centre for the reception of evacuees from London.

In total contrast, the *Kent Messenger* of Saturday, 2nd September 1939 ran the headline: 'Five Kent towns evacuating children this weekend'. Rochester, Chatham and Gillingham, Northfleet and Gravesend had not waited for officialdom and had set the ball rolling to protect their children. Those from the Medway Towns travelled to various parts of the country by train and coach whilst the North Kent children travelled by paddle steamer to Suffolk and Norfolk. Each child was labelled and carried a postcard to send home immediately upon arrival at their intended destination. All of this was perhaps a little premature for with no enemy attacks at all over the county during this 'phoney' period, the evacuees began returning home for Christmas 1939.

As the civil defence measures gathered momentum, the part-time men and women in the military machine got onto a wartime footing. Maidstone saw the girls of the 41st Company of the ATS called to full

Evacuees board a train from London to the country. (Kent Messenger)

time duty at Maidstone Barracks. It was somewhat alien to many of them and the odd hiccup came on more than one occasion as the local paper was keen to mention. 'One of the girls marched across the square in true military tradition, arms swinging and head upright. Approaching a soldier, she threw the most magnificent salute ever. An awkward silence followed only to be broken by the soft voice of an embarrassed NCO of the Queen's Own Royal West Kent Regiment. "It's alright miss, you don't have to salute me, only the officers".'

At Detling RAF station, the 19th Company of the WAAFs were mobilised and reported for duty. An offspring of the Royal West Kent Regiment, the 25 girls made up the nucleus of the first WAAFs attached to No 500 (County of Kent) Auxiliary Air Force Squadron. There were no uniforms at first, just armbands but they were as keen as the men to do their bit.

As Kent went to war, much of the local industry was to suffer. With a large paper making industry just outside Maidstone, the shortage of wood pulp developed into a crisis and resulted in fewer pages in magazines and newspapers as well as a shortage of paper bags for wrapping purposes. Of far more importance to the local populace were the constraints in the breweries resulting on occasions in rationing beer

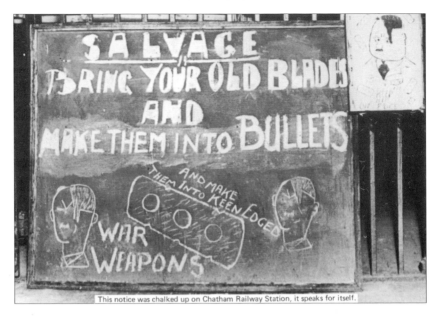

This notice was chalked up on Chatham Railway Station, it speaks for itself.

This notice was chalked up on Chatham railway station. It speaks for itself.

to the public houses. Food supplies were also to be subject to rationing, which began in January 1940 and was to last well into peacetime. The first items to go on ration were butter, sugar, bacon and ham followed by all types of meat in March 1940. In many households, bread and potatoes became the principal diet and the discarding of any bread, however mouldy and stale, sometimes resulted in prosecutions. Civilians were encouraged to turn their flower gardens and lawns into vegetable patches and remember the slogan: 'Dig for Victory'. Rationing, however, was just one inconvenience to the civilians. In addition there was the blackout, the cause of mounting casualties during the early part of the war. The removal of all road signs and the blockading of streets brought further difficulties to the motorist and of course, there were the sleepless nights due to enemy bombing. These and many other inconveniences were to face the Kentish people for many months.

The county in 1940 was also a very dangerous place to live. With the Battle of Britain being fought overhead, many German and British aircraft crashed within its boundaries making the county sometimes resemble a scrap metal yard. Obviously some aircraft did fall on houses with all the dreadful consequences but the majority fell on open

The crater and remains of a Me 109 shot down on 14th September 1940 near Sittingbourne. (Kent Messenger)

countryside. It was the evacuation of Dunkirk that gave Kent an opportunity to show what it was made of when the constant stream of trains from Dover travelled through the county. On board every train were tired and hungry soldiers. At every station that the train stopped at there were refreshments for all. Three of the biggest stations that were ready with tea and food for the troops were Paddock Wood, Tonbridge and Headcorn. Here, women of the WVS, Red Cross and just ordinary housewives were ready to hand out the welcome beverage. It is said 145,000 cups of tea were dispensed at Headcorn alone during the evacuation period.

With Dunkirk over, it appeared as though an invasion of our island was possible. With so many men away in the fighting forces, Anthony Eden, the Secretary of State for War, broadcast an appeal on 14th May for men who for one reason or another, had not been called up for the forces, to form a force to be called 'The Local Defence Volunteers'. The response was phenomenal with 250,000 men volunteering within the first 24 hours. Like the Waafs, the first uniform was just an armband but a full army uniform came later as did the name 'The Home Guard'.

With the Battle of Britain overhead, the first recorded death occurred

The returning Dunkirk troops are given refreshments at Headcorn station.
(Kent Messenger)

Not even the war could stop the Londoners coming hop-picking at the Whitbread Hop Farm, Beltring. (Kent Messenger)

Feldwebel Otto Schoettle surrenders to the police after being shot down on 28th August 1940, at Copt Hill Farm, Capel, near Folkestone. (D. Collyer)

on 3rd July when a bomb dropped at Bekesbourne killing one person. From that time on, death for the civilian population became an everyday occurrence. With the intense fighting now taking place, the sirens were constantly sounding. One day on which they sounded just in time to warn the people was on 27th August 1940. With the naval dockyard at Chatham, it was known that the Medway Towns were an obvious target. It was shortly after midnight that Gillingham was attacked by a force of German bombers. Some scored a direct hit on the Gillingham depot of the Maidstone and District Motor Services Ltd. In one gigantic bang, the entire roof of the garage collapsed burying the majority of the buses beneath it. As the flames began to take hold, the houses either side of the garage and opposite became threatened. Despite valiant efforts by the bus crews, servicemen and civilians alike to get the buses out, the intense heat forced them back. In the end only two buses got out of the inferno. Worst of all, when a roll-call was taken of staff who were in the building at the time, three were found to be unaccounted for. It was only when the blaze had been brought under control and the firemen were able to go inside what was left of the building that they found them, dead in the mess room where they had become trapped. That night was the worst for Gillingham with 20 people killed, a further

A very rare photograph of a bomb exploding at Monktons Avenue, Maidstone on 27th September 1940. (Kent Messenger)

The fuselage of a Ju 88 brought down in Tonbridge Road, Maidstone on the night of 17th September 1940. (Kent Messenger)

22 seriously injured and 18 others with superficial wounds.

Three days prior to that raid, it had been the turn of Ramsgate to suffer its worst raid of the war. Again, with the RAF station at Manston and the fact that the Navy used Ramsgate Harbour, it was an obvious target. It was Saturday and the shopping centre was crowded with people. Around lunchtime, the Luftwaffe attacked Manston, the result of which was to cover the entire area in a blanket of thick smoke. Because of this, the second wave of bombers could not find the airfield so dropped their bombs at random on Ramsgate town centre instead. Thirty one people were killed with 54 others seriously injured, the town's highest death toll of the war. The essential services of gas and water were put out of action for twelve days incurring the positioning of stand pipes at specific places. Some residents of the town had taken shelter during the earlier raid on Manston in tunnels dug into the cliff-face and had preferred to stay there during the second attack. They were the lucky ones!

A Ramsgate resident recalled: 'The sirens had gone and we were all down the tunnel. We heard the bombs dropping on Manston and then suddenly silence. Someone poked their head out of the tunnel and said that the town was covered in a thick black smoke. Should we go out or not? In the end it was decided that we would not venture out just yet when suddenly the sky was full of enemy aircraft dropping bombs all over the town. Terrified that one would hit the tunnel, we huddled together for security and only ventured out when we heard the all clear. As we came out we were sickened by the sight of the devastation and the fact that someone told us that there were many killed. Perhaps we were right to stay in the tunnel after all.'

The end of the Battle of Britain saw no end to the indiscriminate bombing of civilian targets by the Luftwaffe for by the close of 1940 there were to be 22 bomb attacks involving the deaths of civilians. In September of 1940, Gillingham was again the target whilst Ashford, the home of the Southern Railway Engineering Works now involved in manufacturing aircraft components, saw seven people killed with two

Bomb damage at Albion Place, Maidstone in 1940. (Kent Messenger)

*The Mayor of Maidstone walks down Mill Street after the November raid of 1940.
(Kent Messenger)*

injured during a raid on Thursday, 26th September. The next day it was
to be the turn of Maidstone.

It lasted only minutes but the devastation was widespread. Shortly
after midday, 16 aircraft dropped bombs on the county town covering
an area from Barton Road in the south to Allington Park in the north.
St Faith's church next to the museum and the gardens alongside were
badly hit causing the church tower to split from top to bottom. Part of
the museum was damaged and the cottage which was part of the
gardens was totally demolished. A further bomb fell in the goods yard
of the Maidstone East railway station which was adjacent to the gardens
but it was the loss of life that this single attack caused that shook the
community. Ten men, eleven women and a child were killed outright
with 22 men, 22 women and again, one child seriously injured. There
were a further 20 men, 22 women and four children with slight injuries.

1941 and 1942 were to see further civilian deaths and injuries in all
the cities, towns and villages of Kent. In the case of one particular city,
Canterbury, this was to be the target for several of the so-called
Baedeker raids. These were a particular type of raid named after Karl
Baedeker, a German publisher of foreign travel guides. The attacks

were carried out on British cities of architectural interest which were all named in the guides and were reprisal raids for heavy bomber attacks on German cities. On 30th May 1942 a Bomber Command force of 1,046 aircraft destroyed large areas of the city of Cologne. In retaliation, Sunday 31st May saw a Baedeker raid on Canterbury. It occurred around 45 minutes past midnight when an initial force of enemy aircraft dropped parachute flares to illuminate the city. Shortly after, 50 bombers flew in over the Kent coast and attacked in three waves. In all about 100 high explosive and 6,000 incendiary bombs were dropped by the enemy, devastating the city centre. Amidst all of the carnage stood Canterbury Cathedral, rising supreme out of the fire and smoke and destruction that surrounded it. If that were the main target, and it is highly likely that it was, it survived but only just. The Warriors Chapel entrance was demolished as was the Victorian Cathedral Library. The glow from the many fires threw out the outline of the steeple and spires, a sight that could be seen many miles away. The Canterbury National Fire Service together with appliances from all over the county, rushed

An American B17 Flying Fortress that did not make it home and crashed on Romney Marsh. (Kent Messenger)

to the city's aid. They did a magnificent job under the worst of conditions and together with rescue parties, toiled to remove the rubble and look for casualties.

No finer tribute could have been paid to the city and its people than that spoken by Lord Monsell, the Regional Commissioner. 'Canterbury is proud of her people. Under a cruel battering they have shown the same brave spirit which emanates from all Britishers. Their quiet patience is a sure presage of Victory.' In addition, many messages of sympathy were received by the Mayor, who expressed his gratitude to the Regional authorities who had worked so magnificently. A total of 43 people died that night with 48 seriously injured and 50 slightly hurt. Many firemen and rescue parties worked over 24 hours without sleep recovering the bodies and damping down the fires. Daylight saw the city workers and city dwellers wandering around in a daze as Canterbury struggled to get back to normality. It also revealed the extent of the damage. St George's Place and church were in ruins with another area of destruction around St Dunstan's. It soon became

Aircraft were put on display to raise funds during 'Wings For Victory' weeks – here a Vickers Wellington at Rootes of Maidstone's car park, 1943. (Kent Messenger)

obvious that bombs had destroyed around 400 buildings, seriously damaged a further 1,500 and slightly damaged 2,000 others. Clearance was to take until and beyond the end of the war.

Not content with one Baedeker, the night of 2nd/3rd June saw another raid and four nights later, yet another. Whilst these were small in comparison to the 31st May attack, they caused further damage to buildings and killed another five people. Yet somehow, despite all the destruction, Canterbury with its ancient history and Cathedral, survived. The Duke of Kent on a later visit to the devastated city had nothing but praise for its civilians. 'We shall win – keep your chins up,' were his words of encouragement to which one woman who had been bombed out of her home answered, 'God bless you, Sir.'

The civilian population of Kent was to suffer air raids every year of the war though it is true to say that they got fewer and fewer as the war progressed. In June 1944, it was the V1 'Doodlebugs' that they had to endure. These raids were heralded by Maidstone being shelled from the German long range guns situated along the Pas de Calais. In these attacks one woman was killed with considerable damage being done to the town. Several hours after the shelling had stopped, the first V1 crossed the coast between Hythe and Dymchurch. It continued inland and crashed at Swanscombe near Gravesend. A new reign of terror had begun.

In the face of this new weapon, the defences were once again strengthened. The sound of the de-synchronised rocket motor and the flame that was emitted from the tail spread terror throughout London and the home counties. In order to reach the capital, the V1s crossed Kent day after day, night after night. Many never reached their intended target and fell in Kent, either running out of fuel or being shot down. Some became entangled in the balloon barrage that had sprung up around the county. In no time at all, Kent once again became a graveyard for metal.

The first fatal V1 incident happened on Saturday, 17th June when a rocket fell on a house at Benenden killing three people. On the 24th came the worst loss of life in Kent throughout the campaign when a V1, shot down by a fighter, hit the Newlands Military Camp at Charing near Ashford. Forty seven men were killed with 28 seriously injured. With the rockets now coming over at five minute intervals, another crashed just down the road at Smarden. This time it fell on a bungalow killing four of the occupants and injuring a further two. Every day a tragedy unfurled in one Kent village or town. Maidstone was to see three bad attacks on Thursday, 3rd August when one rocket crashed on

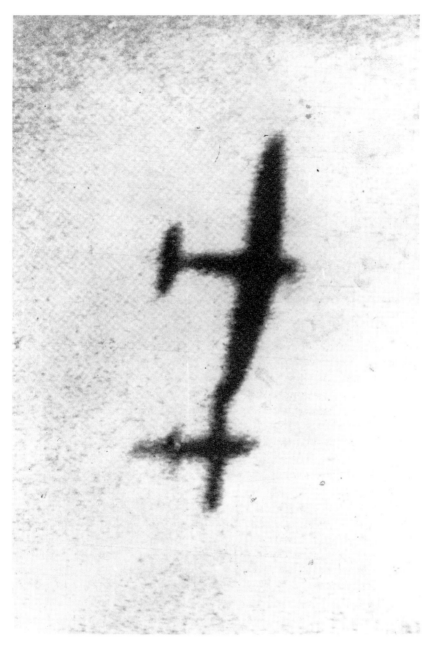

A Typhoon formates on a V1 Doodlebug over Kent. (Flight)

Friday 30th June 1944 saw a V1 shot down by the ack-ack battery on the North Downs. Sadly it crashed on Weald House, then a nursery, and 22 children and 11 nurses were killed. (Kent Messenger)

a golf course seriously injuring three women and damaging 450 houses whilst an hour later, another fell at Allington and a third came down in Maidstone West railway station. In the latter, five people were killed and seven seriously injured. Forty were slightly hurt. Snodland near Maidstone was also to see further tragic deaths together with Dartford and Ashford. Not one town or village was left unscathed.

By 1st September 1944, the V1 attacks were all but over as the advancing Allies overran the launch sites. But a new and more sinister weapon, the V2 Rocket was to appear and once again Kent was to see many deaths and much destruction.

The first V2 to fall in Kent was at Field Crouch Farm at Crockenhill. It landed in an orchard with no damage to property or people. It did, however, ruin a bumper apple crop! From that time on the population were to suffer badly from this deadly silent weapon that fell from the edge of space. The first serious incident involving the V2 happened on 13th November when one landed on a house in Gravesend killing five people. From then until March 1945, hundreds of V2s were to rain down on Kent with many deaths and much destruction. When it was all over,

GIs manning the guns on Romney Marsh during the V1 attacks. (Kent Messenger)

figures revealed that Kent had 2,400 flying bombs or V1s crash onto its soil, 100 more than London. There were nearly the same number of V2s. This together with the constant bombing and the battles that were fought overhead justly earned Kent the unenviable label of 'Hellfire Corner'.

There are still today reminders of the damage caused to property and the civilian population by the rocket campaign. One of the most poignant must be the remains of the Church of St Mary of the Holy Rood at Little Chart, two miles south of Charing. On 15th August 1944 it was destroyed by a V1 coming down after it had been attacked by a fighter. The rocket continued its flight for half a mile before finally crashing into the top of the church tower. Whilst the building succumbed, there was no loss of life. When it was decided to build a new church in 1956, it was on a new site leaving the remains of Little Chart church to stand as a symbol of defiance in the face of adversity.

The incidents that I have recorded here are just a fraction of the whole story. The memories of that time are still vivid to many people, proof if it were needed that as well as a military war, it was also a civilians' war.

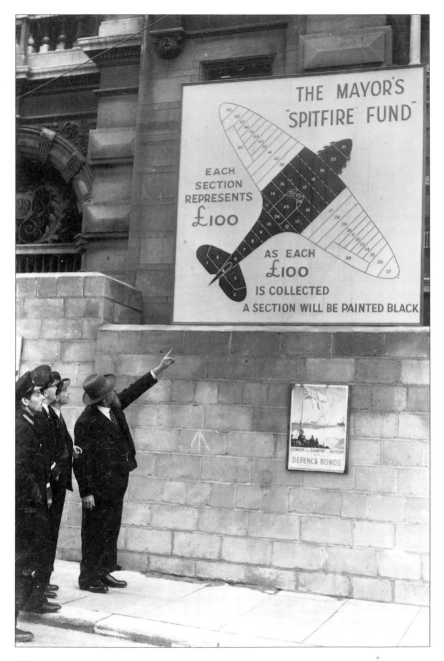

The Mayor's Spitfire Fund, outside Maidstone Town Hall. (Kent Messenger)

POSTSCRIPT

The past few years have seen much controversy over the activities of so-called 'Aviation Archaeology' groups who go around digging up the remains of crashed British and German wartime aircraft. Most of these 'digs' have taken place in Kent and with the discovery of human remains in some of the sites, the Ministry of Defence have felt it necessary to issue strict guidelines on these activities under the title of *Notes of Guidance for the Recovery of Crashed Military Aircraft*. In it they firmly state that all crashed aircraft remain the property of the Crown until such time as the MOD decides to dispose of them. Any group wishing to recover the wreckage of a military aircraft must first obtain a licence from the MOD. If with this requisition the dig goes ahead and human remains are found, all activity must stop. The remains must not be touched and the discovery must be reported immediately to the local police and the MOD. Where the MOD know or suspect that human remains are contained in the crash, a licence may be issued with the stipulation that a member of the RAF be in attendance at all times.

Despite these guidelines however, certain groups and individuals do not obtain a licence and worse still, some human remains are removed and placed in very undesirable containers before their discovery is reported. This is inclined to tarnish the image of all archaeology groups, especially when it comes to the attention of the national media. Recent incidents in Kent have resulted in prosecutions although it must be stated that no charges were preferred as it was the wish of the deceased persons' relatives that their loved ones were removed from their crashed aircraft and given a military funeral.

It is to say the least a very delicate matter and one that must be handled with compassion. Let us hope that the recovery groups and the MOD can bring such incidents to a dignified and Christian conclusion for the benefit of the relatives concerned.

Appendix A

THE SQUADRONS OF THE ROYAL AIR FORCE THAT WERE BASED AT KENT AIRFIELDS BEFORE, DURING AND AFTER THE SECOND WORLD WAR

BIGGIN HILL – 1, 3, 19, 23, 32, 37, 39, 41, 56, 64, 66, 72, 74, 79, 91, 92, 124, 133, 140, 141, 154, 213, 242, 264, 322, 340, 341, 345, 600, 601, 602, 609, 610, 611, 615.

DETLING – 1, 4, 26, 50, 53, 59, 80, 118, 124, 132, 143, 165, 184, 229, 235, 239, 274, 280, 318, 500, 504, 567, 602.

EASTCHURCH – 4, 12, 21, 33, 48, 53, 65, 100, 122, 124, 132, 142, 174, 175, 181, 183, 184, 207, 245, 247, 263, 266.

GRAVESEND – 2, 4, 19, 21, 32, 56, 64, 65, 66, 71, 72, 74, 85, 92, 111, 122, 124, 132, 133, 141, 165, 174, 181, 193, 245, 247, 257, 264, 266, 277, 284, 306, 350, 501, 604, 609, 610.

HAWKINGE – 1, 2, 3, 4, 16, 17, 25, 26, 38, 41, 56, 65, 66, 79, 83, 91, 120, 124, 132, 234, 245, 277, 278, 313, 322, 350, 501, 504, 567, 605, 611.

LYMPNE – 1, 2, 16, 21, 26, 33, 34, 41, 53, 59, 65, 72, 74, 91, 98, 102, 108, 120, 127, 130, 137, 165, 186, 310, 312, 313, 350, 609, 610.

MANSTON – 1, 2, 3, 9, 18, 21, 23, 26, 29, 32, 46, 48, 56, 59, 62, 63, 74, 77, 79, 80, 91, 92, 110, 118, 119, 124, 130, 137, 139, 143, 151, 164, 174, 175, 181, 183, 184, 193, 197, 198, 206, 219, 222, 224, 229, 235, 242, 253, 263, 266, 274, 310, 312, 313, 331, 332, 500, 501, 504, 567, 600, 601, 604, 607, 609, 615, 616.

WEST MALLING – 3, 25, 26, 29, 32, 64, 80, 85, 91, 96, 98, 124, 130, 141, 153, 157, 234, 264, 274, 287, 316, 322, 350, 500, 531, 567, 616.

In addition, Rochester was the Short Brothers factory manufacturing the Short Stirling bomber and the Sunderland Flying Boat.

Appendix B

THE SQUADRONS OF THE ROYAL AIR FORCE, ROYAL
CANADIAN AIR FORCE AND THE UNITED STATES ARMY AIR
FORCE THAT WERE BASED AT THE ADVANCED LANDING
GROUNDS IN KENT

ASHFORD (GREAT CHART) – 65, 122 (RAF). 414, 430 (RCAF). 406th
Bomb Group comprising 512th, 513th, 515th Fighter Squadrons.

BRENZETT – 122, 129, 306, 315.

HEADCORN (EGERTON) – 17th Fighter Wing (RCAF) comprising 403,
421 Squadrons and 405 Repair and Salvage Unit. 362nd Fighter Group,
100 Fighter Wing comprising 377th, 378th, 379th Squadrons.

HIGH HALDEN – 358th Bomb Group comprising 365th, 366th, 367th
Fighter Squadrons.

KINGSNORTH – 19, 65, 122, 184, 602 (RAF). 36th Fighter Group, 303rd
Fighter Wing comprising 22nd, 23rd, 53rd Fighter Squadrons.

LASHENDEN – 127 (RCAF) Airfield comprising 403, 421. 100th Fighter
Wing. Tactical Air Command comprising 354th, 353rd, 355th, 356th
Fighter Group.

LYDD – 121 Airfield comprising 174, 175, 245 Squadrons (RAF).

NEWCHURCH – 3, 19, 56, 132, 184, 602 Squadrons (RAF).

NEW ROMNEY – 181, 182, 247.

STAPLEHURST – 126 Airfield comprising 401, 411, 412 Squadrons
(RCAF). 363rd Fighter Group USAAF.

WOODCHURCH – 128 Airfield comprising 39, 231 Squadrons (RAF).
400 (RCAF). 373rd Fighter Group comprising 410, 411, 412 Fighter
Squadrons.

Appendix C

THE MAIN LUFTWAFFE UNITS USED IN THE ASSAULT ON THE
AIRFIELDS – ORDER OF BATTLE 13th AUGUST 1940

LUFTFLOTTE 2 – BRUSSELS – Commanded by Generalfeldmarschall
Albert Kesselring.

KAMPFGESCHWADER 1-2-3-4-40-53-76.
Equipment – Heinkel He111 – Dornier Do17 – Focke Wulf FW200.

STUKAGESCHWADER 1.
Equipment – Junkers Ju87B 'Stuka'.

LEHRGESCHWADER 1-2.
Equipment – Junkers Ju87B 'Stuka' – Messerschmitt BF109E.

JAGDGESCHWADER 3-26-51-52-54.
Equipment – Messerschmitt BF109E.

ZERSTORERGESCHWADER 26-27.
Equipment – Messerschmitt BF110.

ERPROBUNGS GRUPPE 210.
Equipment – Messerschmitt BF109E – Messerschmitt BF110.

KAMPFGRUPPE 100-106.
Equipment – Heinkel He111.

KUSTENFLIEGERGRUPPE 106.
Equipment – Heinkel He115 – Dornier Do18 – Junkers Ju88D –
Heinkel He111.

LUFTFLOTTE 3 – PARIS – Commanded by Generalfeldmarschall
Hugo Sperrle.

KAMPFGESCHWADER 1-27-51-54-55.
Equipment – Heinkel He111 – Junkers Ju88A.

STUKAGESCHWADER 1-2-3-77.
Equipment Junkers Ju87B 'Stuka' – Dornier Do17 – Heinkel He111.

LEHRGESCHWADER 1-2.
Equipment – Junkers Ju88A – Messerschmitt BF110 – Dorner Do17F.

JAGDGESCHWADER 2-27-53.
Equipment – Messerschmitt BF109E.

ZERSTORERGESCHWADER 2.
   Equipment – Messerschmitt BF110.

KAMPFGRUPPE 806.
   Equipment – Junkers Ju88A – Messerschmitt BF110 – Dornier Do17
   – Henschell 126A.

In addition to the two main Luftflottes, Luftflotte 5 operated from
Stavanger in Norway for attacks on East Coast shipping and the East
Coast airfields.

Appendix D

GLOSSARY FOR LUFTWAFFE UNITS

Jagdgeschwader – Fighter Units.
Kampfgeschwader – Bomber Units.
Zerstorergeschwader – Long Range Fighter Groups.
Erprobungs Gruppe 210 – Experimental Test Wing 210.
Lehrgeschwader – Instructional/Operational Development Group.
Stukageschwader – Dive-bombing Groups.
Kustenfliegergruppe – Maritime Luftwaffe Units.
Kampfgruppe – Coastal Units.

GLOSSARY FOR GERMAN AIR CREW RANKS

Oberst (Obst) – Colonel.
Oberstleutnant (Obstlt) – Lieutenant Colonel.
Major (Maj) – Major
Hauptmann (Hpt) – Captain.
Oberleutnant (Oblt) – 1st Lieutenant.
Leutnant (Lt) – 2nd Lieutenant.
Fahnenjunkeroffizier (Fhnjr) – Officer cadet.
Hauptfeldwebel (Hptfw) – Sergeant Major.
Oberfeldwebel (Ofw) – Flight Sergeant.
Feldwebel (Fw) – Sergeant.
Unteroffizier (Uffz) – Corporal.
Flieger (Flg) – Aircraftsman.

GLOSSARY OF TERMS

AFC	Air Force Cross
ALG	Advanced Landing Ground
ASR	Air Sea Rescue
BEF	British Expeditionary Force
CH	Chain Home (Radar)
CHL	Chain Home Low (Radar)
CIRCUS	Fighter escorted bombing raid to attract the enemy
CO	Commanding Officer
DFC	Distinguished Flying Cross
DIVER	Operations against the V1 Rocket
DSO	Distinguished Service Order
EFTS	Elementary Flying Training School
ELG	Emergency Landing Ground
E&RFTS	Elementary and Reserve Flying Training School
FL/LT	Flight Lieutenant
F/O	Flying Officer
G/CPT	Group Captain
LT/CDR	Lieutenant Commander
NOBALL	Rocket and Flying Bomb Sites
P/O	Pilot Officer
RAMROD	Day Bomber Raids escorted by fighters
RANGER	Deep penetration flights for targets of opportunity
RCAF	Royal Canadian Air Force
RDF	Radio Directing Finding
RHUBARB	Low level strike operation carried out in Occupied Europe
ROC	Royal Observer Corps
RODEO	Fighter Sweep
SQD/LDR	Squadron Leader
TAF	Tactical Air Force
USAAF	United States Army Air Force
USAF	United States Air Force
WG/CDR	Wing Commander

ACKNOWLEDGEMENTS

I acknowledge with thanks all the individuals and organisations who have assisted me in the writing of this book: Group Captain John Cunningham; LAC Fred Brinton; Imperial War Museum; RAF Museum Hendon; Air Historical Branch (RAF); Public Records Office Kew; Bundesarchiv; Militararchiv; Mr C. Samson; Mr Tony Moor (Brenzett Museum); Mr W. G. Ramsey; Mr Vic Baker (Staplehurst); Roy Humphreys; *Kent Messenger*; *Sevenoaks Chronicle*; Maidstone Springfield Library; Kent Aviation and Historical Research Society; 500 Squadron (Old Comrades) Association.

If I have omitted to mention any person or organisation or incorrectly credited any photographs, please accept my sincere apologies. My final thanks must go to Len Pilkington for allowing me access to his vast photographic collection and to my wife, Barbara, as much for her patience as for her help and correcting.

BIBLIOGRAPHY

During my research I consulted various other works. I list them below with grateful thanks to the authors.

Ashworth, C., *Action Stations 8*, Patrick Stephens 1985
Bowyer, Chaz, *Fighter Command*, J M Dent and Son 1980
Collier, Richard, *Eagle Day*, Hodder and Stoughton 1966
Galland, Adolf, *The First and the Last*, Methuen and Co Ltd 1955
Halley, James J., *Squadrons of the RAF*, Air Britain 1980
Hyndman, Oonagh, *Wartime Kent*, Meresborough Books 1990
Jefford, Wg/Cdr C. G., *RAF Squadrons*, Airlife 1980
Ogley, Bob, *Biggin on the Bump*, Froglets 1990
Potter, John Deane, *Fiasco*, William Heinemann Ltd 1970
Ramsey, W. G., *The Blitz – Then and Now Volumes 1 and 3*, Plaistow
  Pictorial 1987
Robertson, Terence, *Channel Dash*, Evans Brothers 1958
Rootes, Andrew, *Front Line County*, Robert Hale
Shaw, Michael, *No 1 Squadron*, Ian Allen 1971
Thetford, Owen, *Aircraft of the RAF*, Putnam 1962
Wood, D. and Dempster, D., *The Narrow Margin*, Hutchinson 1961

INDEX

SQUADRONS